D0850811

THE ORDINARY AND
THE FABULOUS

THE
ORDINARY
AND THE
FABULOUS

AN INTRODUCTION TO MYTHS
LEGENDS AND FAIRY TALES

BY

ELIZABETH COOK
Senior Lecturer in English
Homerton College, Cambridge

SECOND EDITION

CAMBRIDGE UNIVERSITY PRESS

CAMBRIDGE
LONDON · NEW YORK · MELBOURNE

Published by the Syndics of the Cambridge University Press
The Pitt Building, Trumpington Street, Cambridge CB2 1RP
Bentley House, 200 Euston Road, London NW1 2DB
32 East 57th Street, New York, NY 10022, USA
296 Beaconsfield Parade, Middle Park, Melbourne 3206, Australia

© Cambridge University Press 1969, 1976

First published 1969
Reprinted 1971
Second edition 1976
Reprinted 1977
Reprinted with Addendum 1978

Printed in Great Britain at the
University Press, Cambridge

Library of Congress Cataloguing in Publication Data
Cook, Elizabeth
    The ordinary and the fabulous
    Bibliography: p.
    Includes index
    1. Books and reading for children. 2. Story-telling. I. Title
Z1037.C767   1975   028.5   75–7213
ISBN 0 521 20825 4 hard covers
ISBN 0 521 09961 7 paperback
(First edition ISBN 0 521 07346 4 hard covers
             ISBN 0 521 09586 7 paperback)

Contents

[iii]

Contents

Preface to the First Edition

This small book has been written for teachers, for students who intend to be teachers or librarians, and for parents, cousins, aunts and all other storytellers. It is an attempt to show that a grown-up understanding of life is incomplete without an understanding of myths, legends and fairy tales; that the process of growing up would be harder and drearier without them; that there is an abundance of fabulous stories that are enjoyed by children of different ages, and that there are innumerable ways of presenting them so that they become part and parcel of children's lives.

Edwin Muir said that the Orkney of his childhood was 'a place where there was no great distinction between the ordinary and the fabulous', and to a lyric on what he owed to legend, as a man and as an artist, he gave the title of *The Debtor*. In a sophisticated, urban and secular society the ordinary is often divorced from the fabulous; people either day-dream, or else attend to the hard facts. Throughout my argument I have tried to emphasize that fabulous stories illuminate the ordinary world, and that if they also illuminate a 'world to come', it is not like the world of day-dreaming.

The Why of my subject is discussed specifically in chapter I, the What in chapter II, the How in chapter III, and the Where in chapter IV and the Short List of Books. In chapter I I have given a brief account of some old and new methods of interpreting myths and fairy tales, and indicated the importance of mythological tradition in European art; I have also given some reasons for believing that these stories fit into the pattern of children's lives, and provide an answer to some modern problems in teaching. Chapter II is a survey of the stories of four main European traditions of myth and fantasy, relating different groups of tales to the different ages at which children respond to them. Chapter III deals with some of the practical problems of the teacher and storyteller, and with some opportunities for creative work that arise from reading or listening to these stories. Chapter IV and the Short List are intended to help the storyteller to find the right book for his purpose. In chapter IV I have reproduced, from children's books and from translations of original sources, parallel passages that describe seven crucial scenes in stories from the four traditions I have considered; I have added a commentary which is meant to illustrate some of the artistic problems of telling fabulous stories to children. The Short List is a classified and annotated list of children's books, together with some other reading that may be useful to teachers or storytellers; it is a personal selection, not an exhaustive bibliography.

This book is for the ignorant, the unconverted, or the recent convert, not for the initiate. It provides no new or recondite information. In historical matters I have tried to represent the present state of scholarly opinion, and to make my statements as accurate as simplified statements can be, when they are made by one non-specialist writing for other non-specialists. Most of what I have said about the stories themselves will be familiar to those who came across them, either in childhood or later in life, in versions imaginative enough to be remembered. I have not made summaries of all the stories that I mention, but I have tried to say enough to make those who do not know them feel that they are worth exploration. I hope that those who have lived with them for many years will forgive this kind of proselytizing, and pass quickly on to anything that may be new.

E. C.

June 1968

Preface to the Second Edition

This edition of *The Ordinary and the Fabulous* has a revised and
enlarged book-list which includes some of the important writing for
children that has appeared in the *genre* of myth and legend since 1968,
and some recent books on the nature of myth and inherited symbols.
I have not materially altered the text of the first edition, apart from a
few small additions, believing that my essential arguments for the
importance of these stories may be as valid now as they may have been
then; but the obstacles and opportunities that present themselves to
a fabulous storyteller in 1974 are perhaps somewhat different from
those of 1968, and call for some comment in a preface.

In many ways the world might be thought kinder now to tales
'building a...loveliness Out of the battles of old times' and creating
'secondary worlds' that mirror inward experience. The past decade
has been marked by a multitude of movements trying to foster inward-
ness, romance and alternatives to merely practical hard-headedness—
transcendental meditation, black and white magic, astrology (surely
a manifestation of uneasy curiosity about that influence of hidden
natural forces upon human life that is imaged in Greek conceptions of
Fates, Titans, Nereids, Dryads and satyrs), Arthurian societies who
joust and banquet, yoga, a taste in clothes that favours drifting folds
and faded colours and even prefers the second-hand to the brand-new,
and a taste in food that favours the brown beans of the fairy-tale woodcutter. These movements have displayed almost every possible per-
mutation of silliness and seriousness; whether more silly or more
serious they may help the teller of tales to catch the ear of an audience.

A display of illustrations from the Lang 'coloured' fairy books,
preferably 'blown up' to poster size, may attract eyes that turn
naturally to Art Nouveau or Pre-Raphaelite line and to romantic
dresses. An invitation to dwell upon the promise of a lost Paradise in
the titles of Macdonald's *At the Back of the North Wind* or Morris's
The Well at the World's End may be more persuasive to people who
have just listened to nostalgic folk-singing. Children who have just
listened to Mervyn Peake or looked at a reenacted joust (if the performance is not too grubby) may be more ready to listen to stories of King
Arthur. A school study of 'conservation' which really encourages
children to feel reverence for life and curiosity about the variety of it
may produce the right climate of opinion for stories which contain
satyrs, or centaurs, or winged horses, or tree-nymphs: these are

creatures who express in their dual nature a faith that the whole earth is alive and that man is not divorced from non-human life.

Another cluster of 'trendy' interests favourable to myth and fable is the amorphous body of fashions known as 'ethnic', ranging from political concern with the Third World through attraction to Indian music to a liking for handloom cotton skirts and Afghan embroidered sheepskins. A sense of moral obligation to recognize the culture of other continents has led teachers who previously ignored the myths of Europe to search out African and Indian myth and folklore, simply because the visual and verbal art of non-European civilizations happens to be largely mythical or non-realistic. This is a beginning, although to my mind it is not enough. Children need to feel that the forests and shores of their own continent are haunted, and that they themselves inherit the great symbols of European culture, even more than they need to picture the gods and goddesses who live in the rain-forests of Burma and the sacred rivers of India. It does seem, however, that at the moment in English schools the stories of black and brown peoples are being taught with more energy and inventiveness than the stories of Europe, and for this reason I have included in the revised book-list a short section of non-European tales in versions for children. A study of the symbolism and significance of these stories should come from a writer whose birthright they are, who has been brought up in the cultural and literary tradition springing from them. Perhaps one of the African or Indian teachers now working in England will satisfy this need.

There is yet another modern preoccupation that can be exploited by the fabulous storyteller, and that is our concern with the education of the eye. Visual modes of communication have become dominant both in the world at large and in the little world of the classroom. Much more criticism of adult literature now pays attention to iconography. The use of television for all kinds of learning, which has undoubtedly reduced our ability to listen intently, to follow the shape of spoken sentences and to catch the evocative resonance of words, may also have increased our readiness to see pictures as symbols, to make connections between them and to distinguish tones of feeling within them. In primary schools 'art' has not usually suffered as badly as 'literature' in the Procrustean bed of the integrated day, and often the curriculum contains a strong or strengthening element of work in paint, clay, polystyrene, pebbles or whatever may be the newest variant of collage. The storyteller is therefore prudent if he remembers that (as Kerenyi pointed out) mythic stories characteristically evolve from seen ritual images, and that a peculiarly visual quality survives in most of the forms in which they have come down to us. In reading the story of Jason one is not listening to the verbal thought-processes of a single human being, or sensing half-verbally the emotional interactions of a group of individual characters: one is *seeing* a ship between a whirl-pool and a monster, or a witch and a warrior standing beside a tree with a serpent coiled round it and a golden sheepskin hanging from it. Children who want visual images to begin from in their own work will find them in these stories, as I have suggested in chapter III section 3: sometimes today it might be helpful to reverse an otherwise natural order of events, beginning with children's own 'art' work (of course with a good display of pictures in the background, and some evocative verbal description of the one figure or scene chosen as a subject or starting-point), and proceeding after that to an exploration of the whole story.

In spite of all these assets, however, one must recognize sadly that there is less storytelling and less fantasy in children's lives in the 1970s than there was in the 1960s. One sign of poverty is the smaller number of distinguished new versions for children published between 1966 and 1974, in comparison with the good crop of books that appeared in the 50s and early 60s. Clearer signs can be seen by anyone who looks into the work done inside a variety of primary schools in any one part of the country. There seem to be two radical causes of this poverty. The first and more powerful, but peculiar to a chosen method of primary education and therefore, with good will, remediable, is the suppression of imaginative literature in the timetabling and arrangement of children's work known as the 'integrated day': the second, less statutory but more insidiously pervasive in many streams of modern thought, is the absolute value given to an increasingly narrow concept of 'relevance'.

It is quite possible for a child who is being educated by the system of the integrated day to spend weeks or months without hearing a single poem, let alone a substantial story. In the 1960s there was a good chance that children heard a short story or a long chapter every day in class 'story time' at the end of the afternoon—the very magical hour of twilight—as well as reading other poetry and prose used in specific 'creative writing' sessions or introduced into a historical or geo-graphical class 'topic'. In 1974 a few poems and opportunities for original writing may be insinuated into the organized individual assignments of the 'day', and a teacher who cares about imaginative literature will of course let stories into the sacred enclave of the project by the most secret postern gate—but even so there will probably be a story once a fortnight instead of a story once a day. The source of this neglect of stories seems to me to lie in a received idea of what an integrated day ought to be, rather than in any failure by teachers in realizing it.

The integrated day varies in detail from any one school to another, like any method of organization, but it nearly always brings with it a number of practices which affect stories like a strong dose of paraquat. A complete list might run: the abolition of 'subject' disciplines and the concentration of the whole of a child's working day upon a 'topic' or 'centre of interest', with the frequent exception of hours devoted to mathematics or physical education: the arrangement of a child's work by an 'assignment' or 'discovery' method, so that he is given written instructions for using books or other material to find the answers to certain questions, and does not listen to a teacher's voice or talk to other children about what he is doing, since no other child knows about the same book: the choice of 'topic' subjects that are largely factual—such as Pollution, or Electricity, or Communications, or Land Use, or A South American Market—since these are the ones that lend themselves most readily to looking up and copying out *verbatim*: a strong emphasis upon each child producing at the end of a few weeks a collection of 'work' that can be exhibited in a folder or upon the wall.

All these things are hostile to the nature of imaginative literature. Poems and stories—notably mythic and legendary stories—are not 'about' the subject named in a title, or the material of which they are composed: in each the relationship between the tangible material and the theme or mood that the story is really 'about' is delicate and tenuous, and a real meaning can often be sensed by children long before they want to talk about it, as I have suggested in chapter III. To direct a child to look up the story of Prometheus in the middle of answering a series of questions about Fire leading up to Coal Mines and the Fuel Crisis is likely to limit his response to it. Subject-matter-linking is destructive because the discipline of literature concerns a mode of apprehension, not an area of apprehension. Nor does the abolition of the teacher's and reader's voice, and of face-to-face conversation, help to create a *milieu* in which stories can flourish. Most stories are better heard than read silently, at least until the inward ear is well trained;

and what a teacher of stories can do, apart from reading well, and providing a good library, good book-lists and a quiet place, consists very much in generating excitement and awareness by constantly saying 'Do you remember...did you notice...don't you think that was...what did *you* think?' The 'appeal for corroboration', as F. R. Leavis called it in adult teaching, can be made only between human beings. Machines and work-sheets are of no use for this job. A well known American storyteller, Laramee Haynes, has said that oral storytelling is the activity in which the child listening is most certain of the speaker's total gift of attention to him, and that it therefore has a healing power in an unloving world. Concentration upon factual topics which can be organized by a straightforward division of child labour (because the organizer knows in advance what answers the child discoverer is going to produce) will obviously not provide many openings for fable and fantasy. And concentration upon children 'having something to shew for it' distracts attention from the real gain that accrues to the hearer of stories, which is a slow, unexaminable growth of scenes and images in the mind; an ability simply to recall what happened last time and an eagerness to know what will happen next are really the only outward and visible signs of it, and they do not make much shew in an end-of-project display.

Convinced storytellers should try to get their daily story time back. Meanwhile teachers who are trapped in Pollution for five weeks can only make the best of a bad job, try to collect a little group of children surreptitiously, and slip in the story of Daedalus and Icarus without labouring the theme of transgressing a natural order—it is not the only theme of the story—and without mixing it up with questions about aircraft noise.

Convinced storytellers might also be able, by persuasion, to alter the allocation of school funds. The system of working by individual assignments upon enormous 'topics' often seems to be connected with an equally enormous outlay upon tape and video recorders and a ban upon all books apart from reference books (such as junior encyclopaedias) and work books (questions and answers in mathematics and 'English'). I recently saw a primary school in new buildings which is treated as a showpiece for visitors; it has impressive shelf-space for films and hardware, but no central or class libraries, no books of poems or stories, and nowhere in the classrooms where they could be kept if they were provided. Books are still the richest and far the cheapest source of children's knowledge of myth and legend. Sydney Bolt, who has done a good deal for children's literature, recognized that the current fashion for 'projects' is producing a new generation of Gradgrinds, and deplored them all too justly in *The Teaching of Fiction in Schools* when he defined 'that current and alluring approach which, claiming that language governs all human activity, serves up as the version of an English lesson a hot-pot of Reality'.

'Relevance' is not a matter of timetables and expenditure, and is indeed rather like Nereus: hard to resist because hard to grasp, so constantly changing are the forms into which it transmutes itself. Of course all greater or lesser stories have greater or lesser relevance to reality: that is a tautology, and in chapter 1 I have tried to suggest reasons for believing that myth and legend embody archetypal patterns of experience in a language that is more universal than any other. The issue lies in the meaning given to the word 'reality'. At the moment it may be useful to emphasize the very 'otherness' of legend as well as its psychological symbolism, since even among men of letters and theologians the only non-factual reality often seems to be a merely personal one; readiness to look 'beyond personality' is becoming rarer among academics, although paradoxically much more common in popular movements. The world can still be roughly divided between natural Platonists and natural anti-Platonists, between those who recognize the transcendental and those who deny it; the presence of the transcendental in myth has been perfectly described by Kathleen Raine in three essays contained in *Defending Ancient Springs*, a collection published in 1967.

Those who decry myth and fairy tale as 'irrelevant to modern industrial civilization' usually rely on still narrower concepts of 'relevance' and 'reality' which exclude even personal reality and psychological symbolism. For them a good children's story has to be about children and adults who wear the same clothes, go to the same schools and do the same jobs as the children in the audience and their parents: they must worry about the identical economic and ethical problems, and must not care about any of the ambitions or distresses that could touch a prince or an artist in the middle ages and will not literally call for decision in the life of a shop steward today. This form of the notion that 'history is bunk' is not confined to teachers and critics of children's stories. It runs through every call that we have heard during the past ten years to leave out 'all that mediaeval stuff' in academic curricula, to cut out 'dead imagery' from theology, to ignore both the common consent of mankind in ethics and the *philosophia perennis* in metaphysics, and above all, to look only at the material or at most the personal content of art, and to forget the meaning of its form. Recently Brian Jackson was heard to castigate a teacher who had been expounding mediaeval farming to a secondary class on the ground that she was indulging neurotically in a fantasy life. A headmaster chosen in a B.B.C. programme to defend modern primary education said that he could not see what 'relevance' Napoleon could possibly have for a child living in Bermondsey. Apart from the social snobbery of supposing that disinterested curiosity is peculiar to those born in certain postal districts, this neo-utilitarianism is inherently destructive: it constricts human experience, instead of enlarging it as it should be enlarged by good schooling at any age. To be locked up within the confines of what can in fact be seen or done or said within one's own generation is to be imprisoned in a very narrow cell. T. S. Eliot has defined the predicament accurately:

It is a provincialism, not of space, but of time; one for which history is merely the chronicle of human devices which have served their turn and been scrapped, one for which the world is the property solely of the living, a property in which the dead hold no shares. The menace of this kind of provincialism is, that we can all, all the peoples on the globe, be provincials together; and those who are not content to be provincials, can only become hermits.

It is *unrealistic* not to be able to see the bucking black ship of a Greek vase-painting, and the brilliantly coloured knight and enchantress in a mediaeval miniature with *mille fleurs* at their feet, as well as the sombre crowds painted by Lowry and the 'real' postman in the frame of the 'real' front door: these pictures exist in museums and are part of the material fabric of the world: moreover they were made by real human beings and therefore contain some of the reality of human nature that we should not otherwise know about. Another testimony to the self-mutilation that results from merely 'contemporary' learning comes from Virginia Woolf when she is advising a young poet to beware of exclusive, partisan modernity:

Once you begin to take yourself seriously as a leader or a follower, as a modern or as a conservative, then you become a self-conscious, biting and scratching little animal whose work is not of the slightest value or importance to anybody. Think of yourself rather as something much humbler and less spectacular, but to my mind far more interesting—a poet in whom live all the poets of the past, from whom all poets in time to come will spring... You are an immensely ancient, complex and continuous character, for which reason please treat yourself with respect and think twice before you dress up as Guy Fawkes.

No better advice could be given to a young teacher.

To make even the slightest inroad into the Problem of Relevance in the preface to a small book on telling myths and fairy tales to children may well seem digressive: it must needs be perfunctory. Yet the problem cannot be forgotten just because it is so large and so ill-defined. The experience of the past few years suggests that many young teachers are not simply unaware of these stories, but positively determined never to look at them and never to bring them into the classroom; and that this is not just because they remember dingy versions from childhood, but because they hold it as a matter of faith that anything fantastic and anything ancient must be 'irrelevant'. Oddly enough this conviction often coexists with violent dislike of the present pattern of society and manners, a dislike which produces a demand for 'alternatives' and ought in all reason to produce a sympathetic interest in those alternatives that exist in history and in fantasy. Reason, however, cannot affect antipathies rooted in faith; I do not think that any militant anti-antiquarian or campaigner for 'relevance' will be much affected by this argument or by any that I have put foward in chapter 1, if only because on principle he would never pick up this book. The availability of traditional tales in schools and at home—apart from their survival in art, which will probably look after itself—can only be fostered by the display of their beauty and significance in places where it is hard to avoid, and by occasional reminders that 'relevance' is an inadequate and contradictory criterion. Once the anti-antiquarian teacher or parent has somehow been inveigled, cheated or trapped into listening to the story of the Odyssey well told (perhaps because he is compelled to supervise a television lesson or help with the homework) he may come near to forgetting his antipathy, want to go on with the story, and go out and buy a book. 'To be moved with desire to know . . .hoc opus, hic labor est.'

There is one particularly interesting development in the recent treatment of traditional stories by writers for children, and it is difficult to predict its effects for good or ill. Among the fairly small number of remarkable publications in this field there are some that have rightly been regarded as breaking new ground and establishing an art form that did not exist before the 1960s. They are virtually teenage or even adult romances or novels built upon plots taken from myth, legend or fairy tale. The extent to which the traditional characters retain their identity and perform their traditional actions varies. Nevertheless the new *genre* is usually recognizable by its combination of archetypal plot with an explicit investigation of individual motive, thought and feeling, and with a style of language and structure that is romantically expansive, sensuous and packed with tactile imagery: the influence of Lawrence seems to dominate the writing of the school, not least in its heavy-handed description of violent aggression and violent sex. The earliest books of the kind were Alan Garner's novels based upon Celtic legend: in *The Weirdstone of Brisingamen*, *The Moon of Gomrath* and *Elidor*, published between 1960 and 1965, the action of the ancient protagonists is watched and entered into by modern children who walk magically through the barrier of time: the age-group of the children is fairly wide, but they are children if childhood is understood as lasting from about five to about fourteen. In *The Owl Service* of 1967 and *The Red Shift* of 1973 the modern people are the protagonists re-enacting an ancient pattern, and they are no longer children but teenagers with growing-up pains of love and jealousy; the publishers classified *The Owl Service* as a 'novel for young people'. Between 1968 and 1974 the weird, strong, allegorical colouring of Alan Garner's earlier books has run through a still proliferating mass of fantasies for older children by other writers: Ursula le Guin, Nina Beachcroft, Penelope Farmer, André Norton, Penelope Lively and Susan Cooper; they make much of the wizardry and time-shifting but less of the legendary action.

James Reeves takes up the thread of this kind of writing in a series of short stories or novellas in which the princes and princesses of the Grimm fairy tales are given the self-questionings, illusions and awakenings of modern adolescents—or at least of adolescents as psychologists see them. *The Cold Flame* of 1967 was followed by *The Path of Gold* in 1972 and *The Forbidden Feast* in 1973. Rosemary Harris deals with traditional stories in much the same way in *The Lotus and the Grail* of 1974, with the same reflective irony, lyricism and analysis of will and motive that characterize her original fantasies of ancient Egypt and Israel, *The Moon in the Cloud*, *The Shadow on the Sun* and *The Bright and Morning Star*, published between 1968 and 1972. (In reading her work one is positively aware, with relief, of the absence of any Lawrentian tint.) Rosemary Sutcliff's *Tristan and Iseult* of 1971 is a more soberly historical romance, more like her earlier version of *Beowulf*, but she too, in her austere, chiselled, rhythmically evocative prose, writes a love story whose protagonists have interacting emotions and personalities.

The God beneath the Sea of 1970 and *The Golden Shadow* of 1973, by Leon Garfield and Edward Blishen, really belong to this *genre* even though they purport to be direct retellings of Greek myth and Legend. Since their fame was increased by exquisitely wrought illustrations by Charles Keeping, and since the Greek stories are unquestionably the ones that children most need to know, these books should perhaps be described here more carefully than the others which are obviously hybrids and not purely and simply 'versions' of traditional stories.

They are both woven into continuous narrative instead of the more usual episodic, story-by-story form; and this continuity is created in each one partly by the structural device of a wandering bardic storyteller who encounters heroes and hears tales of the gods but never sees one until he meets the messenger of Death, and partly by the dominance of a certain character or a certain theme in the tales. The first book is centred upon the contrasted natures of Hephaestus and Ares, the two children of Zeus and Hera who are here seen as embodiments of painful, ugly creativity and glamorous destructiveness; the second upon the gradual ageing of Heracles, who proceeds through the seven ages of man as he executes his labours, and upon the theme of jealousy, contained both in the relationship between Heracles and Peleus and in the image of the serpents which are sent by Hera to kill the infant hero and are transformed into 'snakes in the mind' in his later madness. Charles Keeping's illustrations do not usually represent incidents in the stories; characteristically they repeat the writers' imagery in visual form, consisting in the second book of several drawings of the figure of Heracles shewing its changes into maturity and decrepitude, interspersed with drawings of the venomous snakes advancing or receding. The stories have been given the same kind of visual commentary that plays of Shakespeare receive in productions where dress and setting represent verbal images in the text, not the material environment of the action.

It looks as if this kind of treatment of myth and legend may well be the one that most attracts writers in the immediate future, if only because it is of a piece with modern style in other things. It is doubtful whether it sustains the inherent strength of myth, and whether it is readily accessible to children. In calling *The Owl Service* 'a novel for young people' the publishers may have been identifying an audience from about thirteen to about sixteen, and Leon Garfield and Edward Blishen may have conceived their books in this way, although Ted Hughes reviewed them outright as books for children. I think that the density of the plot and the heaviness of the description demand a reader who would not get lost, for instance, in the short stories of Lawrence or the novels of Hardy. Certainly it is a novelist's amplitude that is imitated by these writers, and their insistence upon loading every rift with metaphor can make their language sound pretentious and eye-catching:

The bronze bolt slid to, and sounds of kisses and laughter and amorous cries were heard for a truly heroic time. At last they died away into a deep and snoring silence. . . Alcestis, lying in a shipwreck of linen and a storm of hair, never stirred.

It is not just a matter of verbal imagery. Hot beauty, grinning fangs, star-bursts of pain, spattering blood and swollen wombs dominate the storytelling and the illustrations. They may serve to give the stories currency among teenagers accustomed to the bludgeoning impact of writing that ranges from Lawrence and Golding at one extreme of seriousness and the women's serial and the horror comic at the other; but I feel that the books are overwritten and that the style emerges not from a sense of fitness but from an effort to please a known taste—always a dangerous origin, especially when the taste is for those 'gross and violent stimulants' that weaken imagination, as Wordsworth knew. Moreover it is foreign to the telling of myth and legend, as I have suggested in chapter IV, to be personal or to be sensuously elaborate, although ritual and ceremonious elaboration does appear in traditional heroic style.

The nature of myth is to invite interpretation, not to provide it. Of course original works like Wagner's *Ring* and Tennyson's *Idylls* have always given a distinct, partial interpretation of legend, but they were conceived and put forward as personal creations; even so Wagner's is more complete and sustained than Tennyson's because he respects the impersonality of his material. Leon Garfield and Edward Blishen are indeed quite open in saying that the pattern they have seen in Greek myth is not the only pattern that is potentially there:

We were aware that about the whole body of these myths there flickered a thousand possibilities of coherence: there must be many ways of weaving together a selection from them that would enable whatever story was so composed to carry the whole weight of significance the myth-makers meant their inventions to bear.

The questionable words are 'meant' and 'inventions', which relate to the craft of the individual, conscious artist.

Their claim that everything in these books is supported by the narratives and references provided in Robert Graves' *The Greek Myths* is perhaps more doubtful. Major events, persons and places certainly tally with Graves' summaries; causality, motive and some minor narrative details do not. The writers give Peleus a 'hapless dread of being surpassed' to account for his conspiracy with Telamon and murder of Eurytion, and make him feel pleasure at the death of Heracles; traditionally the deeds whereby he incurred pollution are unaccountable. The middle-aged Heracles is given a nostalgic relationship with the chance-found boy Iolaus who worships him, whereas the legendary Iolaus was Heracles' nephew, not an urchin hanging about the streets of Mycenae with a new birthday-knife. Hephaestus is made to carve for Thetis a broach of coral consisting of a pair of embracing lovers, which is seen by Zeus and causes the birth of Aphrodite: traditionally Hephaestus made virgins in gold, not lovers in coral, and if he married a 'living work of art' as Kerenyi suggests, his bride was Aglaia, eldest of the Graces. Of course no storyteller is under any obligation to stick to his sources, still less to footnotes upon them: I have mentioned these details only in order to suggest the extent to which the new kind of fabulous romance 'for young people' is novelistic, personal both in invention and interpretation. Its birth and growth are unmistakably phenomena of the present time: its further evolution and its place in the reading of children must be matters of conjecture.

E.C.

January 1976

Acknowledgements

No statement of intangible debts can be complete, and I wish that I could thank by name all the children, students, teachers and friends who have fostered my belief in the importance of myth by their interest, or clarified it by their questioning. In particular, I should like to express my gratitude to four of my Homerton colleagues: Miss Joan Woodard, who watched over my first attempts to talk about introducing myths to children; Mrs Christopher Morris, who suggested that I might try to write a book on the subject; and Mrs L. C. Knights and Mrs D. S. Brewer, who gave me felicitous hints and moral support during the more tiresome stages of its composition. I should also like to mention gratefully the help I received from Miss Janet Tinling, of W. Heffer and Sons Ltd, Cambridge, who put at my disposal not only her professional knowledge of children's books, but also her personal experience of children's reading; from the librarians of the University Library, Cambridge, who have been up and down their impregnable tower hundreds of times, burdened with grievous loads of fairy tales, and have never once complained; from Mrs Shirley Chestney and Mrs Brenda Taylor, who typed a manuscript that was always later than it should have been; and from the editors of the Cambridge University Press, who have made the business of book-production seem much more painless than it must have been in reality.

I felt that what I had to say in chapter IV could be said only as a commentary upon fairly long specimen passages, and I am therefore especially indebted to the following authors and publishers for their permission to quote copyright material: Shirley Goulden and W. H. Allen and Co. for an extract from *The Nightingale* in *More Tales from Hans Andersen*; J. R. Clark Hall and George Allen and Unwin Ltd for an extract from *Beowulf*; Amabel Williams-Ellis and Barrie Books Ltd for an extract from *Cinderella* in *Princesses and Trolls*; Basil Blackwell and Mott Ltd for the Gavin Bone translation of *Beowulf*; Rosemary Sutcliff, The Bodley Head and E. P. Dutton & Co. Inc. for an extract from *Beowulf*; R. P. Keigwin and Flensteds Forlag for an extract from *The Nightingale* by Hans Christian Andersen; The Hamlyn Group for an extract from *My Book of Cinderella* in the Odhams All Colour Book Series; M. R. Ridley and Kaye & Ward Ltd for an extract from *Sir Gawain and the Green Knight* in the Golden Legend Series; Rex Warner, MacGibbon & Kee Ltd and Farrar, Straus & Giroux Inc. for the extracts from *Men and Gods*; Thomas

Nelson & Sons Ltd for an extract from *Cinderella* in their Favourite Books Series; Ian Serraillier, Oxford University Press and Henry Z. Walck Inc. for extracts from *Beowulf the Warrior* and *The Challenge of the Green Knight*; Geoffrey Brereton and Penguin Books Ltd for an extract from *Cendrillon* in *The Fairy Tales of Charles Perrault*, Mary M. Innes and Penguin Books Ltd for extracts from *Metamorphoses*, Brian Stone and Penguin Books Ltd for an extract from *Sir Gawain and the Green Knight*; Wanda Gàg, Curtis Brown Ltd, Putnam's and Coward–McCann for an extract from *Cinderella* in *Tales from Grimm*.

I

Myths, Legends and Fairy Tales in the Lives of Children

I. PAST AND PRESENT FASHIONS

Once upon a time, and not so very far away or long ago, there would have been no need to give reasons for reading to children the stories that are commonly known as fairy tales, legends and myths. It is a pity that there is no one name that can be used for all of them. In rough and ready phrasing myths are about gods, legends are about heroes, and fairy tales are about woodcutters and princesses. A rather more respectable definition might run: myths are about the creation of all things, the origin of evil, and the salvation of man's soul; legends and sagas are about the doings of kings and peoples in the period before records were kept; fairy tales, folk tales and fables are about human behaviour in a world of magic, and often become incorporated in legends. Critics take an endless interest in the finer differences between them, but the common reader is more struck by the ways in which they all look rather like each other, and indeed merge into one another, and by the much more obvious differences that separate them from nineteenth-century novels, or stories about a family of children living in the East End in 1966. They are not realistic; they are almost unlocalized in time and space; they are often supernatural or at least fantastic in character; and the human beings in them are not three-dimensional people with complex motives and temperaments. These stories do hold a mirror up to nature, but they do not reflect the world as we perceive it with our senses at the present moment. J. R. R. Tolkien, who has written fairy tales and legends, sees them as works of 'sub-creation': in reading them we live in a Secondary World which is internally consistent and intricate, and is related to the Primary World (in which we all live for most of the time) by the human prerogative of generalization and abstraction. 'The mind that thought of *light, heavy, grey, yellow, still, swift*, also conceived of magic that would make heavy things light and able to fly, turn grey lead into yellow gold, and the still rock into swift water.'

Until the end of the eighteenth century traditional 'fairy tales' formed, almost by accident, the greater part of storytelling for very young children: uneducated nurses and servants told children the old stories they had been told themselves, because they were the only stories they knew. In the second half of the nineteenth century the work of men like Charles Kingsley and Andrew Lang was diverting the reading of eight- to twelve-year-olds away from drably realistic, moralising Victorian stories into the world of myth and 'faerie'. The Greek and Northern myths had become standard classroom reading by the 1920's. Most educated people of fifty can't remember not knowing who Perseus or Athene or Thor or the Marquis of Carabas were; the stories had 'got into the bloodstream'. Then the impact of the revival lost its force. As more and more convincingly realistic and not at all moral stories for children appeared year by year, the tale of Perseus, as Kingsley told it, looked drab in its turn: it dropped out of the syllabus. Many people of twenty who went to the same schools, and come from similar homes, have never heard of Perseus. Only the other day a student going into a primary school 'on practice' reported to her supervisor, with un- feigned enthusiasm, 'They seem to be doing a story about someone called Odysseus. It's really rather good; have you ever heard of it?'

At the moment there does seem to be a second revival. Since the last war many fresh versions of myths and legends have been made by accomplished and imaginative writers for children; people who love this kind of literature and hope that their children will love it owe a considerable debt to Roger Lancelyn Green, Barbara Leonie Picard and Ian Serraillier. The original work of C. S. Lewis in *The Chronicles of Narnia* and J. R. R. Tolkien in *The Lord of the Rings* shows that the world of 'faerie' is no dead world. The eight- to fourteen-year-olds who are never invited to enter it are, quite literally, deprived children.

2. SIGNIFICANCES AND VALUES

The inherent greatness of myth and fairy tale is a poetic greatness. The best stories are like extended lyrical images of unchanging human predicaments and strong, unchanging hopes and fears, loves and hatreds. Very diverse particular references have been attributed to these images by critics, according to training, or temperamental bias, or the fashions of the age in which they lived. In the nineteenth century philologists and folklorists saw them as pre-scientific, primitive descrip- tions of natural phenomena, of sunrise and sunset, or spring and winter: they supposed that the thunder gods Zeus and Odin were created by men because they did not understand the physical causes of thunder. In this century Freud has seen Zeus and Odin as terrible father figures, who represent sexual jealousies and antagonism between parents and children. Another kind of psychological explanation is given by Jung, for whom myths embody 'race memories' and represent conflicts not between father and son, but between *persona* and *anima* in one human being. Two anthropological theories have left their mark on modern criticism. Jessie Weston sees mythological stories as embroideries upon the actions performed in primitive fertility rituals; Robert Graves sees them as poetic records of the ritual marriage and slaughter of a sacred king, and of traceable historical events, conquests of matriarchal societies by patriarchal invaders, and the subjection of reigning priestesses to invading kings. Even before paganism was extinct, the fathers of the early Christian Church had seen a meaning in its images, interpreting them as Gentile prophecies of the truths of Christianity, and so preparing for the elaborate Christian allegorical readings which were worked out by mediaeval commentators. Hades and Niflheim, it seems, may 'mean' winter, or the womb, or sexual experience, or the dark side of man's soul, or infertility, or foreign conquest, or spiritual torment, or supernatural powers of evil. The testimony of all these witnesses seems to lead only to a paradox: none of them are right separately, and all of them are right collectively (perhaps Jung and the Christian Fathers tell, between them, rather more of the truth than the rest). The fixed point of a myth or a fairy tale lies in its own concrete nature; not in any of the things that it suggests to different readers, and not in its conjectural origins. The human imagination that merged ritual actions into a story, and made the story grow into a particular shape, is certainly as interesting as the imagination that produced the ritual actions. A myth 'is' everything that it has been and everything that it may become; it is like the chestnut-tree vainly asked by the poet to identify itself as one part of its growth:

> O chestnut-tree, great-rooted blossomer,
> Are you the leaf, the blossom or the bole?

There are indeed some fabulous leaves and blossoms that are felt to be artificial; it seems certain that they never grew out of the bole from which the living branches grew. This certainty is aesthetic, not historical. It does not matter if the branches grew into strange curves and contortions, instead of growing straight, as long as they are unmistakeably alive now. Beautiful and evocative stories may quite well be the product of unconscious misunderstanding and deliberate alteration.

A reader who takes his eyes off the story that is in front of him, and looks for something else behind it, will eventually see nothing but the theories he would have held whether he had read the story or not. To a reader who is attending to stories as they are, and above all to a child hearing them for the first time, Hades 'means' anything and everything he knows that can be described by the words *dark, cold, misty, formless*.

The human experience brought to mind by myth and fairy tale extends beyond the situations described by psychologists and anthropologists. It is conscious as well as unconscious, and civilised as well as primitive. In the story of Odysseus is contained both the love of home and a simultaneous love and fear of adventure and the unknown. Perseus and Beowulf and Jack the Giant Killer fight with dragons and monsters, and their battles remind us of any struggle against hostile circumstance—it is a great mistake to feel sorry for the dragon, as some adult readers do if they have not been brought up on fairy tales. The tasks imposed upon Heracles and upon Elisa in *The Wild Swans* recall any test of endurance and alter our understanding of it. The Arthurian quests and the search of the gardener's sons for the Golden Bird suggest any pursuit of an unattainable treasure. Theseus and innumerable tailors' and woodcutters' sons are obscure and ambitious young men with no apparent chance of realizing their ambitions. The Loathly Lady, the Frog Prince and the prince in *Beauty and the Beast* are creatures who are both fair and foul and remind us of any people or things that awaken love and hatred at one and the same time; and it may not be accidental that the theme of the breaking of a spell that has turned fair into foul is nearly always linked with the theme of the keeping of promises. The Secondary World of myth and fairy tale is a world of fighting, of sudden reverses of fortune, of promises kept and broken, of commands obeyed and disobeyed, of wanderings and quests, of testing and judgement, gratitude and ingratitude, and light and darkness. It is clearly impressed with patterns that anyone can trace more uncertainly in his own experience of the primary world. The realistic, localized story of Mrs Hodgson-Burnett's *The Secret Garden* shows a child what it is like for one little girl, very different from himself, to feel afraid: the story of *Beowulf* shows him fear in itself.

Childhood reading of symbolic and fantastic tales contributes something irreplaceable to any later experience of literature. It is not so much a matter of recognizing the more obscure classical references in

Paradise Lost as of accepting a whole mode of expression as both natural and serious. The realistic novel and play is, after all, a very recent part of our European inheritance. The whole world of epic, romance and allegory is open to a reader who has always taken fantasy for granted, and the way into it may be hard for one who never heard fairy tales as a child. An obvious route leads from the fairy tales of Grimm, and the *Chronicles of Narnia*, through the Northern myths and the Arthurian stories to Tolkien's *The Hobbit* and *The Lord of the Rings* and thence to *The Faerie Queene*.

There are advantages in knowing who's who and what happens in Greek and Northern myths and legends, if one is to be free to appreciate what individual writers have done with them; and because of their poetic fertility these stories have engendered countless original works of art, which give new motivation to the characters, or show new philosophical significance in the shape of the narrative, or create a new mood through the landscape against which the characters move—the 'tales twice told' without any tediousness range from Chaucer's *Troilus and Criseyde* to Wagner's *Ring* and Prokoviev's *Cinderella*. But it is much more important to be able to recognize *the kind of thing* that Wagner is doing in the *Ring*, and to realize that the plots of Shakespeare's *King Lear* and *The Winter's Tale* are by no means vestigial absurdities.

There is another door that can be opened by reading legends and fairy tales, and for some children, at the present time, there may be no other key to it. *Religio*, in one Latin sense of the word, implies a sense of the strange, the numinous, the totally Other, of what lies quite beyond human personality and cannot be found in any human relationships. This kind of 'religion' is an indestructible part of the experience of many human minds, even though the temper of a secular society does not encourage it, and the whole movement of modern theology runs counter to it. In Christian 'religious instruction' there is likely to be less and less *religio*: it may very well be in reading about a vision of the flashing-eyed Athene or the rosy-fingered Aphrodite that children first find a satisfying formulation of those queer prickings of delight, excitement and terror that they feel when they first walk by moonlight, or when it snows in May, or when, like the young Wordsworth, they have to touch a wall to make sure that it is really there. Magic is not the same as mysticism, but it may lead towards it; it is mystery 'told to the children'.

The ability to understand mythological references without using notes or a dictionary has been greatly overrated, and I would certainly put it last among the advantages of being brought up on the European tradition of myth and legend. It is not for nothing that students of English literature talk about 'classical *illusions*' when they have nothing better to say. Nevertheless something is lost from the symbolic potency of 'Was there another Troy for her to burn?' or 'Down, down I come, like glistering Phaethon', if one has to turn to the bottom of the page to discover that it was Helen who brought about the burning of Troy, or why Phaethon undertook the manage of his unruly jades. It is in the nature of a symbol to be inscrutable, to awaken overtones in the imagination, and information gathered within the last few seconds cannot awaken any overtones. It is only when the words *Helen*, *Phaethon*, *Siegfried*, *Bluebeard*, have the same untraceable imaginative history in the mind as words like *fire* and *stone* and *green*, that they can exercise their proper power. The greatest names do need to be known in this way: names like Aphrodite, Athene, Achilles, Yggdrasil, Galahad. Very few people in fact remember why Hephaestus fell from heaven 'from morn to noon, from noon to dewy eve, A summer's day', or who married Hermione, or the names of all the nine Muses. This does not matter very much, and it does not mean that the more obscure allusions are wasted upon a modern reader. If one knows most of the greater persons and places and actions, one knows the imaginative world in which the Greek and Northern gods exist. The names which are unknown or faintly remembered are enough to take one back 'far away and long ago', into Greek sunlight or Northern frost, and very often the English poet making the allusion has himself told as much of the story as one needs to know.

3. CHILDREN'S LIKES AND DISLIKES

Almost certainly J. R. R. Tolkien is right when he suggests that fairy tales became the peculiar property of the nursery by historical accident. They were not evolved for telling to children. They were folk tales, traditional stories as they developed in the unlettered classes of society, often retaining the skeleton plots of more poetic myths and legends. The uneducated nurses and servants who looked after the children of the upper and middle classes brought their stories with them. Myths about the gods, and legends about heroes, are even more obviously adult in origin, passing through the highly developed religious rituals and court cultures of the past. Schoolboys had to come across them in learning to read Latin and Greek poetry, but it was not until the nine-teenth century that it occurred to any writer that there was a natural affinity between the childhood of the race and the childhood of the individual human being.

Nevertheless the accidents that gave these stories to children were happy ones. Children under eleven are eager to know what happens next, and impatient with anything that stops them from getting on with the story. They want to listen to conversations only if direct speech is the quickest and clearest method of showing what was transacted between two people as a necessary preliminary to what these two people proceeded to *do*. At about nine or ten they are beginning to be interested in character, but in a very straightforward and moral way: they see people as marked by one particular attribute, cleverness, or kindness, or strictness, or being a good shot, and they mind whether things are right or wrong. They are especially sensitive to the heroic virtue of justice, and they are beginning to notice why people are tempted to be unjust. They are not interested in the long processes of inner debate by which people make difficult decisions, and become very irritated with grown-ups who insist upon giving them not only the practical answer or information they asked for, but also all the reasons for it. They expect a story to be a good yarn, in which the action is swift and the characters are clearly and simply defined. And legends and fairy tales are just like that. Playground games show that children like catastrophes and exhibitions of speed and power, and a clear differentiation between cowboys, cops and spacemen who are good, and Indians, robbers and space monsters who are bad.

Magic has a particular attraction for eight-to-ten-year-olds, but not because it is pretty or 'innocent'. They delight, in more senses than the usual one, in seeing how far they can go. If some people are taller than others, how tall could anyone conceivably be? If some people are cleverer than others at making things, could someone alter what things are actually made of? If there are different languages which different people understand, could there be a secret language that affected things and people against their will? Such speculations carried *ad infinitum* are given concrete form in giants, and the enchantments of elves and dwarfs, and the magic of runes and spells. The 'if' kind of question always requires consistency in the answer, and children of this age are often fascinated by consistency for its own sake, liking patterns because they are patterns, and working out for themselves intricate maps of imaginary islands and imaginary towns. The whole visual world of the

Greek myths (or the Northern myths, or the Arthurian romances)
satisfies this appetite imaginatively, because of the consistent mood,
form and colouring of its landscapes. So does the detail of most
mythical conceptions. If the moon were a goddess, or if a goddess were
the moon, where would she move, and what creatures would draw her
chariot?

One problem that has arisen quite recently, over the two last generations, may be partially resolved by the modern revival of myths and
fairy tales. Realistic novelists, whether they write for children or
grown-ups, usually write about what they know best themselves, and
take for granted certain experiences and moral presuppositions in their
readers. Some writers present a wider range of class and locality than
others, and the best writers do not make the mistake of supposing that
all the virtues reside in one class and all the vices in another; but there
is rarely any doubt about what they know from the inside, or about the
kind of people they are writing for. Dickens is not writing for people
who live in Tom All Alone's, and he does not pretend that he has lived
there himself. What happens, though, if one tries to read Eve Garnett's
Family from One End Street to a class of eleven-year-olds in a British
school today? Some of them come from families not unlike the one in the
story; some are Jamaican immigrants living in one room; and there may
also be the children of a well-to-do and modern-minded doctor, a poor
and old-fashioned clergyman, and a brilliant and divorced oboist. It is
impossible for this particular audience to be drawn together in listening
to this particular story; either the events themselves or Eve Garnett's
way of describing them will touch a raw nerve. It is difficult to be sure
of her own attitude to the family she has created: sometimes she seems
to take them for granted, and sometimes they seem to be 'low' characters in a comedy of manners. Contemporary comedy of manners always
requires a homogeneous audience. Children cannot be expected to
share in a *joke* about the lives of people very like some of them and very
unlike others. A recent fashion in secondary school English courses has
encouraged the study of passages which are deliberately chosen in order
to expose and emphasize the social differences between members of one
school class; among fifteen-year-olds some of these passages fall flat
because the humour cannot be shared. Younger children are even more
sensitive about their homes. The situations and emotions which are
represented in myth and fairy tale have some counterpart in their lives
however they have been brought up, and they turn into an audience
that is corporate and unselfconscious.

Stories that lead to doing things are all the more attractive to children, who are active rather than passive creatures. Myths and fairy tales provide an unusually abundant choice of things to do. Largely because they are archetypal and anonymous (in quality, if not in provenance), they will stand reinterpretation in many forms without losing their character. They can be recreated by children not only in words but in drama, in mime, in dance and in painting. Action in them is not fussy, and lends itself to qualitative expression in the movements of the human body and in the shapes and colours of non-figurative painting. I have seen two ten-year-olds playing at Theseus and the Minotaur in a solitary orchard with no grown-up, as they thought, within sight or hearing.

II

From Eight to Fourteen: a
Choice of Myths, Legends and Fairy Tales
for Different Ages

1. THE GREEK MYTHS AND LEGENDS

'All our religion, almost all our law, almost all our arts, almost all that
sets us above savages has come to us from the shores of the Mediter-
ranean'—that was Dr Johnson's tribute to our inheritance from the
world of classical antiquity. Some critics in this century would like to
extend the tribute to the shores of the Baltic, but it remains true that
the myths and legends of the Greeks have remained continuously in
the European mind as no others have (except those of the Bible), that
more of them have survived, and that the Greek and Latin poetry from
which we know them is more varied in narrative style, in mood and
colouring, than the sources of any other mythology that has affected
our civilization. They must provide at least half the literary allusions
in English poetry and half the subjects of the narrative painting and
sculpture of Europe. If the pressure of timetables and a world too full
of information force one to tell children *either* Greek *or* Northern
myths, the Greek myths should tip the balance. There is a hard, alert,
often cheerful objectivity in the way in which most of them were told
in antiquity, whether by early or late writers; it is congenial to many
children between the ages of eight and eleven and the best modern
versions manage to retain it.

Children usually like the same Greek myths that poets like and use
most frequently, especially the ones that are (in one of their 'meanings')
about sun and moon and the seasons and the origins of human crafts;
the ones that can be read in part as lyrical 'just-so-stories'. They are
usually bored by the Greek creation myths, by the genealogies of the
Olympian gods, and the stories of their past battles with Titans and
giants: anyway, these things are much more poetically imaged in
Northern mythology. Nor do they like the tales of the philanderings
of Zeus and Apollo in the guise of bull or swan, and may be bewildered

or shocked by them. These stories have contributed a great deal of elegant ornament and some more serious symbolism to European love poetry, but in themselves they do not have the universality of the stories of Prometheus and Phaethon. Robert Graves has given a limited historical interpretation of them, and if he is right, their natural poetic significance may be equally limited. It takes a new process of allegorizing to be able to write

> And Pan did after Syrinx speed
> Not as a nymph, but for a reed . . .

This idea is not naturally present in the story of Pan and Syrinx, and children would not be interested in it if it were.

It may be worthwhile to recollect that the patterns of Greek mythology are not confined to the Zeus–Europa and Pan–Syrinx *motifs*, because in educational institutions it is still possible to hear complaints about 'all those immoral gods'. Of course, the Olympian gods are *amoral*. They are (like Nature, or accident, or 'life'), indifferent to desert; and although they faithfully take care of men who accept their favours and obey them, they bear grudges against those who unwittingly offend them, and their greatest battles are fought not against the powers of darkness but against each other, or against the men who challenge their supremacy. This is not to say that they are always chasing terrified maidens, or that they are never invested with otherworldly splendour.

The Greek heroic legends are of three kinds: stories of exploration and quests and magical adventures; the stories of the Trojan War, which are about nobility in battle crossed by disloyalty and spite, a dramatic and often deeply moving cycle; and the stories of the two doomed royal houses of Mycenae and Thebes, the first descended from Tantalus and inheriting the curse placed upon him for his unnatural sin, and the second, descended from Cadmus, offending against Tantalus' son Pelops and inheriting a curse from him. Oedipus, Antigone, Agamemnon, Orestes and Electra are all born to misery. The legends of their lives are tales of violent crime within the family, and of guilt and retribution and reconciliation: they have been shaped into the form in which we now know them by the tragic dramatists of fifth-century Athens, and are quite beyond the imaginative grasp of any children under eleven. The tale of Theseus, Phaedra and Hippolytus is very like them; versions of the Theseus stories written for children nearly always leave it out. These legends can be appreciated best through reading, at seventeen or later, the tragedies of Aeschylus and Sophocles and the original plays which T. S. Eliot and O'Neill derived from them.

The first Greek stories that children can take into their imaginative lives seem to be the adventures of Perseus and Jason and Theseus— the stories that Kingsley chose for *The Heroes*, which remained a success for over sixty years after its first publication in 1856; the Victorian storytellers were very shrewd in guessing which of the Greek tales would be best-sellers if only they were told in the right way. Children usually enjoy these heroic legends when they are eight or nine. The years between nine and eleven seem to be about the right age for the more intense legend of Odysseus, and for some of the shorter, more poetic myths about the exploits of the gods, and some of the fables of the early days of men. The long, intricate legend of the Trojan War is a story for over-elevens, and one that should not be missed.

As they exist in the mind today, and as they have always existed in the minds of poets and painters, these diverse Greek stories are inseparable from the character of the Greek and Latin poems in which they have been embodied; it is only a highly modern and highly professional archaeologist's eye that looks behind the poem in order to reconstruct a primitive religious picture. Some feeling for the different kinds of literary art that formed these poems is therefore quite a practical asset to the storyteller who is searching for something that will please this or that group of children. It is by no means a waste of time to read a few episodes in the original sources, when there are good translations; it may make all the difference in the business of finding the right story, and the right version of it, and the right way of thinking and talking about it.

The stories of Perseus, Jason and Theseus are full of marvels and single combats; apart from a more aristocratic temper, and a feeling that journeys are long and hard and really do approach the world's end, they are rather like some of the fairy tales which had always been given to children. Andrew Lang included in his *Blue Fairy Book* a version of the Perseus legend beginning 'Once upon a time'. We know the story of Jason chiefly from Apollonius of Rhodes and Ovid, and that of Perseus from Apollodorus and Ovid—all comparatively late and sophisticated writers. It does not follow (this has often been said) that because they wrote in the third, second and first centuries B.C. they lost symbols from the deep past that Homer might have preserved in the eighth or seventh century. Many traditional details may have been kept by accident, and still more cherished for their picturesqueness. Nevertheless it remains true that Apollonius and Ovid were entertaining their readers; although they included plenty of horror and magic and strange scenes, they told their tales with a certain lightheartedness. This mixture gives younger children exactly what they want. Within Victorian conventions Kingsley caught the Ovidian kind of romancing in his slow, spellbound prose; in a series of recent versions Ian Serraillier catches it in fast language which is too bright for everyday use. Danger and horror is thereby made at once vivid and remote, and this is one way in which children learn to face, without shock, what would otherwise be unendurable.

The stories of Perseus and Jason are both about unrecognized princes who have to prove their royal birth, and about their quests into unexplored lands. Perseus flies to the cold northern wastes to cut off the head of the Gorgon Medusa, and Jason sails northwards to distant Colchis to bring back the Golden Fleece of a magic ram, meeting monsters and savage hosts when he touches unknown shores on his way. In both stories the heroes carry off princesses; Perseus finds Andromeda chained to a rock, waiting to be eaten by a sea monster, and Jason is aided in Colchis by the king's daughter Medea, all the more fascinating because she is a witch. The crucial scenes of action and magic are described by Ovid and Apollonius in minute detail which makes them moving pictures in words, and creates an astringent contrast between the extraordinary thing that is being described and the accurate, down-to-earth method of describing it. No one is ever likely to forget the moment when Perseus sees Medusa reflected in his shield, or when Medea chants her spells over the dragon while the Golden Fleece itself gives the only light in the sacred grove of Ares.

The stories of Theseus are known chiefly from the dull prose summaries compiled by Apollodorus and from the much more detailed prose chronicle written by the biographer Plutarch in the first century A.D. Plutarch is a more sober writer than Ovid or Apollonius, and some of his sceptical spirit seems to have entered the Theseus legends when he put them together. In many ways they are not unlike the stories of Jason and Perseus. Theseus is another unknown prince who has to claim his inheritance, and show that he deserves to be a king by paying out the robbers and giants who molest travellers on the perilous road to Athens. These early episodes of the story are satisfactorily gruesome, but the best and most distinctive part comes later. After he has been recognized as heir to the kingdom of Athens, he offers himself as one of the band of youths and maidens who are paid as tribute to King Minos of Crete, to be eaten by the man-bull, the Minotaur, who is imprisoned in a maze in the palace of Cnossos. From this point there is dramatic tension in the story, and something resembling a plot. Theseus tells King Aegeus of Athens that if he kills the Minotaur he will hoist white sails on his ships, in place of the black ones with which he leaves; the audience therefore share the suspense of the waiting Athenians, and when they hear that Theseus has forgotten this agreement they anticipate the grief of Aegeus, and wonder what he will do. Whatever the origin of the maze may be—a ritual dance floor, or some architectural peculiarity of Cnossos—it makes the wrestling of Theseus and the Minotaur one of the most spectacular of all fights with fantastic monsters. Theseus has to feel his way inward through the dark paths, listening to the terrible sounds at the centre, and it is only because the Cretan princess Ariadne has suddenly fallen in love with him, and given him a ball of thread, that he is able to find his way out again. His elopement with Ariadne and the secret launching of the ships make a swift, romantic ending to the Cretan exploit. Children seem to respond to the suicide of Aegeus as a fitting conclusion to the whole story; sometimes they are disappointed if it is preceded by Theseus' desertion of Ariadne on the island of Naxos. As this is originally a separate legend there is no reason why it should not be cut, if it is likely to make the victor's triumphant forgetfulness seem too far-fetched to be credible. On the other hand the procession of Dionysus and the crowning of Ariadne on Naxos are beautiful in themselves: some children may be attracted by their gleaming images of starriness and leafiness, and the divine elevation of the deserted princess gives this little vignette some likeness to the Cinderella story.

The legends of Heracles are superficially rather like those of Perseus, Jason and Theseus, and they used to be favourites for telling to young children; but I find the Twelve Labours too many by half, and most eight- and nine-year-olds seem to agree with me in thinking that Heracles' adventures are rather flat, and that his career is rather monotonous. As it is, two or three of the Labours are enough, and one should be the killing of the Nemean lion. The visual image of Heracles with his club and lionskin seems to have been more powerful in the minds of post-classical poets than any of the records of what he did.

So far as mere events are concerned, the story of Odysseus is another legend that is rather like the stories of Perseus and Jason and Theseus: on the way home from the Trojan War he is shipwrecked and lost, and encounters hostile giants and monsters, savage rocks and delaying enchantresses. But no one could now tell it in quite the same way, because it is impossible to forget how Homer shaped it, and the vision of life that informs his poem. The eighth or seventh century *Odyssey* is epic, not romance. It was composed orally by a professional minstrel, to be sung or intoned as part of the ceremonial feasts of men who were themselves warriors, although no longer petty kings and vassals. Homer is objective, but the fate of Odysseus matters, and he is a thinking and feeling being. The artificial poetic language gives the story a kind of resonance. The ceremonious dignity of the *Odyssey*, and its sharp humour as well, make it a story for ten-year-olds rather than eight-year-olds. It is a pity to use any version that is not full enough to retain something of its poetic character. Barbara Leonie Picard's is a good one. Wisely, she puts the adventures of Odysseus in straightforward chronological order, instead of the sophisticated flash-back sequence of the original, which is dramatic to a grown-up audience but muddling to children. The Marvin version is very Homeric in language, and useful for quotation [Short List no. 24].

The sea-god Poseidon, whom Odysseus has offended almost as soon as he sets sail, is felt throughout the story as a malignant, baneful power that frustrates human efforts to survive. Storms are described so concretely and accurately that the mass and weight of the waves can be felt as one listens. In the same way, 'Athene put it into his head' is not merely an awkward periphrasis for 'it occurred to him': one is aware of the inspiration and protection of the flashing-eyed goddess as if it were a kind of providence. The gods bicker among themselves, but as E. V. Rieu has said, 'the comic element is introduced almost solely on occasions when [they] are shown together...When dealing with mankind, each in his own capacity, they are far from amusing.'

The strange adventures that befall Odysseus are exciting and all the more convincing because of the circumstantial detail with which they are introduced. The outwitting of the Cyclops Polyphemus and the undoing of Circe's spells are beautifully-shaped tales of fantasy and suspense. The cave of the man-eating Polyphemus is dark, vast and bloodstained in just the right way; that is to say it is both gruesome and entertaining, because of Homer's pictures of the one-eyed giant's huge domestic utensils. Children enjoy the sardonic joke when Odysseus tells him that his own name is 'No one', so that when he is blinded and robbed of his victims he can only shout 'No one is killing me', and they like his cleverness when he binds his men to the bellies of the gigantic sheep as they go out to pasture, and clings to the wool of the last ram himself. Circe first drugs her guests with magic wine and then turns them into tame beasts. Her story became in time an allegory of the sensationalism that first turns sour and then destroys the human free-will of those who seek it. Her actions are repeated, with many changes of name and reversals of role, in the actions of Spenser's Acrasia and Busirane, and Milton's Comus. Children often have more intuitive understanding of this unhappy 'hooked' enchantment than one might suppose. They nearly always see the point of Christina Rossetti's *Goblin Market*, which was written for a child audience and says virtually the same about the effect of a magic juice instead of a magic wine. In the defeat of Homer's Circe hints of these deeper ideas are balanced by practical things which can be enjoyed in a different way. The furniture of the palace is described exactly, with delight in its fine workmanship; Odysseus remembers to use his magic herb rightly, and forces Circe to turn the pigs back into men while remaining entirely courteous to her.[1] The story moves quickly to this second climax, and ends in the satisfaction of peaceful, unbewitched feasting by Circe and Odysseus and all their followers.

The temptations of Odysseus by the Lotos-Eaters and the Sirens are magic tales of a similar kind, very like fairy tales in pattern and almost certainly separate in origin from the story of a Greek prince returning from Troy. Yet even when the magic is most magical, and the action most exciting, one is aware of what goes on in Odysseus' head as he lays his plans to save himself or his men. The character of Odysseus is a force in the story, and binds its episodes together. He is not what we would call a 'real' human being; he is more of an embodiment of prudence, craftiness and single-minded determination. Nevertheless he is a being whose actions invite comment and discussion, and Perseus is not.

The princess Nausicaa, too, is quite different from the faceless Andromeda. Nausicaa is the daughter of the king of the Phaeacians, a civilized, gentle people on whose island Odysseus is washed up after a cruel storm. She comes to the mouth of a river to wash clothes in preparation for her coming marriage; not knowing that Odysseus is hidden under leaves in a thicket, asleep, she plays ball with her maidens, and a shout when the ball rolls away wakes him up. Instead of running away and shrieking, she goes to meet the alarming naked castaway,

---

[1] Of course the stratagem of *Odyssey* X, 325 ff., has to be bowdlerized in telling the story to any children. It is modified quite satisfactorily in good recent versions.

and decorously shows him how he can win the protection of her parents. He had better not accompany her on the road, she suggests, since she may be thought to be supercilious towards her Phaeacian suitors. She has a mind, but she is no romantic. She watches Odysseus sadly from behind a pillar when she knows that he has to return home, and in her parting words recognizes that she will have to marry a Phaeacian in the long run.

When Odysseus reaches Ithaca at last the story is dominated by shrewdly observed human feelings and practical contrivances. Athene tells him that his wife Penelope is being molested by a rabble of suitors, and miraculously transforms him into a beggar so that he can get into his own house with the support of his one loyal servant, the swineherd Eumaeus. His son also returns, and the conduct of the suitors towards all these unwanted persons shows them for what they are. Penelope has already appointed the next day for her choice of a second husband: she is going to take the first man who can use the supposedly dead hero's bow, so Odysseus is only just in time to disarm the suitors by stealth and then reveal himself. During these crowded days Penelope and Eumaeus and the nurse Eurycleia behave like credible, although simple human beings; and the final plot and battle has all the attractiveness of a police hunt that ends in the mopping up of the gang. The story of the *Odyssey* is fantastic, and became symbolic in the mind of James Joyce: the telling of it comes near to realism.

The right age for hearing about Odysseus is probably the right age for hearing some of the shorter myths about the gods. The ones that children of ten like best seem to be among those that appear most constantly in the themes and images of English poets—the stories of Demeter and Persephone, Orpheus and Eurydice, Prometheus, and Phaethon. Since these are such short stories, and since they contain the seeds of so many ideas and experiences, they need to be told rather slowly, with a good deal of word-painting. Roger Lancelyn Green's *Old Greek Fairy Tales* are free variations on classical narratives, and suit children of eight and nine. Rex Warner's versions, which are too detailed for children when he is retelling the longer myths and legends, are sometimes quite right for reading these stories aloud to ten- and eleven-year-olds; sometimes passages from his work, or from a translation of Ovid (or Vergil, for the story of Orpheus) can be interpolated into a reading from the shorter versions of Graves or Genest, or into an informal narrative in one's own words. The visual, leisured story-telling of Ovid is the channel through which most of the Greek myths of the gods flowed into European tradition. There are earlier, Greek sources for many of them in the Homeric hymns, in Hesiod's *Theogony*, and in other writings: references to the literary origins now known have made been easily available by H. J. Rose, Carl Kerenyi and Robert Graves [Short List nos. 56, 52–3, 50]. Some of these are no more than allusions or summaries, and the style of the Homeric hymns, although beautiful, is too glancing to be followed by anyone writing for children. The myths that were not touched by the Latin poets did not as a rule survive in European art. A good deal of modern re-discovery of primitive Greek myth depends upon looking at archaic vase-paintings and reliefs, which were unknown to the creative artists of the Renascence and the Romantic period.

The story of the abduction of Persephone by Hades has been explained as one of the myths in which a priestess is defeated by a king, or as one of those which describe the annual burying of a corn-puppet; it has been said that the story of Orpheus stems from a myth of ritual placation of the Great Goddess, in which Eurydice does not appear at all. Other critical interpretations are closer to poetic tradition, in which both these stories are images of rebirth; the theme of release from death is linked with the theme of a divine command that must be obeyed implicitly. The snatching of Persephone into the underworld for three months and her return in spring symbolizes the death and reawakening of the earth (and of anything that dies), and the length of her imprison-ment is determined by her disobedience when she forgets Hades' pro-hibition. The return to earth of Eurydice suggests the release of the human soul, and she, too, has to go back to the underworld because she disobeys Hades. It is hardly surprising that these stories have been told over and over again; they are lyrical in form, and in both there is a climax that invites dramatic treatment. At the last moment Orpheus looks back at Eurydice, only to see her fading into the underworld just as she was about to step into the light: Vergil's vision of her 'like smoke merging with thin air' has become part of the story. The malignant Ascalaphus threatens to hold Persephone in the underworld even after Demeter has searched her out 'with all that pain', when he reveals that she has eaten the three pomegranate seeds.

Modern critics are divided about the importance of the stories of Prometheus and Phaethon, and about the original meaning of them; they have grown into myths which are important to poets, because they are images of rebellion against authority. The Titan Prometheus is an ambivalent figure in Greek versions of the story; he becomes a hero in

Romantic poetry. By stealing the heavenly fire for the benefit of mankind and incurring the punishment of Zeus for his sacrilege, he represents human independence and free-will and the suffering that goes with it. The myth of Prometheus is not so much a story as a single haunting image—the figure of Prometheus chained to a rock, 'ages of hopeless end', while every day vultures tear out his liver and every night the wounds heal to perpetuate his torture. It haunted Blake when he drew the purgation of Oothoon, and is so horrible in its closeness to much ordinary human pain that it may seem too horrible for children. Some are in fact revolted by it; others, if it is told sharply and objectively, show the same kind of interest that they show in the Genesis myth of the Fall. There are eleven-year-olds who want to see whether the knowledge of good really is 'dear bought by knowing ill', and who argue fiercely about the sentence of Zeus.

The story of Phaethon presents no moral dilemma. Phaethon is the child of Helios, the sun, and a mortal mother, Clymene, and he is goaded into begging Helios to let him drive the magnificent chariot of the sun across the sky. Helios gives in reluctantly, leaving him with precise instructions about steering the right course and controlling the horses; in his excitement he forgets them, and Zeus destroys him before he can destroy the earth. It is a clear case of just retribution for vanity, and has even been seen as a patriarchal allegory warning men against listening to female advice. But it is not a trite fable. There is a natural poetic force in the sequence of Phaethon's moods—in his passionate longing to take the place that only a god can fill, followed by empty-headed conceit, excitement and panic. As Ovid tells the story, the chariot of the sun creates burnt deserts and icy wastes when Phaethon cannot stop the horses from plunging too near the earth or rearing too high above it, and children like these ingenious 'just-so-story' details. At the beginning Ovid's descriptions of the palace and chariot of Helios give them clever, intricate visual images of pure heat and light.

Among other shorter myths and fables that are known successes with ten- and eleven-year-olds are the stories of Daedalus and Icarus, Dionysus and Pan and Midas, Epimetheus and Pandora, Athene and Arachne, and Eros and Psyche.

The story of Daedalus and Icarus is loosely attached to the story of Theseus and the Minotaur, since Daedalus was the exiled Athenian master-craftsman who built the maze in which the Minotaur was kept. It is a complete story, and worth telling on its own. The sequence of event and mood is not unlike that of the Phaethon myth; when Daedalus wants to return to Greece he is in danger from Minos, either because his services are invaluable or because Theseus has already escaped and his work is suspect. He makes feathered wings for himself and his son Icarus, copying the pattern from the wings of birds; he warns Icarus to steer a middle course between the sun and the sea, but Icarus is intoxicated by the first excitement of flying, the wax that holds the feathers melts, and he drops into the sea and drowns. The first part of the story reflects a curiosity which is common to children and myth-makers and fabulists. They all like speculating about the way in which things were first found or first made—and children of ten and eleven seem to have no difficulty in knowing whether the question is historical or poetic. They can see quite well that a just-so-story is different from a photograph of a Stone Age pot. The second part of the Daedalus story expresses a basic emotional pattern in the immediate terms of movement; confidence gives way to terror as the wing-beats become more and more rapid, and then begin to fail and lose their rhythm.

The stories of Pandora, Arachne and Pan all bring in the beginnings of things. Pandora is the Eve of the Greek stories of the origin of evil; she is brought to man by Epimetheus the Heedless, as an exact counter-part of the gift of fire brought by his brother Prometheus. The tale of the box which she is forbidden to open, and does open, is an anti-feminist fable, but there is a further (perhaps later) theme in the con-tents of the box; after all its blights and diseases have flown out to spoil the world of man, Hope comes from the bottom to remain with him. The story of Arachne takes us back to Athene's gift of the art of weaving, showing a contest between the inventor goddess and a mortal girl who is skilful and stupid enough to beat her at her own game. The story of Midas' rash judgement between the piping of Pan and the lyre-playing of Apollo takes us back to the invention of musical instruments; it became in time a poetic image of two kinds of art which can be enchanting, the simple and primitive no less than the sophisticated. Midas is certainly punished for awarding the prize to Pan, but this is one of the stories that can be 'adopted by both parties'. Our understanding of the natural world would be much the poorer if there were no figure of the goat-god Pan in our minds, suggesting a power which is both humble and strange, intimate and terrifying. King Midas is less impor-tant to us than Pan, but he is a symbolic figure of affluence and acquisi-tiveness, and he has become a byword for many of the defects of Very Important People. He looks forward to showing off and does not bother to think before he speaks when he asks Dionysus for the gift of turning everything that he touches into gold; when he grows ass's ears as a punishment for his bad taste in music he still has not learnt to hold his tongue. He has to tell the reeds about them, and the reeds repeat his words for ever.

The story of Eros and Psyche was told by Apuleius in the second century A.D., and it is so unlike anything else in myth and legend that some mythographers exclude it from their canon. It has a fairy-tale plot, and the characters are consciously conceived as symbols, as figures representing Love and the Soul. Earlier readers made no such distinction; for them it was just one of the classical stories, and among the most evocative of them. At the most Psyche was the

latest born and loveliest vision far
Of all Olympus' faded hierarchy.

The tale *is* lovely, and some children respond to its loveliness. There is no need to talk about the 'meaning' of the allegory; it is sufficiently embodied in Psyche's promise not to look at her mysterious husband who comes only in darkness, her mistrust, and her penances when she has lost him through her own curiosity.

The 'tale of Troy divine' is the most complex of Greek heroic legends but it is so important in European tradition and so moving in its greatest scenes that children ought to hear it when they can. It is a story for the years between eleven and fourteen, and cannot be told earlier, even with skilful cutting. It is a mistake to isolate the apparently 'fairy tale-ish' episode of the Wooden Horse and tell it as a nursery story; if the treachery of Sinon and Helen's mimicry of the voices of Penelope and Clytemnestra are left out, it isn't even a very good story.

As Homer records it in the *Iliad*, the siege of Troy is a saga of jealousy, revenge and occasional nobility and compassion among both gods and men: it is founded upon the wrath of Achilles when he thinks that his deserts are slighted by his own leader Agamemnon, and upon the Olympian feud between Apollo and Aphrodite on the one hand, and Hera and Athene on the other. These enmities lead to the substitution of Patroclus for Achilles in a sortie against Trojan raiders, and his death at the hands of Hector; to the inflamed hatred of Achilles towards Hector which makes him fight again, kill Hector and mangle his dead body; and to his final relenting when Priam begs him to restore the body of his son. Achilles is the tragic hero of the poem. From his wrath, stung by the wrath of the gods, the other events proceed inexorably. The single combats and mêlées are marked by the helplessness of human warriors when the gods intervene, and the realization that defeat and misery may be lying in wait for any man.

The *Iliad* does not include the story of the Judgement of Paris, which gives a more remote origin to the feud between Aphrodite and Athene, and a divine sanction to the rape of Helen, which causes the war in the first place; nor does it continue the history of the war to the fall of Troy—it ends with the ending of Achilles' wrath. The stories of the death of Achilles, the trick of the Wooden Horse, and the capture and sack of Troy are known from the reminiscences of Helen and Menelaus in the *Odyssey*, from Vergil's *Aeneid*, and from classical mythographers: the fate of the Trojan captives and the returning Greek princes are the subject of fifth-century tragedies. Most people suppose that these tales of the origins and consequences of the war were told in Homer's time, and earlier, in epics or short heroic poems that have been lost.

Since the legend of the Trojan War is not episodic like the legend of the wanderings of Odysseus, and is especially close-knit in the *Iliad*, it does not fall easily into a series of self-contained lessons or broadcasts. Anyone who sets out to tell it to children needs to make plain the threads of fate and cause and effect, and the dominating attributes of the *dramatis personae*: the jealousy of Hera, the corrupted nobility of Achilles, the canniness of Odysseus, the pliability of Helen. To do this it is usually necessary to leave out a good many of the raids, sorties and repulses described by Homer and included in many modern versions for children, and to abolish some of the subordinate warriors altogether. The eighth-century audience of the *Iliad* felt an intense personal interest in the technique of hand-to-hand fighting, which no one, except perhaps a professional wrestler, could feel today. What is described should be described at leisure, in concrete detail, in order to make the events clear in the mind's eye and suggest the heroic magnitude of the legend. Without necessarily using a full translation, one needs to say almost *as much as* Homer says about the first long angry speech of Achilles, or the complaint of Achilles to Thetis by the shore, or Hector's farewell to Andromache, or the horses of Achilles weeping for their dead master, or Priam's words to Achilles when he asks him to think of the isolation of his own aging father, and says 'I have raised to my lips the hand of the man who killed my son.'

Roger Lancelyn Green's *The Tale of Troy* [Short List nos. 16 and 17] is a coherent and dignified version of the whole Trojan cycle; in reading aloud from it one might make quite extensive cuts at some points and use a translation of the *Iliad* at others.

2. THE NORTHERN MYTHS AND LEGENDS

European civilization and literature are not visibly rooted in the traditional stories of Germany and Scandinavia, as they are in the stories of Greece; but the Northern myths and legends have a significance of their own, and a beauty to which some children are especially sensitive. C. S. Lewis read these stories at some time before he was ten and 'was uplifted into huge regions of northern sky...desired with almost sickening intensity something never to be described (except that it is cold, spacious, severe, pale, and remote)'. In *Varieties of Parable* Louis MacNeice gives the same kind of testimony to his feelings about them as a child.

By now it is something of a commonplace to say that Scandinavian sagas and Old English poems express nostalgia and a delight in natural beauty; and that these emotions are both foreign to the classical world, and yet so strong in later English literature that they must flow into it from some 'tap root' in Northern legend, even though the names of the heroes of the North are hardly mentioned until the Romantic and Philological Revivals brought them to light in the nineteenth century.[1] It may not be accidental that in the later poetry of Latin countries there is nothing like 'black Tennyson's articulate despair', or the passionate loyalty of *In Memoriam* and its agonizing over the grounds for belief in personal immortality. In Valhalla the heroic dead lived and feasted; it was only the cowards who died a straw death that went into the misty darkness of Niflheim. In the *Odyssey* it is the shadowy form of the hero Achilles who says 'rather would I live on ground as the hireling of another...than bear sway among all the dead that be departed'.

It is less of a commonplace to say, as J. R. R. Tolkien does, that the Northern gods and the Olympians take a different place in the processes of time, and that in Northern myths the gods have a peculiar relationship both with men and with the equally supernatural powers of darkness. They are all subject to Fate. The Olympians were unpredictable and immutable, and no longer much bothered by the giants they superseded, but the Northern gods are allied with man in perpetual war against the frost-giants, even though they know that the giants will win

---

[1] The 'Romantic Revival' is a name often given to the literature of the period 1780–1830, which gave new importance to evocative imagery, to imaginative perception, and to picturesque settings and stories from the remote past. The 'Philological Revival' is a name for the movement in nineteenth-century scholarship which renewed interest in the development of languages and in their relationships to one another and to a common root. It was centred in Germany.

in the end. 'In Norse...the gods are within time, doomed with their allies to death. Their battle is with the monsters and the outer darkness.' They are on the same side as 'man alien in a hostile world'. It is integrity that counts, not success, and it is worth fighting for lost causes.

The Northern stories therefore intensify the heroic ideal of courage and loyalty. The hero must keep his promises and justify his boast-words. Courage and loyalty are virtues which children of ten can appreciate as virtues. They seem to see, more clearly than their sophisti-cated elders, that these qualities are, in sober fact, the foundation of any human goodness. A coward will only be kind or truthful as long as he is not frightened, and a promise-breaker will change his mind regardless of the wreckage of someone else's life, which may be unknown to him. Human relationships do depend upon the exact and literal keeping of promises.

During the last two centuries Northern myths and legends have been consciously present in the imagination of Europe. Wagner is the greatest of the rediscoverers, a myth-maker in his own right: in England the world-picture of this mythology meant a great deal to Carlyle and William Morris: more recently it has gone into the making of *The Lord of the Rings*.

The strongest imaginative conceptions of the Northern stories lie in pictures, not in events, and for this reason children usually come to them a year or two later than they come to classical stories. They some-times enjoy them at nine or ten, but more often begin to be excited by them at about eleven. The figure of Thor, with his red beard and huge hands and magic hammer Miollnir, is really more stirring than anything he does in his conflicts with the giants. Even more impressive than the figures of gods and goddesses are the cosmological symbols: the chasm from which the world of men was created, filled with ice, with Niflheim to the North and burning Muspelheim to the South; the separate habitations of gods and men and giants and elves and dwarfs; the world-tree Yggdrasil, with its three roots in Asgard, in Niflheim and in Middle-Earth, its branches holding up the sky and its trunk con-stantly gnawed by a dragon; the world-serpent Jormungand, offspring of the half-god Loki and a giant-maiden, encircling the earth and waiting to devour it.

The best Northern myths are the ones about the beginning and end of the created world. These stories contain some genealogy which bores children, and should be cut, but they like the idea of the two beings that first took shape in the white rime, the frost-giant Ymir and the cow Audumla whose warm tongue licked the ice and so released the first of the gods. The struggle between frost and warmth, between evil and good, is carried on throughout the age of gods and men. The downfall of their world is brought about by the treachery of Loki, the god of the kindled fire which may save man or destroy him, the being who is not perfectly of one kind and therefore knows no loyalty.

The stories of the theft of the apples of Iduna and of the death of Balder can be told to show how the end comes out of the beginning. Loki sacrifices Iduna and her apples, and with them the perpetual youth of the gods, in order to save his own skin; but Fate allows his tricks to succeed, and he is able to rescue her. Fire is jealous of the sun; Loki contrives the death of Balder, the most beautiful of the gods and the protector of light. This story is the most dramatic of the Northern myths. It embodies the theme of conflict between light and darkness, since like Persephone Balder has to go down to Niflheim—but unlike Persephone, not to return until the end of the world; and it unites it with the theme of an unsuspected weakness in the preparations of any-one who tries to frustrate the working of Fate. Balder is killed by the weak mistletoe, the one creature that had not been asked to swear not to harm him, just as Achilles was killed by a wound in the heel that had not been dipped in Styx, and Sigurd by a wound in the shoulder that had not been bathed in the dragon's blood.

The death of light means the death of the natural world, and the last battle of gods and men is a tragic consequence of the death of Balder. Loki first shuns the gods, and then sneers at them and is imprisoned under the ground. When he breaks loose he is joined by all his mon-strous offspring and by all the giants. In Ragnarok, the last battle, the gods perish, but not before they have killed their enemies of Ymir's line. The world burns in the fire of Muspelheim, and Balder and Hod, the only gods absent from Middle Earth, return to begin a new order among a new race of gods and men. The story of Ragnarok does not have very much plot, but it is full of wonderful pictures, and infused with the ideas of unconquerable time and the predicament of 'man alien in a hostile world.'

In the brief space of time that the world lasts the gods often pit their cunning or magic against the strength of the giants, and they win for the time being. It would be tedious to tell more than two or three of these stories consecutively, because the pattern of events is repetitive. The most vital are perhaps those of Odin's purchase of wisdom from Mimir at the cost of his right eye, building of the walls of Asgard, and the theft of Thor's hammer. There are also some good fables of the visits of the gods to Middle Earth: the wanderings of Heimdall, and the begetting of the first peasant, the first craftsman, and the first warrior; the goddess Frigg's gift of the first seed and blue flowers of flax to the peasant Awed; Odin's fostering of two young brothers, the liar Geirrod and the generous Agnar, and his final judgement of them.

The stories of the Northern gods have survived in a very consistent form, in comparison with the Greek myths. They were written down in the thirteenth century, when paganism was already dying, and outside Iceland and Scandinavia they dropped out of the repertoire of European poets. They come from a highly-developed pagan religious tradition. The more primitive stories and rituals from which they grew are largely a matter of conjecture.

At two points, in talking to children, it may be necessary to remember that these myths are not primitive. They are not exactly what the Vikings who invaded England in the eighth, ninth and tenth centuries would have told their children, although it is possible to say 'and they told them a story rather like ...' Even more certainly they are not what Englishmen in the eighth century remembered of the creation myths of their forefathers in Germany and Scandinavia in the fourth and fifth centuries. This last distinction may be important. There are two great Northern heroic legends, and one of them, the story of Beowulf, is told in an eighth-century English Christian poem, composed for singing or chanting, in the same oral tradition as the poetry of Homer. The other, the story of the Volsungs, survives in two forms: a thirteenth-century Icelandic prose version of older poems, the *Volsungasaga*, and a thirteenth-century German poem, the *Nibelungenlied*.

The story of Beowulf is an almost unfailing success with audiences of eight-to-ten-year-olds, at least if it is told with some of the descriptive detail and evocative epic phrases of the original poem. *Beowulf* creates scenes which are as dramatic and universal as anything in Northern myth and legend, but it is as simple in outline as the shorter Greek myths. There is a courteous and generous warrior hero, and four monsters: a fierce sea-serpent, the misshapen giant Grendel, his even more loathsome mother, and a fire-breathing dragon guarding a hoard of treasure. There are none of the complicated sequences of cause and effect that make it difficult for children to follow the legends of the Volsungs or the Trojan War. Beowulf fights all the monsters, and kills them; the rest of the poem shows how he came to encounter them, and how his victories were rewarded and celebrated. Yet it is not a repetitive story like the Labours of Heracles. Beowulf fights Grendel as a young man, coming to the assistance of a neighbouring king to whom he is bound in gratitude, and he leaves for home with gifts that prove his courage; he fights the dragon as an old man, the king of his own people, and the few followers he has chosen hang back, so that in killing the dragon he receives his own death-wound. This time his reward is the splendid burial given to his body, and the dragon hoard that is thrown upon the pyre.

It has been said more than once that the poet of *Beowulf* deliberately chose a legend of single combat with monsters, ending in the death of the hero, instead of a more involved heroic tale of human jealousy and revenge. He wanted to dwell lyrically upon a few events, instead of moving swiftly over many. It enabled him to see the monsters as fiends, and to show the weakness of man, together with his capacity for loyalty or disloyalty. He was a Christian, looking back upon paganism, and Grendel is treated with much greater intensity than any of the classical monsters were. Anyone telling the story to children needs to show them not only that Grendel drank his victims' blood, but that he was joyless, and hated the sound of joy in Hygelac's hall. The misty moors and fens and the splendour of Heorot are an essential part of the story, and so is the ceremony of feasting and gift-giving and burial. There are two good versions for children, one by Ian Serraillier and one by Rosemary Sutcliff [Short List nos. 65 and 67].

The story of the Volsungs and the curse on Andvari's gold is one of the most inherently symbolic of all legends: it is hardly surprising that when it emerged from obscurity William Morris found it more power-ful than the legends of the Trojan War. It is as swift and complex as *Beowulf* is simple and slow; in the Icelandic version it covers the lives of two generations, not counting the forbears and descendants of the *dramatis personae*, and a short list of *dramatis personae* would have to run to at least twenty. It contains pretty strong stuff: treachery, thirteen killings (most of them justified blood-vengeances), incest, and jealousy in love. Because of the complexity of the plot and the violence displayed in entirely human feuds it is obviously not a story for young children. Some of it is so reminiscent of the Greek tragic legends that it might seem absurd to suggest that children who are not ready for the Greek stories might be ready for this one. Nevertheless some children of eleven do follow the action breathlessly, and appreciate the weird power of scenes like the forging of Sigurd's sword, the slaughter of the dragon, and the awakening of Brynhild. They are excited by the story without being frightened. In the *Volsungasaga* there is no brooding upon sacrilege or perversion, and it puts horror at a distance by mixing human motives with the power of magic. The stress of the story lies upon courage and generosity, and upon greed for wealth and power. Odin moves through it to protect the heroes, or to end their earthly lives, not to catch them out or send them mad. Some of the villains are human—the false Siggeir, the witch-queen Grimhild, the crafty Attli. Their evil flows into the evil magic that derives from Loki, and runs through the gold ring in the hoard stolen from Andvari, the ring which is capable of changing the human Fafnir into a dragon—'and he lay down on it'—and of wrecking the love of Sigurd and Brynhild as soon as they touch it.

The story falls naturally into four parts. In telling it to children it is possible to keep them fairly distinct, and to begin at the beginning; but the concatenation of events must not be forgotten, for it is part of the character of the story, and a large part of the symbolism that Wagner both found and created within it. The first part is the tale of Loki's killing of Otter for sport, of his theft of the dwarf Andvari's hoard in order to cover the otter-skin with gold as a blood-price, and of the subsequent acquisition of the gold by Otter's miserly brother Fafnir.

The second part is the story of the magic sword given by Odin to Sigmund, son of Volsung, of his sister Signy's marriage to Siggeir, who treacherously murders Volsung, and of the vengeance Sigmund and Signy bring upon Siggeir with the help of their son Sinfiotli, who is conceived while Sigmund is hiding in the forest. Most of the savagery of this part can be left out in telling the story to children. Omission here scarcely counts as bowdlerization, since the stories attached to Sigmund were probably not connected with the stories attached to Sigurd in earlier forms of the legend. Roger Lancelyn Green has contrived an almost unnoticeable transition in *The Curse of Andvari's Gold*, in his *Saga of Asgard*. Odin's gift of the sword to Sigmund is necessary to the next part of the story, but the incestuous birth of Sinfiotli and the exploits of Sigmund and Sinfiotli as werewolves are not.

The third part contains the magical adventures of Sigurd, the son born posthumously to Sigmund by his queen Hiordis. He is saved from Sigmund's last battlefield by Danish raiders, and brought up at a Danish court by the smith Reginn, the younger brother of Otter and Fafnir. Reginn forges Sigmund's broken sword afresh, and with it Sigurd avenges his father and kills Fafnir, thus acquiring the accursed gold. Through bathing in Fafnir's blood he learns the speech of birds, and they send him to a 'shield-castle' on a hill, surrounded by flames, where the Valkyr Brynhild lies asleep. She is waiting for a hero brave enough to ride through them. This central section deserves to be re-created in detail; the adventures are just what children like, and they seem to feel the poetic shape of the legend.

The last part is more intricate. It consists of the human feuds that arise from the curse of the ring with which Sigurd plights his troth to Brynhild. The storyteller may be able to simplify the chain of events in this part, concentrating on the magic potion which makes Sigurd forget Brynhild, and not only marry Gudrun of the Giukings but use magic to trick Brynhild into marrying his brother-in-law Gunnar. The saga carries the chain of murder and revenge 'unto the third and fourth generation' in historical times: in telling it to children it is probably best to end upon a climax—the murder of Sigurd instigated by Bryn-hild, her suicide, and the burial of Andvari's gold in the waters of the Rhine.

Another tragic, sometimes brutal story that can stir the thought and emotion of older children was told in an Icelandic poem of Viking times, the *Lay of Volund* (the English Weland or Wayland), and again in a Norwegian saga of the late Middle Ages; it seized the imagination of the nineteenth-century Danish poet Oehlenschlager, and it is from his Romantic version of it, the *Vaulundurssaga*, that it is best known today. The bones of the story are constant, although names and episodes vary. Volund is a cunning smith, one of three brothers who marry Valkyrie brides coming to them in the form of swans and so departing after seven years. (Oehlenschlager says that when they leave for the last time Volund's wife Alvite, or Hervor, gives him the keys to three magic caverns of ore and gems.) Volund's deprivations con-tinue with the loss of his two brothers, who are too impatient to wait for the return of their wives, and are killed on their separate adventures. Alone in the forest, Volund is cheated by the treacherous King Nidud and his two sons. He is lamed, and held as a solitary captive on an island; one of the rings he has fashioned (possibly for Alvite) is given by Nidud to his own daughter Baudvild; Oehlenschlager adds that Baudvild herself puts out one of his eyes, and that he is cheated out of Alvite's gift of the keys. He executes his revenge upon his persecutors by tricking Nidud into drinking out of precious bowls fashioned around the skulls of his own murdered sons, and by drugging and seducing Baudvild—her resistance being ambiguous in the Lay. In the end he takes wings—either Alvite's feathers or bird-wings he has constructed himself—taunts Nidud, and escapes from his country. The story is highly patterned and full of evocative correspondences; the two families of three members, one loyal and one treacherous; the recurrent *motif* of the fashioning of metal into weapons or ornaments to be used for opposite ends; Volund's contrasted bonds with Alvite and with Baudvild; in Oehlenschlager's saga, the three caves which reveal secrets of one kind to Volund and another to the sons of Nidud. Above all it carries the characteristic Northern theme of resistant endurance of unmerited suffering, and survival when everything cherished has been stripped away; it is also a significantly English story, as Kipling shewed when he brought Weland into *Puck of Pook's Hill* as the most persistently lingering of the English 'Old Things'— a smith of the gods is important in most Bronze and Iron Age cultures, and Wayland is ours, as many place-names proclaim. The ferocity of the story has probably kept it out of most books for children, but it has now been impressively reconstructed by Ursula Synge in her *Weland: Smith of the Gods*. This is a very free, detailed version after the fashion of the 1970s, but her rearrangement of the ending and of the Baudvild relationship seems aesthetically justified; she reveals the shape of the legend.

3. THE ARTHURIAN ROMANCES

King Arthur and his knights have been, at sundry times, very severely reprimanded by teachers and scholars. In about 1568 Roger Ascham, who taught Queen Elizabeth, complained of the 'bold bawdry' of Malory's *Morte d'Arthur*, 'in which book those be accounted the noblest knights that do kill the most men without any quarrel and commit foulest adulteries by subtlest shifts'. In 1954 Robert Graves complained that the historical and legendary material that got into the Arthurian stories was sadly jumbled, and not at all as pure and primitive as a modern mythographer would like it to be. As for the King, though he 'permitted a few knights of the Round Table—those with beautiful Germanic souls and a pleasure in living virginally on bread and water— to ride off in quest of the Holy Grail, he himself never joined them. Living heartily in feasting...he attended church parade like an Edwardian cavalry colonel, largely to set his captains and other ranks a good example'. He had become, for the British, 'a national obsession'.

Yet in the twelfth century it was possible to ask 'Whither has not flying fame spread and familiarised the name of Arthur the Briton, even as far as the empire of Christendom extends?' The Arthurian stories were the legends of England, France and Germany in the Middle Ages; they are the last mythology, or body of fantasies approximating to a mythology, that has ever come to birth in Europe. They not only incorporated a new Christian mysticism and a new conception of romantic or 'courtly' love; they helped to shape and disseminate them. They flowed into the epic poetry of the Italian Renascence, and thence into *The Faerie Queene*. Milton began a poem on King Arthur when he first felt his vocation to write an English epic. In later centuries Tennyson and Charles Williams wrote on Arthurian themes because to their eyes images and significances spontaneously appeared within them. In Wagner's mythopoeic imagination they produced *Parsifal* and *Tristan und Isolde*. The first revival of myth and legend in children's books eventually brought them back to the schoolroom from which Ascham tried to banish them. Since the beginning of this century they have formed a Secondary World for many children in the years between eight and twelve. Jonathan Miller recently described how their dream-like sequences fascinated him before he was ten, and 'somehow disseminated a vague kind of piety'.

There must be something in the stories themselves to account for their power over the imagination of poets and children, and for the paradox that they seem to disseminate vague piety and unmistakeable immorality at one and the same time.

Like the Northern myths, the Arthurian stories create places and persons which are often more memorable than what happens to this or that person in this or that place. One of the strongest impressions that they leave in the mind is a shifting picture of 'forests and enchantments drear'. In this continent, which could not be mapped, any road or stream may meet any other road or stream, islands do not stay in the same place, and fountains, lakes, hermitages and castles may spring into view in any clearing between the trees. Either in the saddle or at the feast, the knight is likely to be surprised by running hounds, or deer, or ladies pursued by churls. Everything is in movement. This is the world of dreaming, and it is also reminiscent of the changes and chances of this fleeting life in their more hopeful guise. Homer saw them as a sombre threat to human prosperity; in the Arthurian stories they may bring either disaster or unforeseeable opportunity and joy.

In much the same way colours and forms of speech remain in the mind's eye and ear. Ceremony is important both for its inherent seemliness and for what it communicates. Black and red knights are overcome by white knights; the gold of court and castle is set against the green

and black of wild nature (which does not mean that the poet of *Gawain*
wrote an allegory in which Instinct overcame Courtesy). In some of the
later stories the knights do not think or deliberate, but they still
speak in a manner characteristic of this imaginary Britain, or Logres.
Their words are simple and grave and scrupulous; not at all heroic, and
yet possessing a kind of ritual formality. They make ordinary greetings
and farewells into expressions of pure delight and melancholy, and
laments over the dead into epitaphs. Christ and the Virgin are named
as naturally as the green grass and the roaring rivers.

The form of the whole cycle of Arthurian legends is likewise expressive of 'a vague kind of piety'. Arthur appears providentially to save
his people from the heathens; the fellowship he gathers round him
flourishes for a while, flowers in the vision of the Grail given to Galahad,
Percival and Bors, and is broken by the love of Lancelot and Guinevere
and the worse sin of the traitor who reveals it; the King is whirled
downwards on Fortune's wheel, but in his last battle he fights on when
the field is lost, and is carried away to the magic Vale of Avalon, to be
healed of his wounds and perhaps to return to Logres. It is a pattern of
flawed goodness, restoration and hope. The characteristic pattern of
the single Arthurian story is the quest. A knight pledges himself to
some far-fetched or ideal task for the love of his king or his lady. He
is not defending himself against fearful odds, but choosing to go out
to look for beauty or holiness, and often finding them. These are the
legends of an age of faith.

Courtesy and piety and hope differentiate the Arthurian stories from
any other heroic legends, and so does the fellowship of Arthur's
knights, which takes the place of the earlier hero, or heroic family,
or band of seafarers. The knights may have magic powers, and they
are not often represented as individual human beings, but they are not
very much larger than life; they are tempted and beguiled, and their
errors are treated with compassion. It is appropriate that these stories
should have come to be known as 'romances', and thereby differen-
tiated from earlier myths and legends. 'Romance' has also come to be
associated with the tangled structure of the Arthurian cycles, and with
the odd mixture of narrative material that was absorbed into them.

For however enchanting the Arthurian forests may be, it is undeniable
that some bewildering things take place in them. Nothing can explain
the loves of Lancelot and Guinevere, and Tristram and Iseult, because
Courtly Love is itself one of the unresolved paradoxes of the Middle
Ages. Nor did the history and myth and fantasy and psychological

realism that went into the Arthurian mixture blend together perfectly, except in the work of a very few writers.

Children of nine, ten and eleven usually fall under the spell of the forests. They are ready to put up with a few absurdities, if a writer does his best to choose the stories that do not present too many moral ambiguities, and to stress the moral patterns that can be felt even in the paradoxes. Roger Lancelyn Green and Barbara Leonie Picard have both moved in the enormous mass of Arthurian sources with a kind of imaginative sure-footedness. Roger Lancelyn Green 'interferes' more often and more insistently in order to stress inner patterns, especially what he calls the 'one fixed pattern. . . the Realm of Logres, the model of chivalry and right striving against the barbarism and evil which surrounded and at length engulfed it.' His version is therefore the easier to understand, although—or perhaps because—his language is more modern and less severely restrained than Barbara Leonie Picard's.

It used to be impossible for any but the most expert mediaevalist to enter the Serbonian bog of Arthurian tradition without sinking and perishing miserably. R. S. Loomis has recently written a small book which takes the common reader across the bog in safety. One's judgement of Arthurian stories for children is certainly improved by a better understanding of origins and sources.

The romances have three very incongruous points of origin: memories of a historical, Romano–British Christian leader who defeated the heathen Saxons in a series of battles *circa* 500; Welsh myths about the exploits of the gods and Welsh legends of a prophet and enchanter; and the beliefs and customs of French court cultures in the eleventh, twelfth and thirteenth centuries. The stories that we know have passed through a succession of mediaeval writings: the gay verse tales which Chrétien de Troyes wrote to please the Countess of Champagne and the Count of Flanders in the late twelfth century; the serious poetry of the German Wolfram von Eschenbach, and the romantic poetry of the Anglo–Norman Thomas and the German Gottfried, at the end of the century; 'the Vulgate cycle', French prose romances of the early thirteenth century, probably written in part by Cistercians, and a later continuation of them, the 'Merlin'; a series of verse romances and ballads written in England between 1300 and 1500, including the most perfect work of art in the Arthurian tradition, *Sir Gawain and the Green Knight*; and Malory's *Morte d'Arthur*, translated and adapted from various French and English sources, and finished in 1470.

Children under ten usually like the form of Arthurian romance that first appeared in the work of Chrétien; the story of a single knight who sets out from Arthur's court in search of adventure or in fulfilment of a vow. They are puzzled by the Lancelot–Guinevere theme that Chrétien initiated. Some of the best stories to begin with are those of Uwaine and the Lady of the Fountain, Gareth and Linette, Geraint and Enid, the quest of the hart, the brachet and the damsel (Arthur's marriage feast), and Lancelot and Turquin. In introducing these one must say something about Arthur and the Round Table and its vows of chivalry, and try to recreate the chivalric world of castles and tournaments and hunting and enchanters, but it is not necessary to tell the whole story of how Arthur came into his kingdom.

The story of Balin and Balan is almost as self-contained as these, and just as simple and humane in its revelation of motives. But it is more serious, even tragic: it comes from the 'Merlin', and the prophecies of Merlin himself sound through the story like the blast of the horn that blows for Balin's coming death 'as it had been the death of a beast'. Balin is able to draw from its scabbard a magic sword which a damsel brings to Arthur's court from the Lady of the Lake (there is some confusion about the purposes of the damsel and the Lady, and throughout the romances the figures of Morgana le Fay, Nimue and the Lady are ambiguous; the storyteller needs to show that they are fairies, and that fairies are dangerous). The sword bears a curse, and Balin is too proud to give it up. Under its influence he snatches the holy spear of the Grail Castle, inflicting an incurable wound upon King Pelles, the guardian of the Grail, and laying waste all his lands. With it he kills his brother Balan unknowingly, meeting his own death in the combat. By Merlin's magic it is preserved for the coming of Galahad, and transformed into the weapon by which the quest of the Grail is achieved and King Pelles is healed.

The story of Balin and Balan is obviously a story for children of eleven rather than children of nine. It leads towards the Grail stories, and could be told as an introduction to them. The years between ten and thirteen are probably about the right time for hearing both the Grail legends and the legends that centre upon Arthur himself and show the rise and fall of his kingdom. These sequences are comparatively complex in plot and mysterious or tragic in feeling.

The Grail stories are the most evocative of the Arthurian romances, despite the queer process of misunderstanding by which they came into being. They are about mystic vision. Even when the original writers are muddled about the sacramental objects that convey the vision, they succeed in creating an experience of fear and wonder. Some transcendent thing is expected in the Chapel in the midst of the waste lands, its door 'waste and broken', its altar 'arrayed with cloth of clean silk', and its great candlestick alight; and in the Grail Castle of Carbonek, guarded by lions that lie down like lambs, where all doors open themselves except that of the chapel, from which 'came out a great clearness, that the house was as bright as all the torches in the world had been there'; and in the procession of white Grail Maidens. Fear and wonder are present even in the wanderings of Lancelot and Percival and Galahad; they do seem to wander, not to ride straight ahead as they do on other quests.

The Grail maidens carry a spear, a dish, and a veiled vessel; sometimes the veiled vessel is itself a dish or platter. According to some writers the appearance of the Grail procession makes every knight see all his fellows as fairer than they usually look, and feel as if he were eating and drinking all the things he likes best. When Galahad sees the vessel unveiled, he sees first the Christ Child and then the crucified Christ.

In primitive Grail stories the vessel was probably a Celtic dish of plenty from which the gods fed, or else—which is more unlikely—a ritual phallic symbol, in association with the lance. Wolfram von Eschenbach filled it with a small white stone, perhaps a symbol of humility. The Cistercian writer of the Vulgate cycle began to identify its contents with the consecrated Host, but still saw it as the dish from which Christ ate the paschal lamb, not the bread, at the Last Supper. The slightly earlier continuation of Chrétien's Grail story makes the vessel a cup in which Joseph of Arimathea collected the blood that fell from the body of Christ on the Cross, and leaves the first platter as the dish used at the Last Supper. Identification with the consecrated elements of the Mass was a natural movement of the imagination, even though women continued to be Grail-Bearers long after Naciens the Hermit was invented to teach the mysteries of the Grail. The two vessels came to be represented pictorially as paten and chalice.

In telling the story to children one has to make up one's mind about what the Grail is, and looks like, as an object. It is probably best to keep to the late tradition of the spear, the dish of bread and the cup of wine, which have known or at least faintly guessed associations with holiness. The concrete description will make its own effect. The important thing is what the Grail does to the knights who see it; how it awakens infinite longing. If children are curious about what the spear and the two vessels are, one can say that they were the cup and the dish used by

Christ at the Last Supper, and the spear by which his side was pierced when he was crucified; the Vulgate story of Joseph of Arimathea's custody of the sacred objects and his arrival at Glastonbury is extremely tedious and should certainly be left out.

There are other inconsistencies. The birth of Galahad, the perfect virgin knight, is symbolically most unsatisfactory: he was conceived through a trick played by the daughter of King Pelles upon Lancelot, whereby Lancelot thought he was sleeping with Guinevere. Chrétien's Blanchefleur, the wanton lady of Percival the Pure, was likewise an anomaly. These artistic blunders can be quite simply obliterated in telling the story: if not, it may well be justifiable to treat them as freely as Roger Lancelyn Green does, in order to give children a coherent imaginative impression of these legends. Bowdlerization is an ugly word; but the case of a story that has passed through many works of art is surely different from that of a story that belongs to one work of art alone. No one can say what the 'real' story of the Grail is. One can only say that the Grail stories are unique, and worth telling.

The secret love of Lancelot and the Queen dominates the romances that describe the breaking of the fellowship of the Round Table, and the mysterious passing of the King. It was regarded as an ideal state by Chrétien, even though he made fun of its exaggerated manifestations. The mediaeval marriage of convenience did not permit the marriage of true minds, which could be celebrated only outside its bonds. Nevertheless the vows of secrecy and fidelity exchanged between true romantic lovers involved the breaking of marriage vows; and since people in the Middle Ages really believed that 'truth is the highest thing a man may keep', they were fixed upon the horns of a dilemma. In the Vulgate *Lancelot* the affair is meritorious. In the Vulgate *Grail* and *Mort Artu* it becomes a mortal sin which prevents Lancelot from achieving the Quest, and causes the fall of Arthur's kingdom. Yet Lancelot is all the nobler for his scrupulous fidelity to Guinevere. When he is dislodged from his precarious foothold by the jealousy of Agravain and the treachery of Mordred, he is at first tragically divided between loyalty to Guinevere and loyalty to the king, and then tragically incapacitated by his unbroken love of his friend Gawain, Mordred's half-brother, who has turned against him.

Children of eight cannot begin to understand the idea of an action or state which is itself erroneous, and yet produces some good, and cannot be annihilated as if it had never been. It makes a kind of sense to some children of eleven and twelve, at least in this concrete form.

The paradox of romantic love constantly appears in the story of Tristram and Iseult, but there it is softened by the magic potion which is intended for Iseult and her future husband Mark of Cornwall, and drunk in error by Iseult and Tristram. They cannot help loving one another. The Tristram romances are only loosely attached to the Arthurian cycle; they tell an independent love story, in which everything leads towards Tristram's involuntary devotion to Iseult of Ireland, or follows from it. His fight with the Irish dragon gives him the right to claim Iseult as the bride of Mark. He marries Iseult of Brittany because of her name, and dies because his wife is too jealous to let Iseult of Ireland heal his wound. He is a strangely fascinating figure; a forest creature, born in the woods, and brought up to be a perfect huntsman and a perfect harpist, he disguises himself as a minstrel, and in some versions of the story takes Iseult away from Mark to live in the forest again, as if it were Arcadia. Some children of eleven and twelve feel this fascination: others are bored because all love stories are boring, especially tragic ones. *Tristram and Iseult* is probably a story to be discovered on one's own.

One Arthurian quest story was told so minutely and beautifully in the late fourteenth century that it should not be simplified for eight-year-olds. The versions of *Sir Gawain and the Green Knight* that have been made for children by M. R. Ridley and Ian Serraillier both retain the significant plot of the original poem and give some idea of its moral sensitiveness and descriptive loveliness. They can be read to eleven- and twelve-year-olds; it is worth waiting until children are ready to hear them.

Sir Gawain is a poem about the difficulty of keeping one's word. Gawain has to be strong-minded even to set out to keep an assignation with a green giant who can pick up his own severed head and ride off with it. Almost at the end of a bitter journey through frost and hail, he finds a welcoming host who goes out hunting on three successive days and leaves him to resist the lures of his young wife; he not only resists her, but does it so delicately that he seems to be paying her a compliment. Only the fear of death by the Green Knight's axe drives him to accept her green girdle, which she describes as a magic talisman; and to conceal it, instead of restoring it to the huntsman when he comes home, even though they had promised to exchange the winnings of each day, and before this he had faithfully restored the lady's kisses. When the Green Knight lets his third blow graze Gawain's neck, and lets him see that he is himself the huntsman who tested him and has now judged him for his one venial fault, Gawain is angry and ashamed. He feels like a coward and a traitor, but the Green Knight honours him, and so does the Round Table when he returns.

The plot loses its meaning if one does not feel that Gawain's temptations are almost more than he can stand; and this is the effect of the poet's long, elaborate descriptions. He wants us to appreciate the horrifying colour of the Knight himself, green from top to toe, the cold and loneliness of the winter journey, the decorous merriment of the huntsman's castle and the subtle wit of his beautiful wife.

4. A NOTE ON CELTIC MYTHS AND ON THE OLD TESTAMENT

Celtic myths and legends survived in abundance in Ireland. Many modern readers, children and grown-ups alike, find them dull or ridiculous. A mythographer can take an interest in their skeleton plots, but the stories as they have actually been told are rarely poetic; they are, as Louis MacNiece said, 'unpromising material...except for grotesque farce'. Although Yeats 'tried throughout his life to make something of' the Irish hero Cuchulain, it was no good: the legend was too distorted. 'What happens to Cuchulain when he gets into his battle frenzy? He twists himself inside his skin so that his heels and buttocks appear in front...And a dark column of blood rises from the top of his head like the mast of a great ship.' Our real inheritance from Celtic mythology was transmitted through the Arthurian romances.

The myths and legends of the Old Testament are as poetic and dramatic as anything in Greek or Northern mythology, and they have exercised an even greater power over the imagination of Europe. They were the only highly developed, literary mythological stories that were heard by uneducated people in the Christian period, and they meant as much as the Greek stories to poets and men of letters.

Nothing is said about them here, for the simple reason that in Christian tradition they have been regarded, in a multitude of conflicting or overlapping definitions, either as uniquely significant history, or as a uniquely true mythology. In pagan tradition myths were at first regarded as history, and later accepted as true fantasy. Most recent Christian theologians have been so intent upon demythologizing that the truth of Biblical fantasy does not seem to interest them, even when they make a few grudging acknowledgements that an inferior, 'poetic' kind of virtue may reside in it. Old Testament stories are still told in some 'religious instruction', but they are quickly dropping out of it, and the text of the Bible in any version will soon be unknown to most children.

Before very long it will be the work of teachers of literature to tell the stories of the Old Testament, and perhaps the New as well—if it is not already theirs. No other myths or legends give children more exciting themes for their own dance and drama. Our long-standing need for a coherent, seriously written version of them for children of eight and nine has been largely satisfied by the publication in 1968 of Roger Lancelyn Green's *Tale of Ancient Israel*, which is accessible to believers and unbelievers alike. In the past ten years there have been a few other children's books that help to reveal our Hebraic inheritance of stories, notably Philip Turner's *Bible Story* with memorable illustrations by Brian Wildsmith, and the adaptations from the Jerusalem Bible made in the *Bible Stories for Children* illustrated by Brother Eric of Taizé; I have included six books in a section on the Old Testament in the book-list at the end of this revised edition. It is a conspicuously small list in comparison with those devoted to our Hellenic and Northern inheritance, and it remains unfortunately probable that there is more bad writing in Bible stories for children than in versions of any other traditional stories. Even so, storytellers might well be more bold and more responsible in making use of the good material that is available.

5. FAIRY TALES

Children find many kinds of delight and excitement in fairy tales, if a strong initial sales-resistance can be overcome. The teller of fairy tales is bound to be in the wrong. If he tells them to children of six and seven, he is accused of frightening them out of their lives with such grown-up horrors: if he tries to tell them to children of nine and ten, the children themselves protest that they are much too grown up for such babyish stuff. Fairy tales have come to belong to the nursery, but there were children of five and children of nine in seventeenth-century nurseries, and a seventeenth-century nurse must have told them different stories, in different ways. Today the craftiest trick is to change the label, and avoid any mention of 'fairy tale'—or 'folk tale', which sounds like a drearier kind of fairy tale, associated with folk dancing and other such unfashionable pursuits. 'A very old story of magic and adventure', or 'a story about a mermaid written over a hundred years ago' are clumsy, long-winded phrases, but they do not arouse suspicion.

A few fairy tales can still be told to seven-year-olds successfully.

Kathleen Lines and Sara and Stephen Corrin have collected some of them. There are also any number of picture-books on the market that turn naturally strong, significant parables into sweet and cosy whimsies for five-year-olds. They should be avoided like the plague.[1] They persist and still reappear every Christmas, even though during the last ten years a new kind of publication, the 'quality' fairy-tale picture-book, has begun to appear in significant and still growing numbers. (See *Short List of Books* nos. 160 to 182). Some of these new books manage to be not too expensive, scholarly, lovely to look at, and really attractive to five- to eight-year-olds: some indulge in visual stylistic clichés that seem to be directed towards an ever-fashionable adult audience; in some the pictures seem too sophisticated for the text, or *vice versa*. On the whole they do represent a healthy reaction against the sentimentalization which is still with us, and which can do real damage. Sentimentalization is quite different from the reinterpretation that a serious writer for children feels justified in making in order to bring traditional stories 'freshly and more vividly before a new generation'. The choice of fairy tales for under-sevens ought to be determined by the degree to which they are inherently alarming. Children are frightened of giants or dogs with eyes like mill-wheels as long as they feel that what happens in a story might literally happen to them. Usually, at about five, six or seven, they come to realize with sudden and complete clarity that what happened hundreds of years ago, and what happens in Never-Never-Land, are equally different from what happens at home. J. R. R. Tolkien has interpreted 'Is is true?' quite rightly. 'They mean: "I like this, but is it contemporary? Am I safe in my bed?" The answer "There is certainly no dragon in England today", is all that they want to hear.' After this realization, it is usually visual images of maimed or deformed living creatures that cause nightmares: the severed head of the talking horse in *The Goosegirl*, or the feet that dance for ever even when the executioner has chopped them off, in Andersen's *The Red Shoes*—itself a product of a child's guilty nightmares of divine retribution. In comparison with these stories *Bluebeard* is good clean fun, even if it is an image of every man's desire to kill the thing he loves.

There is one other cause of fear that may persist throughout a child's life until he begins to see fairy tales as an anthropologist sees them, and may still affect the imagination of an anthropologist of fifty. In the

---

[1] One fairly safe rule-of-thumb is: never use a book that does not give the name of the translator, adaptor or reteller of the stories on the title-page.

heroic legends and romances one starts with the warrior who rescues the helplessly doomed or enchanted maiden—with Perseus or Sigurd, not with Andromeda or Brynhild. In traditional fairy tales one starts with the helpless maiden, with Snow White or the Sleeping Beauty, or—worse still—with the helpless child who is degraded or turned out of doors by the cruel stepmother. One knows that she is going to be rescued, but identification with her present helplessness may be too much to bear.[1] (In one interesting pattern that develops in fairy tale the rescuer of the persecuted or bewitched characters has himself (or herself) been bewitched or persecuted—Beauty in *Beauty and the Beast*, and Elisa in *The Wild Swans*.) The nearest equivalent in legend is the position of the royal hero, like Theseus or Arthur, who is obscurely fostered and has to prove his royal birth; but the centaur Cheiron and Ector were excellent foster-fathers. No one in antiquity seems to have given much thought to the sufferings of the baby Oedipus exposed on the mountainside, or the baby Perseus exposed in a chest on the high seas. The one figure who resembles Cinderella is Electra, as Sophocles saw her.

Fairy tales have always hovered between the fully-grown poetic imagination and the imagination of children. Our present uncertainty about their proper place in the lives of children can be explained only by their odd history in written literature.

It begins with the appearance of Charles Perrault's *Histoires ou contes du temps passé* in 1697. This collection of 'old' stories included *Cinderella*, *Red-Riding-Hood*, *Bluebeard*, *Puss-in-Boots*, *The Sleeping Beauty* and seven others. Perrault said that they were 'composed' by his own son as a child; we know that this son had to write them out as exercises in composition, and presumably as quite a little boy he had repeated them to his father. The book was published with a frontispiece showing an old woman with a distaff sitting in front of a fire and telling stories to three children. It is natural to guess that she represents the nurse that Perrault employed, who told the stories to the child in the first place. They obviously come from folklore, from tales that were told among fully-grown men and women of the poorer classes. Like myths and legends, they reveal patterns of adult feeling and behaviour,

---

[1] Some stories can be made both less alarming and less babyish to modern eight- and nine-year-olds by showing very clearly that the persecuted characters are young people of about twenty: see James Reeves' treatment of *Jorinda and Joringel* [Short List no. 132]. Two stories that cannot be handled in this way are *Hansel and Gretel* and *The Babes in the Wood*; these should be absolutely banned.

On persecution, see also p. 108 and note 2.

or patterns in history—escape from a cruel tyrant, a test that distinguishes the innocent from the guilty, love and death, a death-in-life which can end in rebirth if a mysterious condition is fulfilled.

Yet one recalls the engraving of the nurse looking at the children's faces as soon as one attends to the detail of the stories. Cinderella is taken to the ball by a fairy godmother who turns a pumpkin into a coach and lizards into footmen. Her equipage is exactly what the boy would have seen when his own parents went out, since the Perraults moved in distinguished circles. The coachman has 'the finest moustaches in the district'.

The refrain-phrases of folklore are still there in many of the tales, phrases like 'Sister Anne, sister Anne, do you see anyone coming?' and 'What big arms you have, grandmother!' But there are also natural and very childlike snatches of dialogue. While the fairy 'was wondering how she could make a coachman', it is left to Cinderella herself to say 'I will go and see whether there is a rat in the rat-trap; we could make a coachman of him'. It is usual to ascribe these touches to the literary art of Perrault; but surely the first ideas for them might have come from an old upper servant who had 'improved herself' in an upper-middle-class family, and knew exactly what her children liked to hear?

Perrault's book started a fashion in France. Hundreds of fairy tales were written during the eighteenth century, many with some foundation in oral tradition, often overlaid with moral allegory. They were not usually written for children, but they must have enlarged and altered the storytelling that still went on in nurseries. The best is Mme Leprince de Beaumont's lovely and morally sensitive *Beauty and the Beast*, which has the strength of folklore behind it, and has been made more poetic, not less so, by a civilized intelligence. Mme d'Aulnoy's *Goldilocks*, *The Bluebird* and *The White Cat* are more artificial, but they are good tales, and it is not hard to see why children enjoyed them.[1]

A new movement to write down the stories of the peasant in his hut, and the nurse in her nursery, began just after revolution destroyed the French culture that had sheltered the Perrault tradition. It radiated from Germany and Scandinavia; it was a part of the whole Romantic Movement in European literature, and of the philological and anthropological movement in German scholarship.[2] Once again adult interests were inextricably confused with interest in what children really liked, and once again the publication of traditional fairy tales inspired writers to invent new ones.

[1] Short List nos. 125–6 and 122–4.   [2] See note, p. 23.

Jacob and Wilhelm Grimm were philologists and historians who went out to collect stories from illiterate men and women, believing that they could reconstruct a forgotten European mythology from these long-buried fragments, and shed light on the earliest migrations of European peoples. They knew, however, that their stories had already been partially appropriated by children: they called the collections which began to appear in 1812 *Kinder und Haus-Märchen*, and they expected them to be read to a mixed audience of children and grown-ups.[1]

They wrote as scholars, not as storytellers, and were obviously more concerned to preserve evidence for future anthropologists than to put their stories into words that would hold the attention of children. They wrote down events and details as they heard them, making alterations only if they sounded incoherent. After reading the lively French fairy tales it is dull to read their narrative; but their sequences of magical adventures, objects, persons, and places are in themselves significant and beautiful. It is only the language that is dull; Roger Lancelyn Green's version of *The Brave Little Tailor* shows how these bare twigs burst into leaf when the stories are told as a clever nurse would have told them by word of mouth. Characteristically they are stories of persecuted children and maidens, ambitious young men who have to pass magic tests to marry a princess, and small brainy men who get the better of big brawny men. There are few fairy godmothers, and these few may derive from Perrault: their place is taken by magic birds and beasts, and there are some dwarfs. The Grimm collections preserved for us the stories of *Rumpelstiltskin*, *Rapunzel*, *Snow White*, *The Golden Bird*, *Hansel and Gretel*, *The Dancing Princesses* and *The House in the Wood*.

Hans Andersen had read these fairy tales before he first published his own in 1837, but his inspiration lay in what he had heard as a child from the old women in the almshouse at Odense, where his grandmother looked after the garden. Unlike the Grimm brothers, he was born among the poor who still told stories, and unlike them, he was a master of the spoken word. In his work every word is in its place, and could be in no other; at least that is what Danish critics say, and that is the impression made by an idiomatic translation like those of M. R. James, R. P. Keigwin and L. W. Kingsland. His friend and benefactor Edvard Collin left this record of his behaviour with children:

In several of the circles in which he moved every day there were young children with whom he occupied himself; he told them stories, part of which he made up on the spur of the moment and part of which he took from fairy tales we all know...the children were enchanted...He gave life even to the driest of sentences: he did not say, 'The children got into the carriage and then they drove off', but 'Then they got into the carriage, bye-bye daddy, bye-bye mummy, the whip cracked, smick smack, and off they went, gee-up there.'

His first published stories were traditional, although he improvised as much as he liked in matters of detail. *The Princess and the Pea, The Tinder Box* and *The Wild Swans* still hold children of eight and nine spellbound. The ideas and experiences contained within these stories seem to fall exactly within their range. They like the magic tests which prove so entertainingly that the claimant to royal birth must be genuine, because 'no-one but a princess could possibly be so sensitive', and fall so cruelly upon Elisa, weaving the shirts of nettles and forced to remain dumb even when her own prince believes that she is a witch. Andersen creates his own suspense; *The Tinder Box* opens with the soldier already on his way—'A soldier came marching down the road— left, right! left, right! He had a pack upon his back, and a sword by his side'...He creates the fairy-tale world for us, if we do not know it already: 'The eleven brothers—they were princes, of course—went to school with stars upon their breasts and swords by their sides'...His bantering humour may suggest to modern ears that he does not believe in the paraphernalia of stars and swords, but as he reaches the climax of his story there is no doubt that he takes his magic seriously.

But the youngest had a swan's wing in place of one arm, because a sleeve was missing from his shirt which she had not completely finished. 'Now I can speak!' she said. 'I am innocent!' And the people who saw what had happened bowed before her...At the top was one flower, white and gleaming, which shone like a star: the king plucked it and placed in on Elisa's breast, and then she woke with peace and happiness in her heart.

The Emperor's New Clothes is a traditional fantasy or parable, but not exactly a fairy tale. Andersen took it from a mediaeval Spanish story which exactly suited his wry humour and talent for mimicry. It is a certain success among children of eight and nine. The slick, tongue-twisting Impostors, the nervously self-important Courtiers, and the insistently candid Child all come to life in his hands. The satire, which is aimed at the idiocy of VIPs, must have appealed to him as a self-made man; it certainly appeals to children, who see reflected in it the natural idiocy of all grown-ups.

Andersen was not only a man with unusual insight into traditional stories and an unusual talent for getting every inflection of the voice onto paper: he was also a Romantic. This last attribute sometimes takes his later work out of the reach of children, even though everything else conspires to make it delightful to them. After 1843 he invented his own plots, allowing an emotional interpretation of life to determine the shape of his stories. One of his strongest feelings is nostalgia, and two of his strongest themes are the plight of the outsider, and the primacy of Love over Reason. Sad, tender yearning and sob-stuff of any kind are disgusting to most children, even though they appreciate supernatural mystery and rejoice in it. *The Staunch Tin Soldier*, *The Fir Tree*, *The Ugly Duckling* and *The Little Mermaid* are all parables of the sufferings of a soul that has not found its home; but with a little cutting they can all be read to children. *The Ugly Duckling* is told with plenty of humour, and the duckling does turn into a swan in the end. Most children's experiences of loneliness and teasing are enough to make them take to this story. *The Little Mermaid* is perhaps the most perfectly formed of Andersen's fairy tales; it contains Romanticism in a nutshell, and goes as far as any story can go in representing a longing for Otherness, without passing quite beyond the apprehension of children. Some ten-year-olds are not merely bored by it: they are positively repelled. Others are strangely attached to it. I have heard two people recollect, in later life, how this story reflected their hatred of school and longing for home, and became a consolation to them.

The Snow Queen, another great and seminal fairy tale, could be read throughout as a Romantic allegory personifying Love and Reason. It is virtually a narrative extension of Wordsworth's image of the wizard who 'by simple waving of a wand . . . dissolves Palace or grove' just as he himself 'unsouled . . . by syllogistic words' the mysteries of Passion. The passage about little Kay's obsession with the mathematical jig-saw puzzle of ice pieces is overtly allegorical. But the greater part of *The Snow Queen*, to a reader who is not perversely searching for 'meanings', is a tale of magic and adventure. In it Andersen returns to the traditional fairy-tale figures of the lost children, the witch, the robber band and the talking beasts, and gives them new life. The Snow Queen herself is the best witch in the whole of fairy-tale literature. Children of ten and eleven can be enthralled by the central section of the story, if the sentiment of the opening and closing sections is toned down by severe cutting. They can also be enthralled by *The Nightingale* which is another extended image of the life-giving power of nature, and the death-bringing power of the intellect. It is not an allegory, and there is no need to explain the song of the real nightingale and the song of the mechanical bird. The court of the Emperor of China is represented just as a child would like to see it, and in fact just as Andersen had represented it to himself as a child, when he saw it at the bottom of the stream behind his home. Yet this story, too, is coloured by more melancholy than some children like. 'The Nightingale' was Andersen's name for the singer Jenny Lind, who did not return his love, and autobiography has come into fairy tale. Cutting may be necessary at the end in reading it to children.

Andersen was fully aware that he was using the fairy tale to communicate his own understanding of life, and that he was communicating it to an adult reader. But he never forgot that he was trying to please children. He said that he would 'get hold of an idea for the older folks, and then tell a story for the young folks, remembering all the time that father and mother often listen, and we must give them something to think about, too!'

A Grimm tradition and an Andersen tradition both flourished in the nineteenth century; and in both of them writers fluctuated between interest in what children liked, and interest in what adults ought to know, and interest in what they wanted to say themselves. Throughout the century anthropologists were busily collecting evidence all over Europe, and eventually all over the world, knowing that the triumph of literacy would soon destroy it. One of the most prolific workers in the movement was Andrew Lang, who published in 1889 *The Blue Fairy Book*, the first of a series of 'coloured' books that ended in 1910. They were intended for children; Lang refused to 'soften' his traditional stories, and insisted that with all their magic and horror they were more sustaining to the imagination of children than the improving realistic stories which had taken possession of Victorian nursery bookshelves. If there were any nurses of the old kind left in the England of 1850, the Gradgrinds would have dismissed them. The *Fairy Books* sold well. Like the *English Fairy Tales* of another folklorist, Joseph Jacobs,[1] they are still valuable for their original illustrations, and for some good stories that are otherwise hard to come by.

Andersen's stories were models for a host of 'invented' fairy tales. Some of them, notably Oscar Wilde's and George Macdonald's, have

[1] Short List no. 153.

never quite fallen out of our repertoire for children, and are either being revived at the moment, or seem to be due for revival. Macdonald's fantasies, together with Andersen's, lie beneath the *Chronicles of Narnia* which C. S. Lewis published between 1950 and 1956; these stories have proved an almost invariable success with eight- to eleven-year-olds of every kind.

The work of all these writers embodies, quite unmistakeably, their experiences and beliefs as fully-grown human beings: biography and autobiography exist to be used as a standard of comparison. The *dramatis personae* are traditional—kings and queens, enchanted children, giants and witches and dwarfs and elves: the ideas are not. Wilde's *The Happy Prince, The Selfish Giant* and *The Star-Child*[1] are parables in which the love of rich and rare possessions comes to shut out human charity; they mirror the tension between Beauty and Goodness that Wilde felt in his own life. Yet Wilde told these stories to his own small son; and children today seem to see the Giant's dilemma without any difficulty, and delight in the fantastic descriptions of his flowering tree, and of the bewitched Star-Child in his ugliness. Macdonald's stories express an individual understanding of religion.[2] The mysterious woman who may be young or old, and lives in a tower that may or may not be there, or at the Back of the North Wind, represents an elusive, redemptive, sometimes painful vision; the goblins are a race that manifest the darkness of man's heart. Children at the end of the last century loved *The Princess and the Goblin*, and it can be revived for modern ten-year-olds, if some passages touched by Victorian sentiment are cut. C. S. Lewis's Narnian stories are likewise parables of redemption and of spiritual regress and progress;[3] he said that he wrote the because at the time a children's story seemed to be the right form for what he wanted to say. Yet they are real children's stories; nine-year-olds are fascinated by Narnia, which owes something to the planets of science fiction, and by the White Witch—a reincarnation of Andersen's Snow Queen—and by the diverse races of rational beings, dwarfs and Talking Beasts and Marsh-Wiggles.

In Narnia there are creatures from Northern legend and Arthurian romance, as well as creatures from fairy tale. The Narnian stories cannot be classified neatly as 'invented fairy-tales'; they might just as well be called invented myths or invented legends. The same could be said of J. R. R. Tolkien's short tale, *The Hobbit*, and his long, elaborate

[1] Short List no. 154.   [2] Short List nos. 144–6.
[3] Short List no. 232.

trilogy *The Lord of the Rings*.[1] Strands of old material of every kind are always appearing in them, but they are a new fabric. They continually suggest interpretations of good and evil, but they are not moral or dogmatic allegories. Nearly all ten-, eleven- and twelve-year-olds like *The Hobbit*, and many children with a growing taste for fantasy will begin to read *The Lord of the Rings* compulsively at some time in the years between eleven and sixteen.

It seems that traditional and 'invented' fairy tales are alike in presenting adult experience in childlike form, which may account for the way in which different children take to them at such different ages. It would doubtless be convenient if one could find in them a bridge between the world of straightforward children's stories like *Peter Rabbit* and *A Bear Called Paddington*, and the world of Perseus and Sigurd, but there is no bridge. There will always be a chasm, and the kings and queens of fairy tale live on the other side of it.

The first step is always a leap. Many children find it easier to leap into legend and romance than to leap into fairy tale. If fairy tales do come first, one might begin with something like *The Emperor's New Clothes*, or the Grimm *Fisherman and His Wife*, which are tartly humorous and set in a world that is not strange. Alison Uttley's *The Spice-Woman's Basket* and Eleanor Farjeon's *Bertha Goldfoot*[2] bring in traditional fairy-tale characters in a comfortable, solid form, and point a moral that fits into the lives of seven-year-olds.

The really powerful poetic fairy tale may be more accessible to eight-year-olds in Perrault and his successors than in Grimm and Andersen. *The Sleeping Beauty* and *Beauty and the Beast* contain less distressing material than *Hansel and Gretel* or *The Snow Queen*. They are told imaginatively enough to create their own world, whereas the Grimm stories need to be filled out by a creative storyteller, and they are shrewd enough to appeal to the modern eight-year-old who finds a gingerbread house babyish. Perrault's *Red-Riding-Hood* is an exception, of course; it is peculiarly nursery-ish in manner and peculiarly savage in content, even if one doesn't suspect it of imaging sadism or originating in ritual murder.

The trouble is that Perrault's stories have usually been spoiled in children's minds and visual memories by bad nursery picture-books. They can sometimes be rescued by being read in a good translation (with appropriate cutting), and by being introduced as eighteenth-century stories. After accepting *Beauty and the Beast* children can go

---

[1] Short List nos. 237 and 239.   [2] Short List nos. 205 and 184.

anywhere they like among fairy tales. The reader might say 'You all know something about this story, but I don't expect you've ever heard the *whole* of it as it used to be told in France two hundred and fifty years ago, when gentlemen wore'...and proceed rather as Beatrix Potter did in beginning *The Tailor of Gloucester*.

Quite often older children who have never liked fairy tales begin to like them after reading *The Chronicles of Narnia*. C. S. Lewis takes them into Narnia in the company of modern children who are not disposed to believe in magic or Secondary Time; and he writes in the language of their own period, which he turns into brisk, firm prose, untainted by the dying fall of Romantic cadences.

III

Presentation and Creation in
the Classroom

1. A NOTE ON NAMES

It is always tiring to listen to a story which is cluttered with unknown names, especially if they are in a foreign tongue. In reading myths and legends to children, or in telling them in one's own words, minor characters can be called 'the king his brother' or 'the third knight, the one in red', or 'a nymph'. In the oral tradition of fairy tale most characters are anonymous anyway. Of course one would not speak of Poseidon and Hades as 'the two gods'; these names should be acquiring their proper symbolic powers in the imagination of children.

When children possess a book themselves, and read and re-read it, the effect is quite different: they enjoy picking up threads from other stories, and discovering interrelationships in a Secondary World. There is no reason why a *writer* should leave his minor characters without their traditional names.

It is often helpful, in reading a story aloud, to break off from time to time, even if one does not want to cut any of the written text. In talking to children about what has just happened, or in telling them the next part of the story shortly and simply, one can remind them that Fafnir is the name of the dragon they heard about last week, without appearing to ask tiresome questions: one need only say 'Now Reginn the smith was the younger brother of Fafnir—do you remember how Fafnir grabbed Andvari's gold and loved it so much that he went and lay down on it to keep it safe, and turned into a dragon? So Reginn told'...

Some of the figures in myth and legend are known by more than one name, and one has to decide which form to use, and use it consistently. The gods and heroes of the Greeks were taken over by the Romans; some of their names were Latinized, and some were exchanged with those of earlier Latin divinities. Nearly all later poets call them by their Latin names, and there is a good case for introducing them to children like this, as Rex Warner does. Nevertheless every other recent writer for children uses the Greek names, so it is better for the reader and storyteller to use them too. The characters in the story of the Volsungs are better known by their Icelandic names than by their German ones, and as Wagner is no guide, using a mixture of both, one should probably say 'Sigurd and Gudrun', not 'Siegfried and Kriemhild'. Hearing Poseidon called Neptune does interrupt the growth of a child's pattern of images, but as need arises the alternative name can be picked up without too much fuss. Blackboard lists of the Greek and Roman pantheon are a distraction, and they kill the whole idea of listening to stories. Three or four names on a blackboard may help children to strengthen an aural memory with a visual one; if there are more than that, they are a nuisance.

The names of mythical and legendary characters have created a bugbear for the reader and teller of stories, as well as for the children listening to him. They are often difficult to pronounce. I think that this bugbear has grown larger in recent years, and I know that it is now large enough to frighten off some teachers who have no other reason for fearing myths and legends. For some strange reason, they feel ashamed of not being able to utter these words, very much as two generations ago 'genteel' English people felt ashamed if they were caught in the act of mispronouncing some of the more oddly spelt names of titled families. Of course it would be a delight and a privilege to know Greek, Latin, Anglo-Saxon, Old Norse, Old French, Middle English, French, German and Danish—the languages in which the stories I have been describing were originally composed; it would also be a reward for a great deal of hard work. But there is nothing to be ashamed of in not knowing them, especially at a time when it is becoming increasingly hard to pick up even a modicum of Latin at school. And if one need not be ashamed of not knowing the languages, one need not be ashamed of not knowing how to pronounce certain words in them. Paradoxically it is often the very people who press most strongly for the abolition of 'classics' who are the most embarrassed if they are faced with a classical name that they cannot utter, as if they felt that knowledge of this sort ought to be be infused by supernatural grace.

As soon as irrational shame has been dispersed, one can set about the business of learning; there really is something to be ashamed of in neglecting to make proper enquiries. The most satisfactory method is to ask someone who has a grounding in the language concerned, because it is always easier to pick up sounds by ear than to recreate them from marks on paper. Sixth-form Latin usually provides familiarity with 'the ordinary English pronunciation' of Greek names, which did not change when the old pronunciation was reformed. Most people with a degree in English will be able to help with Anglo–Saxon and Norse names. If human aid is not available one must turn to books, and it is unfortunately true that books are not as helpful as they might be. The Americans are more realistic than the English; some of their translations, the Kennedy *Beowulf* for instance [Short List no. 72], provide indexes of proper names in which pronunciation is shown by putting the sounds into ordinary modern English spelling: thus the Geats appear as 'Gaý ats' and Queen Wealtheow as 'Waýalh thay o'. This is a much easier method for the common reader than the use of scientific phonetic symbols. Wanda Gàg showed the way by giving children English rhymes for German words in charming postscripts to her collections of Grimm stories [Short List nos. 129 and 130]. The *Oxford English Dictionary* gives phonetic equivalents for the Greek names that have been used metaphorically enough to qualify as common nouns. The *Oxford Companion to Classical Literature* [Short List no. 51] and the Marvin versions of Homer [Short List nos. 23 and 24] indicate the stressing and the long and short vowels in Greek names.

Recent children's books give no clues whatsoever to pronunciation— a sin of omission which is absurd as well as wicked. We need a simple grown-up pronouncing dictionary of mythology, and all writers for children ought to demonstrate the pronunciation of the names they have used.

2. THE VISUAL IMAGE AND THE HISTORICAL SETTING

Illustrations in children's own books, and pictures on the classroom wall, can make or mar their understanding of myth and fairy tale. To enter into the world of any story one has to see the characters and their clothes and houses in the mind's eye, and be able to watch them as they go about their business. If the story has a realistic contemporary setting, the words *refrigerator* or *theatre* are enough to recall the refrigerators and theatres that children have seen. In a historical novel by Rosemary Sutcliff descriptions of a tunic or a shield are complete enough for some children to be able to work out what the tunic or shield looked like—illustrations are a great help, but they are not a *sine qua non*.

No one has ever seen a giant or a dragon or a fairy with his bodily eyes, and their appearance is rarely described in detail in traditional stories. The Odysseus of history and the Arthur of history were once visible, but no one ever saw the Odysseus of Homer or the Arthur of the romances, and they have never been described completely either. Without a picture to look at, children either see nothing in their minds, or else collect an assembly of incongruous visual images. Heorot, the *hall* of Hrothgar, is the school hall or the hall of their own little house; the *barge* in which Arthur is carried to Avalon is one of the barges they saw when they visited a busy seaport.

It is foolish to illustrate myth and fairy tale impressionistically, because there are no concrete memories for the impression to recall. The sketchy, spiky, smudgy style of drawing that has recently become fashionable is of no use for books of this kind. It is precisely because no one has ever seen the Odysseus of Homer that children need to be shown how his hair is arranged, how his clothes are cut and sewn, and how his weapons are made and ornamented. The more imaginary the subject, the more precise the illustrations need to be. Buildings, clothes, armour and weapons are the things that above all need to be drawn clearly.

It seems that it is possible to have a wrong visual image; but is it possible to have a right one? What did Odysseus and Arthur look like? Or, even more unanswerably, what did Demeter and Thor and the Sleeping Beauty look like? The tellers and writers of all myths, legends and fairy tales were looking into 'the dark backward abysm of time', and discerning memories of different historical periods, some quite clear and others so faint that they were little more than ghosts. 'Accuracy' in illustration may require the mingling of two or three periods, if they are mingled in the original writings. Precision is required for aesthetic, not for historical reasons.

The best illustrators of myth and fairy tale for children have already satisfied this need for imaginative, pseudo-historical accuracy. Some of the rather expensive picture-books that have appeared recently are especially useful, even if they are too brightly coloured. Wall-pictures for children to look at while a story is being told or read aloud can be made from good illustrations; it is not difficult to scale them up, selecting the two or three most important figures and simplifying the lines of the drawing. Pictures should be large enough for everyone to see: at least full-imperial overall, with human figures eighteen inches high, or more. Line should be emphatic; broad felt pens are particularly useful.

This is a teacher's job, not a child's. Since children cannot see the characters of legend without the help of illustrations, it would be absurd to ask them to 'imagine' King Arthur. There are countless imaginative activities that arise naturally from listening to legends, but this is not one of them.

Teachers who can draw, however simply, usually like to go beyond mere copying. One's own figures can be clothed and armed and housed by comparison with reproductions or diagrams of the drawing and sculpture of relevant periods. It might therefore be useful to give a rough idea of dates.

The heroes of the Trojan War of about 1200 B.C. were described by Homer in about 750 (or 750 and 650, if there were two Homers), more or less in the fashion of 1000–800, with some very faint recollections of 1200. They were drawn as recognizable and recognizably clothed human beings on Greek vases from 650 to 300, in the changing styles of contemporary dress; they were also represented in reliefs and statues of that period. As comparatively little is known of Greek dress in 1000–800 or 1200, and it is dangerous to bring in Cretan dress of 1450 by analogy, it seems justifiable to draw them now in the dress of either 650 or 400, making allowances for the bronze weapons that Homer names. Stories about the gods and other heroes of the Greeks were written between 700 B.C. and A.D. 300, and continuously represented in painting and sculpture, always in contemporary dress. Again, it seems justifiable to choose any fashion in this long period that is aesthetically satisfying. Perhaps the clothes of 650 B.C. do suggest archetypal images better than those of fifth-century Athens or first-century Rome.

The men who wrote the Icelandic sagas were looking back to the heyday of a dying religion, and so it is natural to think of the Northern gods in the dress of 300–400 or 800–900 A.D., not that of 1250. On the other hand the poet of *Beowulf*, who was looking back to a period before 550, described in about 750 treasure and weapons which correspond with treasure and weapons buried in about 650; it is obviously right to illustrate the poem in that style. The writers of the Arthurian romances have entirely forgotten the Romano–British life of 500, and are seeing idealized pictures of their own castles and clothes of 1170–1470. In illustrating a series of Arthurian stories one might as well choose a late point in this long period and take advantage of the elegant and exuberant French and English fashions of 1350–1400. *Sir Gawain* is exceptional in giving minutely detailed descriptions of the clothes and armour of 1385, and *must* be illustrated accordingly.

Writers of fairy tales who were in any way artists themselves seem to have thought of their characters in a modified contemporary setting.

The characters of French fairy tales obviously wear eighteenth-century clothes, including the fairy godmothers, who are never described as small and ought to be drawn the same size as the ordinary human beings. They are human beings themselves; not creatures of another race, but Wise Women who are learned in magic and can enter the world 'of faerye'. Andersen's characters seem to wear the dress of his time, and the illustrator he chose himself, Vilhelm Pedersen, shows them in a simplified form of it which is subtly timeless. The traditional tales of peasant origin collected in the nineteenth century rarely give much indication of setting. The post-Pre-Raphaelite illustrators that Lang collected for his *Fairy Books* concocted a quite unhistorical pseudo-mediaeval, pseudo-classical kind of drapery that suited these traditional stories perfectly, and they worked in microscopic detail inside a frame. Among recent illustrators of fairy tale who suggest a timeless past there are E. H. Shepard, Pauline Baynes, Harold Jones and Edward Ardizzone. We have by now got rid of the innovated, prettified winged toddlers of E. M. Tarrant who had nothing to do either with the pastness of the past or with any description of fairies earlier than *Peter Pan*; but our present distorted rag-and-bone-women may be worse, and Disneyland has yet to be laid waste.

Since myths and legends are so tenuously attached to historical times and geographical places, it is usually misleading to bring them into a history or geography lesson, or a 'project' on Greece or Scandinavia. Mythology is storytelling, and the genius of the storyteller is rebuked by the genius of the historian. It spoils the story of Odysseus to make it an introduction to a study of 'real' eighth-century armour. The one natural point of contact is the historical date of writer or listener. There is nothing wrong in saying 'And just at the time we were learning about, Homer told the story of Odysseus—or Hans Andersen told the story of the Mermaid—which had happened a long, long time ago even then, and I'm going to read it to you now', or 'This boy in the castle in 1350 would have heard the old stories about the court of King Arthur, and I'll tell you some next time'. Even so it is better not to read too many legends of the same kind consecutively: children under eleven listen to them in the right spirit more easily if they are not assembled historically, but scattered over the syllabus and mixed up like poems in an anthology.

In a lesson on the historical tellers of unhistorical tales the question 'Is it true?' will probably emerge. In this context a child of ten or eleven usually means more than 'Are there dragons in England today?

Am I safe in my bed?' He wants to know whether the story is important. All too often I have heard the answers 'No, it's *only* a legend', or
'Legends aren't *true*', or 'Legends are about things that never *really*
happened'. A teacher who makes these replies is destroying in one
clumsy blow all the delicate fabric that the story has itself created.
Real and *true* are words of value, not words of definition and measure-
ment, and *only* is here a term of disparagement. He has said, to all
intents and purposes, 'This story doesn't matter; it has no value'.
Listening to myths and fantasies is an education in thinking in images
and symbols, and in thinking about things that cannot be apprehended
in any other way; it should be the foundation of a grown-up awareness
that
                    the mind of man becomes
        A thousand times more beautiful than the earth
        On which he dwells.

The point that must be made, somehow, in talking to older children
who ask 'Is it true?' is that when they 'make up' stories and pictures
themselves, what goes on inside their heads is 'real' just because it is
'really' going on there; if it wasn't, they wouldn't be able to write the
stories or paint the pictures. An idea of relationship between fact and
fantasy can sometimes be suggested by reminding children of a previous
lesson on some historical event or historical conditions, for instance
a battle or the building of houses that stand up against ice and snow,
and asking them to think what it felt like to fight in the battle or live in
the houses, and then saying 'Suppose you wanted to tell a story about
the fear without telling the story of the battle—or to describe the cold
without describing the houses?' Visual images will sometimes communicate an idea of multiple 'reality' and 'truth' to curious eleven-
year-olds. If the teacher brings an enlargement of a formal but fairly
individualized mediaeval or Renascence portrait, and asks them to
think about the clothes, and the hair, and the book or lute or pet monkey
in the hands, and the expression on the face, they see that it is a 'real'
picture of a 'real' person. If one of the children goes up to the picture
and puts her hair against the painted hair, and her hands against the
painted hands, they see that her hairs are not golden wires and that her
hands are not pinkish-white—and yet the painting continues to tell
them about a 'real' person.

The problem of 'reality' should never be forced upon children.
Their curiosity should be satisfied as it arises, but they will not continually want to know 'What does this particular story mean?' as long

as they are interested in it as a story, and feel assured that 'made-up' stories are important, and have nothing to do with 'fibs' and lies; the lamentably proverbial phrase 'Don't tell fairy stories' affects some children quite deeply.

Stories should be left to make their own imaginative effect with as little interference as possible by the storyteller. Information about the transmission of myths is of no use to children, and neither are theories about the interpretation of them. The more a teacher knows of these things, the better; knowledge will deepen his imaginative understanding of the stories, and understanding will make him a better storyteller.

3. WORDS, COLOURS, SHAPES AND MOVEMENTS

Just as myths and fairy tales can be recreated *for* children, they can be recreated *by* children; not only in words, but also in movement, shape and colour. Children bring their own experience into the process, just as the classical poets and mediaeval romancers did. They cannot 'imagine' buildings, clothes, armour or weapons (see preceding section): but they can use everything they know about trees, or grass, or ice, or sand, or animals' fur and prickles and hooves, or how people move and think and feel. When they are really familiar with good illustrations, they can begin to think about the texture of white samite, or how you hold a lance, or move in plate armour.

The simple exercise 'Tell the story of. . .' is not dull when the story is mythical, because its meaning does lie in what happens. The stories of Demeter and Persephone and the Death of Balder and Beowulf and Grendel are exciting to tell; and there are plenty of questions to brood over. Persephone is the spirit of spring, so what was she picking, and how did she walk? What sort of noise did Hades' chariot make? What can I say that will show just how dark the darkness was? What words can I find to show just what sort of nastiness there was in Ascalaphus? Retelling a myth or fairy tale is by no means a matter of remembering what a teacher said and writing it down. Of course one would not ask a child of ten to tell the whole story of Jason, or Beauty and the Beast; the story of the sowing of the dragon's teeth, or of Beauty's first day in the Beast's castle, would be enough.

Pretending to be one of the characters in a story is an old-fashioned exercise for ten-year-olds, but none the worse for that. There are plenty of opportunities for it in myth and legend and fairy tale, and of course a large part of the Odyssey was written as the hero's first-person report to Alcinous and Arete. Odysseus can describe his encounter with Circe to one of the men who stayed in the ship, to persuade him that it is safe to go to her palace; the soldier in *The Tinder-Box* can tell the princess how he won his gold and managed to reach her.

Painting in words is often refreshing to children who have got into the habit of writing stories mechanically. One can ask them to suppose that Perseus had a camera when he first saw the Fates, or that Jason had one when he saw the dragon coiled round the tree. What would come out in the photograph (preferably a coloured one)? What lies in the background? What is light, and what is dark? What sort of faces do the Fates have? What sort of noses? What sort of skin?

The success of real painting depends even more upon the narrowing of subject-matter. Any complete scene from myth or legend is a complicated composition, as half the narrative paintings of Europe will attest. There are far too many people and objects for eight- to eleven-year-olds to make into a visual pattern, quite apart from the frustration they feel when they 'can't draw' human figures, or can't imagine what their clothes would look like in different positions. The best ideas that myth and fairy tale give children for painting are abstract; but in some stories there are details that ask to be painted figuratively, especially non-human ones. Dogs with eyes like mill-wheels sitting on chests of gold are very paintable; so are dragons, and so are the sacred trees that they guard—the apple-tree of the Hesperides, the tree on which the Golden Fleece is spread, and the world-tree Yggdrasil. When children have seen enough good pictures of the Greek and Northern gods in an appropriate setting, they may be ready to give an impressionistic, imaginative interpretation of what they have seen and known concretely. The object of their work is exactly the reverse of the object of a teacher's work in making a wall-picture. One can begin with castles or temples at midnight, or at dawn; afterwards might come a head of Grendel, or one-eyed Odin in his broad hat, or the icicle-crowned Snow Queen; or a dark forest glade with Sir Galahad riding away almost out of sight at the end, or the great dark cave of the Cyclops, with Odysseus just escaping into daylight at the mouth.

Children's visual imagery is precious and fragile. It should never be wantonly smashed, as it is if they are asked to draw a picture of Perseus beheading the Gorgon on lined paper 8″ by 5″ in the last five minutes of the lesson. Drawing is not a time-killer.

The most exciting ways of retelling these stories are dramatic ones, either in movement alone or in movement accompanied by words.

They provide innumerable encounters between beings of opposed essences, which are a natural source of group dances to music that expresses the contrast of symbolic opposites—Beowulf and Grendel, Persephone and Hades, the Duckling and the Swan, the Mermaid and the Prince, Rapunzel and the Witch.

There are just as many sequences which can be mimed or half-danced to music, either with groups of children taking the part of each character, or with a class divided into several groups, in each of which a single child takes a single part. Daedalus and Icarus can toil and moil to build the maze for the Minotaur, and then delicately fit feathers into wings, until at last Daedalus soars levelly in the air and Icarus plunges upwards and downwards. Beauty can open one door after another in the strange castle, delighted and frightened by what she finds; the Beast can limp and prowl up to her, let her go, and then grow weaker and weaker and go to look at his roses before he dies. Movement to music is not very unlike movement to words, in which parts of the narrative are read by a teacher; this method works particularly well in recreating Arthurian stories like those of Uwaine and the Lady of the Fountain, and Balin and Balan.

The scripted play is a complex thing. It does not succeed unless children are used to working together persistently, and have plenty of time. If conditions are propitious, there are many legends and fairy tales out of which they can make their own plays; *The Emperor's New Clothes*, *The Dancing Princesses*, and the story of Theseus, Ariadne and the Minotaur are good ones. In bringing a class play up to performance pitch one's worst worry is to know what to do with the children who are not taking leading parts. The provision of a number of minor parts does not solve the problem. The children taking them clutter up the stage and still do not have enough to do to keep them interested. Legends and myths lend themselves to being told by a chorus and a few principal actors, as the Athenian playwrights found. A chorus of Townsfolk, or Sacrificial Victims, or Sailors, or Benevolent Fairies, can be fully engaged in doing most of the storytelling and commenting, thus leaving Theseus free to concentrate upon wrestling with the Minotaur.

Retelling stories is not the only kind of creation that springs from listening to myths and fairy tales. Many of them give, in narrative form, images of elemental qualities that can be translated into non-figurative painting, poetry and dance. The grey, cold wastes where Perseus finds the Gorgons, or the misty chasm that fills with blocks of ice in the Northern creation stories, can be reinterpreted in patterns of cold colour and stiff, angular shapes, or in frozen, angular movements. The towering flames through which Sigurd rides can inspire a fire-dance, or a painting in reds and golds and twisting shapes, or a poem called *Flame*. The forests of Arthurian romance can become a composition of black and green branching shapes in poetry or painting. The wrath of Achilles and the disloyalty of Mordred can turn into dances or poems called *Anger* or *Treachery*.

IV

The Language and Temper
of Fabulous Storytelling: a Critical
Examination of Seven Crucial Scenes
Described in Children's Books and in
Translations of Original Sources

There are times when one stands in a hot bookshop in front of a row of the books enumerated in my Short List, and feels sadly perplexed: they all look attractive and they all seem reasonably authoritative. The following passages show how different writers for children have handled a few of the most intense episodes in certain myths, legends and fairy tales, and what they adopted, altered or rejected in the more important of the original sources from which they worked. By putting several versions side by side here, I hope that I shall enable prospective story-tellers and readers to examine the language of these writers in peace and quiet, and with a cool head. The comparisons and contrasts that are suggested may invite them to dwell for a moment on the truth of a commonplace; the English that children hear deserves at least as much scrutiny as the English that their parents read silently.

Stories are misrepresented worse than any other large works of art when fragments of them are offered for critical inspection. The specimen brick gives a poor idea of the building. Nevertheless it may give some knowledge that the most accurate architectural drawing cannot give, and more feeling of character than is given by a poor diagram. Those who for some reason or other have missed our greater myths and fantastic tales may find in these fragments a persuasive argument for reading them now; certainly a more persuasive argument than any that I could invent. For the sake of brevity, I have had to leave out lines (three dots indicate omissions): for instance, M. R. Ridley and Ian Serraillier (pp. 96–7) both include in their narratives the coming of Christmas, which changes Gawain's weariness to gaiety; but I have omitted the parallel lines describing this from I c, I d and II.

I. MEDEA BEWITCHES THE SERPENT WHILE JASON SNATCHES THE GOLDEN FLEECE FROM THE GROVE OF ARES

1. *Versions for children*

A. That night, Medea led Jason to the temple where the Fleece hung from a pillar and sang magic spells to the serpent, sprinkling poppy juice on its eyes until they closed in sleep. Then Jason stole the Fleece and ran with her to the *Argo*.

— Robert Graves, *Myths of Ancient Greece* [Short List no. 10]

B. Medea again came to Jason, and warned him, and in the night she led him and Orpheus to the magic garden where the Golden Fleece hung on the tree at the world's end, guarded by a dragon—just as the apples of the Hesperides hung in their garden at the world's opposite end.

It was a dim, mysterious place, high-walled and pillared with the dark boles of mighty trees. Through the dappling moonlight Medea the witch-maiden led the way, until they came to the centre where the Golden Fleece shone in the darkness as it hung from a tree round which coiled a dragon larger and more terrible than any in the world.

'Play and sing!' whispered Medea to Orpheus, and she began to murmur a spell while he touched gently on the strings of his lyre and sang in a sweet low voice his Hymn to Sleep...As Orpheus sang it seemed that the very garden slept: the wind grew still; the flowers drooped their heads, and not a leaf stirred. The great gleaming dragon slid slowly from the tree, coil within coil, and, resting its terrible head on a bank of sleeping red poppies, slept for the first and last time in its life.

Only by the charms of Medea did Jason himself remain awake, and when he saw that the dragon slept, he drew near and looked up at the shining Fleece. Then Medea sprinkled the dragon with her magic brew, and whispered to Jason:

'Climb! Climb swiftly up the coils of its back and take down the Fleece, for my charms will not hold it long!'

So Jason, not without dread, mounted that terrible ladder into the great ilex tree and unhooked the Golden Fleece which had hung there ever since Phrixus stripped it from the magic ram; and by its light he found his way through the garden.

— Roger Lancelyn Green, *Tales of the Greek Heroes* [Short List no. 15]

C. Mooring *Argo* to a tree, they hurried along the path to the grove of the war-god where the Fleece was hanging on an oak-tree. They saw it gleaming in the distance and, when they came close, they had to shade their eyes.

The serpent lay coiled at the foot of the tree with its head raised; its eyes were flickering like torches. When it saw them coming it stretched out its neck, flashed its forked tongue and hissed. So loud was the hissing that all the leaves in the wood shook. In Colchis babies were startled out of their sleep, and their mothers picked them up from their cradles and hugged them to their breasts.

The loathsome creature slithered forward on its horny scales and opened its huge jaw. It could have swallowed *Argo* and her crew in one gulp.

But Medea walked right up to it and began to stroke its eyelids with a sprig of juniper leaves, which she had already dipped in her ointment. Then she called to Orpheus to sing.

His fingers swept the harp strings in a dreamy tune...There was not a whisper in the wood.

The cruel jaw sagged. The light in the eyes grew dim as mistletoe. The long coils girdling the tree and twisting far into the darkness beyond relaxed. The hooded eyelids slid down, and the serpent slept.

Then Jason sprang up and seized the Fleece.

As they hurried back through the wood the glow from the Fleece turned Jason's cheeks to fire and the path to liquid gold.

— Ian Serraillier, *The Clashing Rocks* [Short List no. 33]

D. All that remained now was to face the terrible dragon that guarded the Golden Fleece. It was a creature with a great crest on its head, a three-forked tongue and curving hooked teeth. It was coiled around the stem of the tree where, through the thick dark leaves, glowed a gleam of gold, shewing where the fleece was. Jason sprinkled on the dragon some juices from the herbs of forgetfulness which Medea had given him. Then three times he recited a spell strong enough to make stormy seas calm or to force swollen overflowing rivers back into their beds. Gradually and for the first time sleep came over the dragon's eyes. Jason threw the heavy fleece across his shoulder and, fearing some treacherous attack from King Aeetes, hurried to his ship with the Greeks and with Medea, who had saved him.

— Rex Warner, *Men and Gods* [Short List no. 36]

E. Medeia and the heroes ran forward and hurried through the poison wood, among the dark stems of the mighty beeches, guided by the gleam of the golden fleece, until they saw it hanging on one vast tree in the midst. And Jason would have sprung to seize it; but Medeia held him back, and pointed, shuddering, to the tree-foot, where the mighty serpent lay, coiled in and out among the roots, with a body like a mountain pine. His coils stretched many a fathom, spangled with bronze and gold; and half of him they could see, but no more, for the rest lay in the darkness far beyond.

And when he saw them coming he lifted up his head, and watched them with his small bright eyes, and flashed his forked tongue, and roared like the fire among the woodlands, till the forest tossed and groaned. For his cries shook the trees from leaf to root, and swept over the long reaches of the river, and over Aietes' hall, and woke the sleepers in the city, till mothers clasped their children in their fear.

But Medeia called gently to him, and he stretched out his long spotted neck, and licked her hand, and looked up in her face, as if to ask for food. Then she made a sign to Orpheus, and he began his magic song.

And as he sung the forest grew calm again, and the leaves on every tree hung still; and the serpent's head sank down, and his brazen coils grew limp, and his glittering eyes closed lazily, while Orpheus called to pleasant Slumber...

Then Jason leapt forward warily, and stept across that mighty snake, and tore the fleece from off the tree-trunk; and the four rushed down the garden, to the bank where *Argo* lay.

— Charles Kingsley, *The Heroes*, 1856 [Short List no. 20]

II. *Original sources in translation*

A. A path led them to the sacred wood, where they were making for the huge oak on which the fleece was hung, bright as a cloud incarnadined by the fiery beams of the rising sun. But the serpent with his sharp unsleeping eyes had seen them coming and now confronted them, stretching out his long neck and hissing terribly. The high banks of the river and the deep recesses of the wood threw back the sound, and far away from Titanian Aea it reached the ears of Colchians living by the outfall of Lycus, the river that parts from the loud waters of Araxes to unite his sacred stream with that of Phasis and flow in company with him till both debouch into the Caucasian Sea. Babies sleeping in their mothers' arms were startled by the hiss, and their anxious mothers waking in alarm hugged them closer to their breasts.

The monster in his sheath of horny scales rolled forward his interminable coils, like the eddies of black smoke that spring from smouldering logs and chase each other from below in endless convolutions. But as he writhed he saw the maiden take her stand, and heard her in her sweet voice invoking Sleep... The giant snake, enchanted by her song, was soon relaxing the whole length of his serrated spine and smoothing out his multitudinous undulations, like a dark and silent swell rolling across a sluggish sea. Yet his grim head still hovered over them and the cruel jaws threatened to snap them up. But Medea, chanting a spell, dipped a fresh sprig of juniper in her brew and sprinkled his eyes with her most potent drug; and as the all-pervading magic scent spread round his head, sleep fell on him. Stirring no more, he let his jaw sink to the ground, and his innumerable coils lay stretched out far behind, spanning the deep wood. Medea called to Jason and he snatched the golden fleece from the oak. But she herself stayed where she was, smearing the wild one's head with a magic salve, till Jason urged her to come back to the ship and she left the sombre grove of Ares.

Lord Jason held up the great fleece in his arms. The shimmering wool threw a fiery glow on his fair cheeks and forehead; and he rejoiced in it, glad as a girl who catches on her silken gown the lovely light of the full moon as it climbs the sky and looks into her attic room.

— Apollonius of Rhodes, *Argonautica*, trans. E. V. Rieu [Short List no. 40]

B. It remained to lull to sleep with magic drugs the watchful dragon which grimly guarded the golden tree. It was a striking sight, this creature, with its crest and three-forked tongue and curving fangs; but when Jason had sprinkled it with a herb whose juices bring oblivion, and had three times recited spells that produce tranquil slumbers, spells which soothe the tossing sea and raging rivers, then sleep fell upon those eyes which had never known it before, and the heroic son of Aeson gained possession of the gold. Exultant in his spoil, and carrying with him as a further prize the one who had enabled him to win it, he sailed homewards in triumph.

— Ovid, *Metamorphoses* VII, 149–158, trans. Mary M. Innes
[Short List no. 46]

The snatching of the Golden Fleece from its sanctuary is the climax of this tale of quest, just as Medea's enchantment of the dragon is the climax of all the spells which win her Jason's love. A serpent coiled round a tree or rod is a primitive symbol in many religions. The audience therefore needs time; time to see the darkness of the sacred wood, the glimmering of the Fleece, and the enormous coils of the dragon; time to sense the exercise of black and white magic and of ordinary human daring; time to recognize the emotions that in our common experience arise in any raid upon the unknown.

The classical poets who told the story saw the possibilities which this scene offered both for sheer entertainment and for evocative colouring (II A and B); in successful writing for children it is given comparably detailed treatment (I B–E). Passage I A is obviously no more than a summary, giving facts where a storyteller ought to give pictures. As a plain narrative it is firmly written, and may be useful, for instance, as a text to incorporate into a painting, or to speak as an introduction to a movement of a dance-drama. Robert Graves' noticeably (and deliberately) irreverent manner suits some of the Greek stories, but it cannot catch any of the feelings inherent in the pattern of this episode. Characteristically, he changes the sacred wood into a temple and the oak into a pillar.

Roger Lancelyn Green (I B) and Ian Serraillier (I C) have both re-created the scene visually, and both write in English that sounds clear and natural to modern children. The whole impression of I B, however, is more distant and dreamy that that of I C; Roger Lancelyn Green has gone as far as he can in using phrases 'evidently distinguished from common speech' without actually crossing the boundary that divides current language from an archaic or invented language. The rhythms are gliding and repetitive, even soporific, *sempre cantabile*; the phrases either long or running together into one long sentence—'until they came to the centre where the Golden Fleece shone in the darkness as it...' Some of the wording has fallen naturally into decasyllabic lines:

> It was a dim, mysterious place, high-walled...
> The wind grew still; the flowers drooped their heads...
> Slid slowly from the tree, coil within coil....
> Slept for the first and last time in its life.

There are more epithets than there are in IC—some critics would say too many—and they are either expected and traditional, which is justifiable and sometimes necessary in a traditional tale, or else very slightly archaic—'*mighty* trees...*dappling* moonlight...*gleaming* dragon... *sweet low* voice...*sleeping* poppies'. Where IC has 'ointment', IB has 'magic brew'.

The effect of this rhythm and diction is, I think, to make IB a little easier than IC for children to get hold of. They are left in no doubt that the tale is heroic, and that it is a tale 'of faerÿe'. Among the important words there are enough familiar ones for them to keep up with the narrative without being distracted by what is for them a verbal oddity. 'His eyes grew dim *as mistletoe*', or 'his jaw *sagged*' (IC) might stop an eight-year-old from attending to the story.

The cross-reference in IB to the other magic tree of the Hesperides 'at the world's opposite end' seems, out of its context, to be an unnecessary complication of the story, but as the whole of *Tales of the Greek Heroes* is designed to be read as a composite saga, it is an imaginative reminder for the child who is reading from beginning to end and fitting everything into place. The teller of a single tale should of course leave it out.

The freshness of Roger Lancelyn Green's version lies not in any obtrusively original phrasing, but in an original and understanding use of classical sources. In both IB and IC a great deal has been taken from Apollonius (IIA) and in both the enchantment of the dragon by Orpheus, rather than Medea herself, comes from the *Argonautica Orphica* (not reproduced here, as there is no good modern translation). In IB, however, there are also some of the best things from Ovid's story: his 'sleep fell upon those eyes which had never known it before' (IIB) has been sensitively fitted into the pattern and sensitively changed into 'slept for the first and last time in its life'; and some striking lines from a later episode, when Medea is casting her spells in order to procure the murder of Aeson, have likewise been woven into the fabric here as 'the wind grew still: the flowers drooped their heads, and not a leaf stirred'. At one point the action of I B is decidedly more exciting than that of I C. Jason climbs up the dragon in order to reach the Fleece, using it as a ladder, and Roger Lancelyn Green evidently saw that this was one of the most hair-raising details of the story as it was told by Valerius Flaccus in his *Argonautica*. Valerius makes Medea tell Jason, 'Climb up the dragon himself, and plant your feet on his back, where he lies in your path'.

I C is the most demonstrably original of these versions, and its conscious modernity and thrust make it acceptable to tough nine-year-olds who find that anything romantic is 'sissy'. The source-material is more limited than that of I B and I E, being confined to Apollonius (II A) and the *Argonautica Orphica*, with perhaps a touch of Ovid in the 'forked tongue'; but everything that Apollonius can contribute towards a bright, hard-edged effect has been used. The toughness of heroic adventuring has been slightly magnified, and the strangeness of magic slightly diminished. Ian Serraillier seems to have determined not to use more epithets than appear in ordinary workaday prose, even when they are present in his originals: he turns 'bright as a cloud...' into 'they saw it gleaming', 'the shimmering wool' into 'the glow from the Fleece', and 'threw a fiery glow on his fair cheeks' into 'turned Jason's cheeks to fire'. He substitutes the practical remark 'they had to shade their eyes' for the more fanciful image of II A. Most of the weight of sensuous meaning is carried by verbs—by *slithered*, *swallowed*, *sagged*, *girdling*, *twisting*. Even more strongly marked is the quick, emphatic sound of the short sentences, which never fall into verse rhythms. Quite often a brief sensuous image of the vintage of the 1960's is used in place of a more traditional description: 'sharp unsleeping eyes' becomes 'its eyes were flickering like torches' (an ambiguous reference, which might be to oil or naptha flares, or to electric torches), and Apollonius' images of smoke and sea swell are replaced by the entirely new 'the light in its eyes grew dim as mistletoe'. This last image is certainly clever, and striking, and appropriate inasmuch as mistletoe would be growing on the sacred oak. Some children may find it too clever, too modern, and too much like the 'good ideas' they are expected to produce themselves in 'creative writing'. There are children who really prefer the unashamedly formal style of I D and I E.

Serraillier is the only modern writer for children who makes use of Apollonius' picture of babies clinging to their mothers when they hear the dragon hissing. Like most epic and lyric poets, Apollonius (IIA) spends a good deal of time in fashioning detailed vignettes which seem to have very little bearing upon the main subject of his story. He brings in—or drags in—not only babies in distant places, but the course of all the rivers that separate them from the scene of action; smoke eddying from logs on a fire; the swell of a slowly moving sea; a young girl preening herself in a silk dress by moonlight. A first impression suggests that all these images are equally inaccessible to children, and could do nothing but spoil the story, so that anyone reading fragments of Apollonius himself to thirteen-year-olds, or writing the story for eight-year-olds, ought to leave all of them out. In IB there are none of these secondary pictures, which is another reason why it seems to be the easiest passage to listen to. In IE as well as IC the babies have been retained whereas all the rest has been rejected, and this one 'so that...' does not make the passages very much harder. The picture really is different from all the other pictures in that babies living by the outfall of Lycus literally heard the dragon, while the girl in her silk dress had nothing to do with Jason until Apollonius thought of comparing him with her. The girl in the silk dress is a surprising picture to find super-imposed upon the picture of a dragon, a princess and a hero; it is quite a shock to see an ordinary young woman, caught in an act of rather endearing vanity, in a very domestic setting, just after looking at Jason with the fleece on his shoulders in this dark wood, even though it is true that in both pictures someone is delighted by a treasure, and that in both a light is shimmering in darkness. Contrast is stronger than likeness; an adult reader comes back to the story with his taste for marvels refreshed by the small dose of domesticity administered by Apollonius. This is a sophisticated response. A child would think the image silly, if he thought about it at all. On the other hand some older children may appreciate the smoking logs and the swell on a sluggish sea. Eddying smoke is like a dragon in shape and movement, and so is a rolling swell; both are powerful and fascinating. 'Epic similes' of this second kind may be very effective in storytelling for children, whereas those of the first kind are nearly always ruinous. The difference between them creates a problem that will be raised again by the passages in group 2.

Like most of Rex Warner's classical storytelling, ID is almost a translation of Ovid (IIB) without reference to other sources. On this occasion Ovid happens to be less pictorial than usual, because he is saving his most blood-curdling magic for the later episode of Medea's murder of Aeson. Warner has caught the speed and epigrammatic sharpness of the original, and the terse 'three times he recited a spell strong enough to make stormy seas calm or to force swollen over-flowing rivers back to their beds' does as much in its own way as some of the word-painting of I B. Warner turns the ingenious 'sleep fell upon those eyes that had never known it before' into a well contrived *diminuendo* and *rallentando*: 'gradually and for the first time sleep came over the dragon's eyes'. Ovid's most telescopic phrase, *arbor aurea*, is too telescopic to make much effect as the English 'golden tree', and at this point only Warner extends his original, feeling some need, like the other writers for children, of putting 'gleam of gold' against 'dark leaves'. The vocabulary of I D is not difficult, and it would not be difficult for an intelligent ten- or eleven-year-old to understand. Its formality makes it accessible to some older children who are wary of anything that suggests 'telling to the bairns'. It is very obviously grown-up writing. If it is read aloud well it can give children a feeling for one kind of 'classical' style.

I hesitated before including Kingsley's version (I E) either in this selection of passages or in the following Short List of Books. It is Victorian and sounds Victorian, in tempo and rhythm and syntax. It is obviously romantic. Before a modern child could take it in, he would have to grow new ears for nineteenth-century English, as well as new eyes for the world of ancient myth. For most primary-school classes it would be a disastrously wrong choice. Yet in its own kind it is unmistakeably good. It shows that the story is a heroic legend on a larger-than-life scale; details from many different classical poets have been imaginatively remembered and beautifully integrated; it is quite free from the whimsies that make Nathaniel Hawthorne's Greek stories 'sound Victorian' in the popular sense of the phrase—outdated, mawk-ish and false.

Kingsley's use of Apollonius (II A) needs no comment. Like Roger Lancelyn Green (I B) he has taken the spell-binding song of Orpheus from the *Argonautica Orphica* and the idea of Jason treading on the dragon from Valerius. He may be closer to the sense of '*adverso gressus*' *ait* '*imprime dorso*' in making Jason step *across* the dragon, rather than *up* the dragon, since by this time it has been thoroughly hypnotized and has partly slid down the trunk. From Valerius, Kingsley also took its bronze and gold scales, and its recession into the darkness, and its gentle fawning upon Medea as if to ask for its usual food. In a remarkably un-Victorian fashion, he has rejected the words in which Valerius makes Medea feel sorry for the disappointment that her pet will feel when it wakes up and finds that the Fleece is not there. Kingsley, for one, understood that dragons are not to be pitied.

The language of I E is not quite an invented language like that of the Butcher and Lang *Odyssey* (2 II A); the words and most of the syntax are familiar. Nevertheless, it sounds archaic because of the long runs of simple, balanced phrases linked by the recurrent narrative 'and'. Occasionally there are nearly Miltonic expressions such as 'that mighty snake' and 'half of him they could see'. The strongest archaizing and integrating force in the passage is the prose rhythm, which is so incantatory that it is virtually a verse rhythm. For a good deal of the time Kingsley seems to hear the tale in 'fourteeners':

> Shuddering, to the tree foot, where the mighty serpent lay...
> His coils stretched many a fathom, spangled with bronze and gold...
> And when he saw them coming, he lifted up his head...
> The fire among the woodlands, till the forest tossed and groaned...
> And the serpent's head sank down, and his brazen coils grew limp...
> And the four rushed down the garden, to the bank where Argo lay...

Some children may like this kind of thing very much indeed, and the book should be in the classroom library for them to discover. It is too good to send for pulping.

2. ODYSSEUS IS DRIVEN BY STORM
TO THE COAST OF PHAEACIA

I. *Versions for children*

A. Then in a fury Poseidon called up the stormwinds, and whirling Odysseus into the deep, went on his way well pleased, deeming that this was the end. But Odysseus came safely to shore...
— Roger Lancelyn Green, *The Tale of Troy* [Short List no. 16]

B. He had not gone any great distance before an immense wave overturned the raft, and Odysseus never discovered which god to blame for this disaster. Two days later he was washed ashore, naked, near Drepane in Sicily...
— Robert Graves, *The Siege and Fall of Troy* [Short List no. 9]

C. But as he came nearer to the coast, he heard the sea thundering on the reefs, and knew that here were no gently sloping beaches where a tired swimmer might walk ashore; but only sharp rocks and craggy cliffs, and the surf battering against them.

'What now shall I do?' he wondered. 'Weary as I am, I yet dare go no farther in, for I should be torn to pieces on the pitiless rocks.'

At that moment he was seized by a huge breaker which carried him forwards towards the shore, and he would indeed have been killed upon the reef had he not grasped hold of a rock as he was swept along. There he clung while the wave rushed past him, but as it flowed backward again, he was torn from the rock and washed out to sea. With all his might he battled against the incoming waves until he reached the calm water beyond the breakers, and, keeping an eye ever towards the shore for the sight of a shelving beach where he might land, he swam farther along the coast.

Just when it seemed to him as though he could surely go no longer, but must choose between drowning in the deep sea or being dashed to pieces on the crags in a last attempt to land, he caught sight of the mouth of a river, where it flowed into the ocean.

Joyfully he swam to it, and a little way upstream, where the sand and stones sloped gently to the river's edge, he came ashore.

— Barbara Leonie Picard, *The Odyssey of Homer* [Short List no. 26]

D. But when he had swum near enough to hear the thunder of the breakers, and saw that there was no harbour and no shelter and only cliffs and jagged reefs, then at last his knees were loosened and his heart sank within him and he cried,

'Can it be that I have struggled hither against all hope and yet there is no place to land? If I go on, the waves will dash me on the rocks, and the cliffs are so sheer and the water so deep that I can gain no foothold. If I swim along the coast to find some shelter, the winds may bear me out again to sea, or Poseidon may send some monster to devour me, and there are many such.'

At that moment a billow swept him towards the cliffs, and there all his bones would have been broken, had he not thought of clutching at a rock and clinging to it with both hands till the wave had passed. But as it ebbed back again, it dragged him away with it and stripped his hands of skin, as a cuttlefish is dragged from its hole with pebbles clinging to its suckers. But he saved himself by turning and swimming along the shore outside the breakers, till he came to the mouth of a river free from rocks and sheltered from the wind.

He felt the river flowing and prayed to the River-God.

— F. S. Marvin and others, *The Adventures of Odysseus* [Short List no. 24]

E. But when he looked again he saw that there was no place where he could land, for the cliffs rose straight out of the sea, and the waves dashed high against them. And Ulysses thought, 'Now what shall I do? I see the land, indeed, but I cannot set my foot upon it. If I swim to it, then a wave may dash me on the rocks and kill me. And if I swim along the shore till I find a place where I may land, then some monster of the sea may lay hold of me.'

But while he was thinking, a great wave caught him and carried him on towards the cliffs. He caught hold of a jutting rock that was there, and clung to it with all his might till the wave had spent its force, so that he was not dashed against the face of the cliff. Nevertheless, when the water flowed back, he could not keep his hold on the rock, but was carried out to the deep. After this he swam along outside the breakers looking for a place where it was calm, or for a harbor, if such there might be. At last he came to where a river ran into the sea. The place was free from rocks and sheltered from the winds, and Ulysses felt the stream of the river, for it was fresh, in the salt water of the sea. And he prayed to the god of the river, saying, 'Hear me, O King, and help, for I am flying from the anger of the god of the Sea'.

— Alfred J. Church, *The Children's Odyssey*, 1907 [Short List no. 3]

F. On the third day all was calm, and the land was very near, and Odysseus began to swim towards it, through a terrible surf, which crashed and foamed on sheer rocks, where all his bones would be broken. Thrice he clasped a rock, and thrice the backwash of the wave dragged him out to sea. Then he swam outside of the breakers, along the line of land, looking for a safe place, and at last he came to the mouth of the river. Here all was smooth, with a shelving beach, and his feet touched bottom.

— Andrew Lang, *Tales of Troy and Greece*, 1907 [Short List no. 21]

II. *Original source in translation*

A. But when he was within earshot of the shore, and heard now the thunder of the sea against the reefs—for the great wave crashed against the dry land belching in terrible wise, and all was covered with foam of the sea,—for there were no harbours for ships nor shelters, but jutting headlands and reefs and cliffs; then at last the knees of Odysseus were loosened and his heart melted, and in heaviness he spake to his own brave spirit:

'Ah me! now that beyond all hope Zeus hath given me sight of land, and withal I have cloven my way through this gulf of the sea, here there is no place to land on from out of the grey water . . . But if I swim yet further along the coast to find, if I may, spits that take the waves aslant and havens of the sea, I fear lest the storm-winds catch me again and bear me over the teeming deep, making heavy moan; or else some god may even send forth against me a monster from out of the shore water; and many such pastureth the renowned Amphitrite. For I know how wroth against me hath been the great Shaker of the Earth.'

Whilst yet he pondered these things in his heart and mind, a great wave bore him to the rugged shore. There would he have been stript of his skin and all his bones been broken, but that the goddess, grey-eyed Athene, put a thought into his heart. He rushed in, and with both his hands clutched the rock, whereto he clung till the great wave went by. So he escaped that peril, but again with backward wash it leapt on him and smote him and cast him forth into the deep. And as when the cuttlefish is dragged forth from his chamber, the many pebbles clinging to his suckers, even so was the skin stript from his strong hand against the rocks, and the great wave closed over him. There of a truth would luckless Odysseus have perished beyond that which was ordained, had not grey-eyed Athene given him sure counsel. He rose from the line of the breakers that belch upon the shore, and swam outside, ever looking landwards, to find, if he might, spits that take the waves aslant, and havens of the sea. But when he came in his swimming over against the mouth of a fair-flowing river, whereby the place seemed best in his eyes, smooth of rocks, and withal there was a covert from the wind, Odysseus felt the river running, and prayed to him in his heart.

— Homer, *Odyssey* v, trans. Butcher and Lang [Short List no. 41]

B. But when he had come within call of the shore, he heard the thunder of surf on a rocky coast. With an angry roar the great seas were battering at the ironbound land and all was veiled in spray. There were no coves, no harbours that would hold a ship; nothing but headlands jutting out, sheer rock, and jagged reefs. When he realised this, Odysseus' knees quaked and his courage ebbed. He groaned in misery as he summed up the situation to himself:

'When I had given up hope, Zeus let me see the land, and I have taken all the trouble to swim to it across those leagues of water, only to find no way whatever of getting out of this grey surf and making my escape... if I swim farther down the coast on the chance of finding a natural harbour where the beaches take the waves aslant, it is only too likely that another squall will pounce on me and drive me out to join the deep-sea fish, where all my groans would do no good. Or some monster might be inspired to attack me from the depths. Amphitrite has a name for mothering plenty of such creatures in her seas; and I am well aware how the great Earthshaker detests me.'

This inward debate was cut short by a tremendous wave which swept him forward to the rugged shore, where he would have been flayed and all his bones been broken, had not the bright-eyed goddess Athene put it into his head to dash in and lay hold of a rock with both his hands. He clung there groaning while the great wave marched by. But no sooner had he escaped its fury than it struck him once more with the full force of its backward rush and flung him far out to sea. Pieces of skin stripped from his sturdy hands were left sticking to the crag, thick as the pebbles that stick to the suckers of a squid when he is torn from his hole. The great surge passed over Odysseus' head and there the unhappy man would have come to an unpredestined end, if Athene had not inspired him with a wise idea. Getting clear of the coastal breakers as he struggled to the surface, he now swam along outside them, keeping an eye on the land, in the hope of lighting on some natural harbour with shelving beaches. Presently his progress brought him off the mouth of a fast-running stream, and it struck him that this was the best spot he could find, for it was not only clear of rocks but sheltered from the winds. The current told him that he was at a river's mouth, and in his heart he prayed to the god of the stream.

— Homer, *Odyssey* v, trans. E. V. Rieu [Short List no. 43]

Homer gives a very exact account of the storm that nearly drowns Odysseus just before he sets foot safely upon Phaeacia (II A and B), and it is not difficult to see why. It is the last of Odysseus' perils by wind and water, and he is about to be the guest of a king whose court is more civilized, luxurious and accomplished than anything the hero has known among the Greeks. It is the last chance we have to see his powers of endurance, his bodily strength, and his presence of mind. The worse his present exposure seems, the more we shall appreciate the courtesy of King Alcinous' hall and the tales of its minstrels, and among them Odysseus' own tale of the perils already past. He will be found by Nausicaa when he wakes up and crawls out of a heap of leaves, and the more we know of the seas and rocks that have battered him, the more we shall understand how frightened she must be by the naked, salt-caked, torn and bleeding figure that appears before her.

I A and I B are summaries, and this storm is too important to be summarized. Roger Lancelyn Green and Robert Graves have written narratives that keep the threads of the Trojan cycle of legends untangled, and they are useful to the storyteller or the child who wants a guide to the sequence of events, especially the events of the ten years' war. The story of the return of Odysseus is so episodic that there is not much difficulty in remembering what happened or why it happened; if the episodes are not treated in almost Homeric detail all their colour seems to drain away.

I C and I D both succeed in recreating the fury of the storm, and the thoughts and movements of a man resisting the temptation to panic. There are fairy-tale episodes in the *Odyssey*, but this is not one of them; Odysseus is here a real sea-dog, and the word-painting in Homer and in these two passages is not atmospheric or evocative, but practical. In both there is an almost cinematic development from movement to movement. Odysseus' first survey of the coast as he looks for a safe place to walk ashore leads to an immediate reaction of despair and resentment; then follows the unforeseen onslaught of the great breaker, and his painful resistance to it; then a renewed hope and activity of mind when he finds himself in calmer waters and decides to swim parallel with the land until he can see a gap in the cliffs; then realization that he has come to the mouth of a river, and can turn towards the shore without danger. Both I C and I D give some feeling of the power of the wild seas, and a visual image of the coastline; in phrases like 'sharp rocks and craggy cliffs, and the surf battering against them', and 'where the sand and stones sloped gently to the river's edge', I C is visually more clear and emphatic than I D.

I D is obviously more Homeric than I C; I C is obviously more straightforward than I D for children to read—it sounds more modern. In much the same way E. V. Rieu's translation of the original (II B) is more accessible, to some adult readers today, than the Butcher and Lang version (II A). But something has been lost from II B, and from I C, and one is sorry to lose it, even as the price of a style that lets one get on with the story quickly. It is not idiomatic English to say that knees are loosened (I D and II A), but for all that the phrase describes very accurately a sensation that most people have when they are exhausted or shocked, whereas knees very rarely quake (II B) although the expression is an accepted one. Homer's language shows that for him the river and its god are not two distinct entities, which makes his lines difficult to turn into any ordinary English. They communicate, none the less, the immediate physical sensation of being pulled by a current running across the currents of the sea, and there is nothing obscurely primitive in this; it is what would assure any man in Odysseus' situation that his eyes were not deceiving him and that the river was really there. Butcher and Lang are literal in their translation: 'Odysseus felt the river running, and prayed to him'. E. V. Rieu's 'The current told him that he was at a river's mouth' is idiomatic, but it weakens the meaning, since 'the current told him' might be a merely verbal personification. The version for children by Marvin and others gets rid of the Homeric ambiguity and yet keeps the vital sense-experience: 'He felt the river flowing and prayed to the river-God'. The idea has been left out of I C entirely, together with two others that help to create a sense of a world not only savage but pervaded by countless supernatural powers. Amphitrite feeds herds of monsters in the waters, or so Odysseus believes, although he does not know what they are; and the thought of clutching the rock comes into his head because Athene put it there. I D manages to keep the substance of 'many such pastureth the renowned Amphitrite' without introducing the name of yet another divinity; Poseidon, whom we know already, serves adequately as the overlord of the sea-monsters. I D also retains some of Homer's realistic detail of the skin being stripped from Odysseus' fingers and left sticking to the rock—which means something to any child who has scrambled up a cliff or been knocked over by a rough sea—together with his simile of the cuttlefish which is wrenched from its hole with pebbles sticking to it. This comparison is raw and horrible, as the experience was; but there is nothing in it which is difficult to get hold of, and nothing that calls for a sophisticated response (unless the process of likening is pursued to the point at which one reflects that although bits of the living cuttlefish must have been left in the hole, Homer has actually pointed to bits of the hole being left on the cuttlefish). The image seems strange and 'old-fashioned' only because it has been developed so completely, and because of the 'as when...' form in which it is introduced. Its substance is vivid to most children, and some children like the form just because of its strangeness. (Compare pp. 67–70 above.)

I D is shorter than I C, but it contains some trace of all the dominant ideas in the original, and also sounds a little archaic, without becoming as odd or bewildering as II A would be to a child reading alone. The run of the phrases suggests that the story was meant to be intoned:

...and saw that there was no harbour and no shelter and only cliffs and jagged reefs, then at last his knees were loosened and his heart sank within him and he cried...

This retelling by F. S. Marvin and others is in fact an accomplished piece of work, an abridged and simplified free translation in which there are few incongruities or awkward joints. The only edition in which it is available is a textbook, and a textbook of 1920 at that, old enough in typography and style of illustration to look frowsty, but not old enough to look antique. If it could only be made into a well-printed book which looked either ancient or modern it would be a lovely thing for older children to possess. As it is, it contains many passages that can be read to children who are not quite ready for snippets of a full translation. The joint authors preserved the flash-back arrangement of the *Odyssey*, which is always frustrating to children, who like to begin at the beginning of a story: but anyone reading from their work, or from a full translation, can easily rearrange the order of events.

A comparison of I C with I D need not lead to any simple conclusion that one is better than the other; the questions that follow more justifiably are 'Better for which children?' and 'Better for what kind of use?' I C has not superseded I D; but Barbara Leonie Picard's book can be put straight into children's hands, and her avoidance of artificial language and archaic conceptions make the legend entertaining and credible to children who may never have heard any English that departs from the idiom of modern speech. To write within the limits of modern phrasing and yet make a legend sound heroic is no easy matter, and her prose is noticeably severe and dignified, even when comparison with the original suggests that she is consciously avoiding incantation.

I E and I F have been included to show how good the Victorian retelling of classical stories could be (these versions were not published until 1907, but they are still written in the Victorian tradition). Neither would be the right thing for most school classes (compare notes on 1 I E, pp. 69–70 above); if children are ready for a more epic style than Barbara Leonie Picard's, they are usually ready for the Marvin version, but there are a few musical and well-read children of nine and ten who would enjoy the simple, ceremonious prose of Lang and A. J. Church. I E could be read aloud in class *as a quotation*, by a teacher who was telling the story in his own words; Church is particularly imaginative and arresting in dealing with the freshwater current of the river. There is a beautifully printed edition of his version, which is probably the best thing to put into the hands of a bookish child who wants to know more about Odysseus.

A note on the language of storytelling for children is not the place to enter into a long argument (still proceeding among scholars) about the language into which epic poetry ought to be translated for grown-ups. However, the argument cannot be dodged altogether. It has already been introduced, faintly and in miniature, by comparing I c with I D. It may confront, directly and unavoidably, the storyteller who wants to show how some outstanding action or speech or landscape was first put into words, or put into words by the poet who determined its present significance. It is exciting to children of nine or ten to hear the words in which a story was first told, just as it is exciting for them to hear the words of an eyewitness of a battle, or to handle a fifteenth-century bench-end, or a beribboned and ruched Victorian album. These experiences are stirrings of the historical emotion, the feeling of touching the same thing that was touched by human hands centuries or millennia ago. Homer's narrative of the storm could well be plundered by anyone prepared to tell the story in his own words and quote from time to time. The first description of the coast as Odysseus sees it through the rising spray is simple and graphic enough, and so is the coming of the great wave and the simile of the cuttlefish. Such a storyteller is then compelled to decide whether it is II A or II B that gives the more strongly a sense of immediate contact with a poet of the seventh century B.C.

The case against translating early epic poetry into colloquial English has been presented by J. R. R. Tolkien in a preface to his revised edition of the Clark Hall translation of *Beowulf* [Short List no. 69], and this is his conclusion:

Personally you may not like an archaic vocabulary, and word-order artificially maintained as an elevated and literary language. You may prefer the brand new, the lively and the snappy. But whatever may be the case with other poets of past ages (with Homer, for instance) the author of *Beowulf* did not share this preference. If you wish to translate, not rewrite, *Beowulf*, your language must be literary and traditional; not because it is now a long while since the poem was made, or because it speaks of things that have since become ancient, but because the diction of *Beowulf* was poetic, archaic, artificial (if you will) in the day that the poem was made.

The poetry of Homer is here specifically excepted, and the relative naturalness of the *Odyssey* is perhaps indicated by the mere existence of a modern idiomatic prose version which sounds sensible and serious, and can be read easily (IIB); all translations of *Beowulf* into the idiom of modern speech sound inept. However there is some measure of agreement among critics, including E. V. Rieu himself, about the nobility of Homer's diction, and the presence of archaic and conventional expressions within it. The Butcher and Lang version (IIA) was made in the belief that a literal translation was needed at the end of the nineteenth century to transmit 'that half of the truth' of the poem that interested the historian; it was also inspired by a hope that literal translation into 'antiquated prose' would capture some of the feeling of the original. In their preface the translators asserted that

It may be objected, that the employment of language which does not come spontaneously to the lips, is an affectation out of place in a version of the Odyssey. To this we may answer that the Greek Epic dialect, like the English of our Bible, was a thing of slow growth and composite nature, that it was never a spoken language, nor, except for certain poetical purposes, a written language. Thus the Biblical English seems as nearly analogous to the Epic Greek, as anything that our tongue has to offer.

At various times I have tried out IIA and IIB on students of twenty and on children of ten and eleven. Sometimes the students had the text of the passages; the children just listened. Most of the students who just listened preferred IIA. First and foremost, it was easier to follow. Some said that it seemed more consistent in style, or more appropriately remote; or simply that it sounded more interesting. A few voices were raised against 'phoney' antiquity or 'oldë-worldë' sentiment. The students who read silently from a typescript nearly all thought that II B was easier to understand, and some thought that it was more forceful or more 'sincere'. The children nearly all liked II A better. It was 'more like a proper story'; it was 'more glorious', and 'sounded like the sea'. A few said that it sounded 'funny'. One shrewd child observed that it was 'like being in church', which may or may not have been intended as a compliment.

Apparently II A is meant to be heard, while II B is meant to be seen. The differentiation was so marked that some of the students who preferred II B when they read silently changed their minds when the two passages were read aloud. The phrasing of II A does explain this effect; it is hard to recognize a syntactic pattern on first scanning

and swam outside, ever looking landwards, to find, if he might, spits that take the waves aslant, and havens of the sea.

Still more baffling to the eye is

But when he came in his swimming over against the mouth of a fair-flowing river, whereby the place seemed best in his eyes, smooth of rocks, and withal there was a covert from the wind, Odysseus felt the river running...

Yet neither of these sequences presents any difficulty if one is listening to a reader who *has* grasped the pattern. The words are '*plain* and old', as the translators claimed; a sensation of being carried or floated forward on successive waves of sound is created by the voice which is suspended and not allowed to drop, and it is more expressive than the stopping and starting of

Presently his progress brought him off the mouth of a fast-running stream, and it struck him that this was the best spot he could find, for it was not only clear of rocks but sheltered from the winds.

At this point 'it struck him that'... does sound a little inconsequential for a man who has just escaped with his life, in the same way as 'I have taken all the trouble to swim to it' sounds petty by the side of 'I have cloven my way through this gulph of the sea'.

A teacher or storyteller cannot say that 'antiquated prose' or 'idiomatic modern English' is right, or wrong, without thinking of his audience; yet again, he can only ask 'Right for whom, and for what?' The 'Biblical English' of Butcher and Lang certainly makes more impression on modern children than one might expect; but it would be

wise to remember that 'the English of our Bible' is becoming as unfamiliar as Epic Greek to many ears.

3. THE GOLDEN TOUCH OF KING MIDAS
1. *Versions for children*

A. Dionysus gratefully promised to grant Midas any wish he pleased: and
Midas chose the magic power of transforming into gold whatever he touched.
It was great fun at first: making gold roses and golden nightingales out of the
ordinary ones. Then, by mistake, he turned his own daughter into a statue,
and also found that the food he ate and the wine he drank were turning to
gold in his mouth; so that he nearly died of hunger and thirst. Dionysus
laughed loudly at Midas, but let him wash off the 'golden touch' in the
Phrygian river Pactolus—the sands of which are still bright with gold—and
restore his daughter, too.

— Robert Graves, *Myths of Ancient Greece* [Short List no. 10]

B. Did I tell you that, although he was powerful and rich through inheritance,
Midas was not particularly intelligent or witty? In conversation he always
said the obvious thing and he muddled whatever he did say, for not only was
he stupid, but he never stopped to think. So, when he heard what Bacchus
said through the pleasant fumes of wine, he staggered and cried out: 'Oh,
divine Son of Jupiter...turn everything that I touch into gold.'

Scarcely had he heard this wish than Bacchus set about granting it.

Seated in front of a table groaning with delicious food, Midas put out his
hand to help himself; suddenly all the exquisite fish, the delicious meats and
the rare fruit were ·turned into gold. The fool immediately realized his
mistake and, dying from hunger and thirst, he sought out Bacchus, to beseech
him to take back his dangerous gift. Bacchus accordingly ordered him to
bathe in the waters of the Pactolus. The bath saved Midas, but from that time
on the river had an abundance of gold in its sand.

— Emile Genest, *Myths of Ancient Greece and Rome*,
trans. Barbara Whelpton

C. So pleased was Bacchus...that he said to Midas: 'Choose anything you
like for a gift, and it shall be given to you.'

Midas made bad use of the opportunity which the god had given him.
'What I should like', he said, 'is that everything which I touch should be
turned to gold.'

Bacchus granted his prayer, but wished that he had made a better choice,
since what he had asked for would only bring him sorrow. But Midas went
away full of joy and at once decided to try the effects of his new power.
Hardly daring to believe it, he broke off a twig from a small oak-tree.
Immediately the twig turned to gold. He picked up a stone from the ground,

and the stone sparkled and shone with precious metal. He touched a clod of earth, and the clod became a great nugget of gold. He let his hand stray over the ears of growing corn, and the harvest was a harvest of gold. He picked an apple from a tree and, when he held it in his hand, it was like one of the apples of the Hesperides... Then, as he was still rejoicing in his new power, his servants brought out a table covered with fine meats and bread. But when he put out his hand to take the bread, it immediately became hard and stiff. When he put a piece of meat in his mouth and started to bite it, he found that his teeth were biting on hard metal. He mixed water with his wine to drink, but, when he raised the glass to his lips, it was molten metal that flowed into his mouth.

This was far from being what he had expected. He was rich indeed, but also most miserable. Now he longed to escape from his wealth, and hated the very thing for which he had prayed. All the food in the world could not relieve his hunger. His throat was parched with thirst. He was tortured by the hateful gold. Lifting up to the sky his shining arms and hands, he prayed: 'O Father Bacchus, forgive my me mistake! Have pity on me, and take away this gift that seemed so very different from what it really is!'

The gods are kind. Midas had confessed his fault and Bacchus made him as he had been before... Midas did as the god had told him. The golden touch passed from his body into the water. Even to this day the river rolls over golden sands and carries gold dust to the sea.

— Rex Warner, *Men and Gods* [Short List no. 36]

D. Meanwhile, Marygold slowly and disconsolately opened the door, and showed herself with her apron at her eyes, still sobbing as if her heart would break.

'How now, my little lady', cried Midas. 'Pray what is the matter with you, this bright morning?'

Marygold, without taking the apron from her eyes, held out her hand, in which was one of the roses which Midas had so recently transmuted.

'Beautiful!' exclaimed her father. 'And what is there in this magnificent golden rose to make you cry?'

'Ah, dear father!' answered the child, as well as her sobs would let her; 'it is not beautiful, but the ugliest flower that ever grew! As soon as I was dressed, I ran into the garden to gather some roses for you; because I know you like them, and like them the better when gathered by your little daughter. But, oh dear, dear me! What do you think has happened? Such a misfortune! All the beautiful roses, that smelled so sweetly and had so many lovely blushes, are blighted and spoilt! They are grown quite yellow, as you see this one, and have no longer any fragrance! What can have been the matter with them?'

'Poh, my dear little girl—pray don't cry about it!' said Midas, who was ashamed to confess that he himself had wrought the change which so greatly afflicted her. 'Sit down and eat your bread and milk! You will find it easy enough to exchange a golden rose like that (which will last hundreds of years), for an ordinary one, which would wither in a day.'

'I don't care for such roses as this!' cried Marygold, tossing it contemptuously away. 'It has no smell, and the hard petals prick my nose!'...

Midas, meanwhile, had poured out a cup of coffee; and, as a matter of course, the coffee-pot, whatever metal it may have been when he took it up, was gold when he set it down. He thought to himself, that it was rather an extravagant style of splendour, in a king of his simple habits, to breakfast off a service of gold, and began to be puzzled with the difficulty of keeping his treasures safe. The cupboard and the kitchen would no longer be a secure place of deposit for articles so valuable as golden bowls and coffee-pots...

Then, with a sweet and sorrowful impulse to comfort him, she started from her chair, and running to Midas, threw her arms affectionately about his knees. He bent down and kissed her. He felt that his little daughter's love was worth a thousand times more than he had gained by the Golden Touch.

'My precious, precious Marygold!' cried he.

But Marygold made no answer.

Alas, what had he done? How fatal was the gift which the stranger bestowed! The moment the lips of Midas touched Marygold's forehead, a change had taken place. Her sweet, rosy face, so full of affection as it had been, assumed a glittering yellow colour, with yellow tear-drops congealing on her cheeks. Her beautiful brown ringlets took the same tint. Her soft and tender little form grew hard and inflexible within her father's encircling arms. Oh, terrible misfortune! The victim of his insatiable desire for wealth, little Marygold was a human child no longer, but a golden statue!

— Nathaniel Hawthorne, *A Wonder Book*, 1852

E. As he drew near to his own rose-gardens, Midas paused to try his new and wonderful power. He reached up and picked a spray of oak-leaves all fresh and green—and found them a moment later almost too heavy to lift, for they were solid, shining gold. He picked up a stone, and it too was solid gold by the time he was standing upright again with it in his hands. Feeling his sandals grown strangely heavy, he unfastened the straps of thin gold and walked barefoot through the grass—and the grass itself turned to gold, while he left golden footmarks in the dust...

With a horrible fear clutching at his heart, Midas picked up the golden cup of wine. A moment later he was spitting out drops of gold, and choking desperately over golden dust.

'Perhaps in the morning I may find some way of eating and drinking,' thought Midas...

At last, so lame from treading on gold that he could hardly walk, Midas came to the valley where the King was whom the Satyrs served.

'Pardon me!' he cried, falling on his knees in front of the fragrant bower.

'I have done wrong, I know—pardon me my greed, and take away this horrible Golden Touch, for I want never to see gold again!... A moment later he felt ordinary wet clothes clinging about him, and was satisfying his long thirst with icy water more pleasant than any wine. Then he went home again, eating grapes and munching apples happily.

When he reached his lovely rose-gardens he found with delight that not a golden rose remained; all were their own selves of soft scented damask, red or white, as before.

— Roger Lancelyn Green, *Old Greek Fairy Tales* [Short List no. 13]

II. *Original source in translation*

The god... gave Midas the right to choose himself a gift—a privilege which Midas welcomed, but one which did him little good, for he was fated to make poor use of the opportunity he was given. He said to the god: 'Grant that whatever my person touches be turned to yellow gold.' Bacchus, though sorry that Midas had not asked for something better, granted his request, and presented him with this baneful gift. The Phrygian king went off cheerfully, delighted with the misfortune which had befallen him. He tested the good faith of Bacchus' promise by touching this and that, and could scarcely believe his own senses when he broke a green twig from a low-growing branch of oak, and the twig turned to gold. He lifted a stone from the ground and the stone, likewise, gleamed pale gold. He touched a sod of earth and the earth, by the power of his touch, became a lump of ore. The dry ears of corn which he gathered were a harvest of golden metal, and when he plucked an apple from a tree and held it in his hand, you would have thought that the Hesperides had given it him...

So he exulted in his good fortune, while servants set before him tables piled high with meats, and with bread in abundance. But then, when he touched a piece of bread, it grew stiff and hard: if he hungrily tried to bite into the meat, a sheet of gold encased the food, as soon as his teeth came in contact with it. He took some wine, itself the discovery of the god who had endowed him with his power, and adding clear water, mixed himself a drink: the liquid could be seen turning to molten gold as it passed his lips.

Wretched in spite of his riches, dismayed by the strange disaster which had befallen him, Midas prayed for a way of escape from his wealth, loathing what he had lately desired. No amount of food could relieve his hunger, parching thirst burned his throat, and he was tortured, as he deserved, by the gold he now hated. Raising his shining arms, he stretched his hands to heaven and cried: 'Forgive me, father Bacchus! I have sinned, yet pity me, I pray, and save me speedily from this disaster that promised so fair!' The gods are kind: when Midas confessed his fault, Bacchus restored him to his former state...

The king went to the spring as he was bidden: his power to change things into gold passed from his person into the stream, and coloured its waters.

Even today, though the vein of ore is now so ancient, the soil of the fields is hardened by the grains it receives, and gleams with gold where the water from the river moistens its sods.

— Ovid, *Metamorphoses* XI, 100–145, trans. Mary M. Innes

[Short List no. 46]

The tale of Midas is the fable of the Foolish Wish, a story that sprouts everywhere in folklore, as if to prove what Lang called 'the strange identity of human fancy in all places', and to show that one of the truths most firmly embedded in common sense (or perhaps in 'the memory of the race') is the knowledge that human beings are day-dreamers, and that they dream of blessings that would prove to be curses if their dreams 'came true'. The German tale of *The Fisherman and his Wife* is one variant of it, and among many others are the Scandinavian *Why the Sea is Salt* and the English *The Woodcutter's Three Wishes*. Yet as one remembers it, the story of Midas is not like these other folk tales in feeling; it seems more serious, and dignified, and allegorical. Of course this impression is partly caused by the principal source, which is not a peasant fable but an elegant Latin poem. Nevertheless it cannot be quite accidental that legends of a mighty King of Phrygia absorbed a tale of this particular Foolish Wish instead of any other. Midas does not wish for anything as grotesque as a black pudding to stick on his wife's nose, or a quern to grind an endless stream of herrings. He wishes for gold, a universal symbol of wealth and the power that wealth confers. Ovid's account of the manner in which gold became 'hard food for Midas' (II) leaves later poets with a shining instance of the difference between necessities and luxuries, or nature and artifice, or love and power, or any other things brought to mind by the antithetic words *bread* and *gold*. Since the story is funny and simple like a folk tale, and also evocative like a myth, it can be told to quite young children and also to teenagers. In any retelling of it one hopes to find both the peasant shrewdness and the poetic evocativeness.

I A is a good version for seven- or eight-year-olds, if one wants a half-minute story. Robert Graves' cheeky manner is not incongruous here, because Midas really is making a fool of himself. As the facts of the tale are so few anyway, one does not feel that he is rushing on and leaving his audience two or three events behind. There is no attempt to copy Ovid's moving picture of the changes coming over the growing, organic things that Midas touches, but the poetic theme is introduced by the nightingales and roses. Roses do not come into any classical record of this particular story about Midas, but in another place Hyginus says that the king was famous for making the first rose garden in the world. To graft his report on the story of the Golden Touch is easy and felicitous; it is done in I D and I E as well as in I A.

In I B some of Ovid's details are introduced, although the story remains fairly short. The wine and the meat are included, and the writer must be trying to make the episode lively when he turns round to chat to the reader with 'Did I tell you that...?' When a storyteller is really extemporizing, this kind of appeal to the audience often works, especially with young children; but it has to be a real question, addressed to real children at one particular moment. Put into print in this fashion, it sounds heavy and condescending. A version of the shorter classical stories that was intermediate between those of Robert Graves and Rex Warner would be useful for many nine- and ten-year-olds; but I B is too ponderous for them. The material is simple, but the sentences are cumbersome without being resonant. 'Seated in front of a table groaning with delicious food, Midas put out his hand' is more awkward in structure than the equivalent sentence in I c: 'Then, as he was still rejoicing in his new power, his servants brought out a table covered with fine meats and bread'. Nothing in I B is as direct and incisive as 'He picked up a stone from the ground, and the stone sparkled and shone with precious metal'. The easy-going language at the beginning, for instance, in 'he muddled whatever he did say' clashes unpleasantly with the formal, old-fashioned 'he sought out Bacchus, to beseech him to take back his dangerous gift'. The use of 'witty' and 'fool' is not quite English, and suggests literal translation from French.

I B does not give more to the imagination than I A, for all its additional words. As soon as children are ready for something longer and more classical than I A, they are probably ready for I c. Rex Warner's method of freely translating and abridging Ovid can be seen at its best here; the story of Midas is one of Ovid's most delightful flights of fancy, and this is a sparkling version of it. Ten- and eleven-year olds enjoy the minute detail in which Ovid displays the change coming over the twig, the clod, the corn, the apple... the *bread*! As each new object turns up, they can anticipate what is going to happen *this* time. Some cutting may be necessary, but not much. Sometimes I c gives a better impression than II of the original effect. 'He let his hands stray over the ears of growing corn, and the harvest was a harvest of gold' is much lighter and more compact and more rhythmical than 'The dry ears of corn which he gathered were a harvest of gold', which says exactly what Ovid says, but does not suggest his elegance. 'This gift that seemed so very different from what it really is' is not a translation of *speciosum damnum*, but does catch the cleverness and moral thrust of the phrase, and 'this disaster that promised so fair' does not.

ID and IE belong to the same *genre* of retelling. The versions of the story made by Hawthorne and Roger Lancelyn Green are both considerably longer than Ovid's narrative; they are fully-blown short stories, and I have not been able to reproduce completely the sections that correspond with IA to IC; they would take up too much space. Hawthorne's account of Midas' breakfast goes on for pages. ID and IE do not show what has been included or excluded by these two writers. They are given only as specimens of the temper and language of the two versions.

Both ID and IE have been written for quite young children. Hawthorne wrote his Greek stories for a five-year-old and an eight-year-old, and they still suggest an average listening age of six or seven. Roger Lancelyn Green's book is dedicated 'to June, who complained that there were too many names in Greek mythology'. Except for Perrault (compare pp. 41–2), all the other good writers for children represented in this chapter are careful to preserve something of the background and feeling of their original sources. Both these writers have decided to ignore Ovid's poetry, and to write in the personal, unhurried, easy-going style that has always been necessary in telling stories to children under seven. Hawthorne goes farther than this; he invents a daughter of Midas so that there shall be a young child in the story, and gives Midas the full menu and table-setting of an American Civil War breakfast of 'hot cakes, some nice little brook-trout, roasted potatoes, fresh boiled eggs, and coffee... and a bowl of bread and milk for his daughter Marygold'. Hawthorne's stories became so popular that Marygold became part of the Midas legend in many people's memories; she is included in IA, even though Robert Graves must have known that she is not mentioned in any classical source.

It is a risky operation. Turning a poetic tale into a nursery story (as distinct from a child's story) is always likely to end in sentimentality. It seems to me that Hawthorne has fallen over the cliff, and that Roger Lancelyn Green manages very cleverly to keep on a safe cliff-path. There is too much whimsy in Hawthorne's 'the hard petals prick my nose', and too much effusive sentiment about sentiment in 'a sweet and sorrowful impulse to comfort him', and 'her sweet, rosy face, so full of affection as it had been'. Putting a very little girl into the tale may make it acceptable to a five-year-old, but will probably lead to indignant rejection of it at the age of nine, which would be a pity. Hawthorne's Greek stories have been out of fashion for some time, and it would be pointless for an unsympathetic reader to discuss them, if they had not recently (1963) been republished for children with the blessing of Kathleen Lines and also of Roger Lancelyn Green. In their eyes Hawthorne is a nineteenth-century Perrault, putting an old tale into a contemporary setting, and telling it in a personal and humorous way. They are two critics with whom one hesitates to disagree, and it is true that there are likenesses between Perrault's method and Hawthorne's; but there are important differences as well. Perrault took over stories that had no strong associations with any region or culture. The story of Midas has always been remembered as a classical story, however vague or long may be the period of time implied by that term; it is associated with wine, not with mead or beer or coffee. Perrault did not turn grown-up characters into child characters. Perrault's familiar style is terse and witty; a child will not grow out of it and come to dismiss the stories as childish. Young children today still like to hear a good deal about what people eat, but not as much as Hawthorne tells them; the pace of his stories is Victorian, and children now are like their elders in expecting a more rapid narrative style than the Victorians expected in their fiction.

Ie is easy without being childish, and Greek without being severely classical. Everyday experiences of eating and bathing—or falling into a pond—are described in a way that is real to children of seven who know what it is to spit out drops of this or that and choke desperately, or to have ordinary wet clothes clinging round them, or to munch apples happily; but the wine and the grapes and the apples are Greek, and need not be unlearned. The words given to Midas when he thinks 'perhaps in the morning I may find some way of eating and drinking' are very simple, but they are more kingly than 'I don't quite see. . .how I am to get any breakfast'. Two of the things touched by Midas here, and not in any other version, so far as I know, are his sandal straps, and then, when he is barefooted, the blades of grass. These original additions to the story are imaginative, since the inevitable sequence from bad to worse is Ovidian in its cleverness, and also quite right for children, who are acutely aware both of uncomfortable shoes and of the feeling of sharp stones under bare feet. The beauty of growing things is shown in the roses without embarrassing effusiveness. Children of seven like this version, and some children of eight, nine or even ten may find that *Old Greek Fairy Tales* are a good way into a Secondary World.

4. THE LAIR OF GRENDEL'S MOTHER, AND BEOWULF'S FIGHT WITH HER BENEATH THE WATERS OF THE LAKE

I. *Versions for children*

A. Along the base of the cliffs lay black shelving rocks where the sea beasts basked at noontide, and others that were jagged and fanged like sea beasts themselves, and the waves of the open sea, driven into the confined space, boiled and weltered as in a cauldron. At the landward end of this evil place a stream coming down from the high moors had cut for itself through the years a deep gorge overhung with a tangle of sere and salt-burned trees that dripped grey lichen into the grey mists of the falling water and the spume that beat up from the churning waves below. A place of ill-omen; a dreadful place of which men told many stories—stories of giant shapes half glimpsed in the sea mists, of strange sounds echoing and strange lights flaring beneath the water, and storms that blew up out of nowhere and strange tides that set there. . . .

Down and down sank Beowulf into the cold swinging depths; down and down for what seemed the whole of a day. From all sides the tusked sea beasts rushed in upon him, striving to gore him to pieces; and ever as he sank he fought them off with stroke and lunge of the great sword Hrunting. At last his feet touched the sea floor, and instantly an enemy far more dire was upon him, as the Sea-Hag leapt to fling her arms about him, clutching him to her with claws as terrible as her son's had been. He was being rushed through the black depths, close-locked in her dreadful embrace, and now, still together, they were diving upward through the under-water mouth of a cave.

Up and up. . . They were in a vast sea-hall above the tide-line, white sand underfoot, and the faint light of day falling in shafts from some opening to the cliff top far above. Beowulf tore himself free and springing clear for a sword stroke, brought Hrunting whistling down on her head. The cave rang with the blow, but for the first time since it was forged the blade refused to bite, and next instant she was upon him once more.

— Rosemary Sutcliff, *Beowulf* [Short List no. 67]

B.   . . . the lonely land
Where dwell the dark spirits, by paths of peril,
By cloud-haunted hills where wolves go hunting,
By windy cliffs where swollen torrents tumbling
Plunge headlong into the misty deep,
The grumbling under-water. A mile beyond
There lies an evil lake no plummet has sounded,
The margin all along with the roots entangled

Of tall trees; in gloomy splendour they rise,
Their branches feathered with frost. Yonder at night
A horror can be seen—the cold flood on fire,
With candles kindling the dark till quenched at dawning
To a grey smoulder...
                    O weird and evil
Is the Grendel lake! When stormy wind is stirring,
The angry wave leaps up to lash the cloud
And the air darkens and the bloated heavens weep...
                    He dived into the surge;
The dark wave swallowed him, downward he sank.
Many a savage monster fastened upon him,
With cruel tusk and talon ripped and slashed
His mailcoat—while Grendel's mother, tyrant queen
Of that dismal realm, laughed in her lurking place
Deep at the bottom of the lake. Minded to slay him,
Suddenly lo! with arm outstretched she launched
Upward, straight for Beowulf, and clutched him in her claw
And hugged him to her hairy chest so smothering-close
He could not swing his sword, then downward dragged him,
Deep down to her den.
                    When the rushing ceased,
He beheld a paved floor unrolling at his feet.
Under the lake in a lofty hall he stood
Whose roof, buttressed with stout rafters, upheld
The weight of water...
                    a shape
More massy than the rest, dark-shouldered,
Towering high, like a mountain hiding the sun.
'Twas the foul she-monster, were-wolf of the deep.
Then drew he his sword, Hrunting, the death-dealer,
Prince of a thousand fights. The edge of steel
Slashed home; with clash upon clash it dinned
Its greedy battle-cry into her skull—yet failed him,
Crumpling like a reed.
              — Ian Serraillier, *Beowulf the Warrior* [Short List no. 65]

II. *Original source in translation*

A. They dwell in a land unknown, wolf-haunted slopes, wind-swept headlands, perilous marsh-paths, where the mountain stream goes down under the
mists of the cliffs,—a flood under the earth. It is not far hence, in miles, that
the lake stands over which hang groves covered with frost: the wood, firm-
rooted, overshadows the water.

There may be seen each night a fearful wonder,—fire on the flood!...
That is no pleasant spot. Thence rises up the surging water darkly to the
clouds, when the wind stirs up baleful storms, until the air grows misty, the
heavens weep...

The surging water received the warrior. It was a good part of the day
before he could descry the solid bottom. Quickly she who, fiercely ravenous,
had ranged the watery realm for fifty years, greedy and grim, found that one
of the human kind was there, examining from above the home of monsters.
Then she clutched at him, she seized the warrior with her horrid claws...
when she came to the bottom, bore the ring-clad lord to her own dwelling, so
that, however brave he was, he could not wield his weapons; for so many of
the weird creatures hampered him in swimming. Many a sea-beast tried to break
through his shirt of mail with its warlike tusks,—the monsters pursued him.

Then the chief perceived that he was in some unfriendly hall or other,
where no water harmed him in any way, nor might the sudden rush of the
flood touch him, by reason of the vaulted chamber;—a fiery light he saw,
a glaring flame shine brightly. Then the brave man perceived the accursed
monster of the deep, the mighty mere-wife. He gave a forceful impulse to his
battle-sword; his hand did not hold back the blow,—so that the patterned
blade sang out a greedy war-song on her head. Then the stranger found that
the shining weapon would not bite, could do no harm to life; but the blade
failed the chieftain in his need.

— *Beowulf* 1357–76, 1494–1525, trans. J. R. Clark Hall [Short List no. 69]

B.   They dwell in lands of hiding,
     Wolf-slopes, windy nesses, paths of risk
     Between bogs, where mountain streams go sliding,
     Dropping down the headlands under the mist;
     Pools below the earth. Not far off
     Measured in miles, stands the lake:
     Over it hang boughs of frost;
     Firm by the roots, on the water leans the brake.
     There each night a dangerous splendour
     Can be seen—fire on the flood!...
                    It is no pleasing place:
     The waves of the mingle beat up together
     Wan to the clouds, when the wind stirs
     The horrible dripping weather;
     The sky weeps and the welkin smurrs...
     The whelming brim received him brief.
     It was great part of day ere bottom he could spy.
     But the one who still did keep
     For half a hundred years,
     Grim and greedy, the compass of the deep,

Found that a man from above was trying to get in
The nest of ill creatures. Then she clutched at him, and wound
The man in desperate grips. . .
              The she-wolf of the mere
As she came to bottom, bore and blustered him
To her courts, that he, though strong, could not drag clear
His weapons; but many horrors clustered at him,
Many beasts of the wave, his sark of war to burst
With battailous tusks: they crowded hot
At the soldier.
             Then saw the hero first
That he was in some enemy hall—I know not what—
Where no water hurt him, nor, in the roofed hall, might
The flood touch him with sudden drench.
Then he saw firelight—a strong flame shine bright—
By that the brave man found the bottom-wench,
The pond-wolf mighty; his sword he sped
Wigh vigour behind it,—hand withheld not its dash,—
That the ring-iron sang on her head
A greedy song of war. But the battleflash
(As found the stranger) bit, nor would attain
Her life—the edge at need betrayed its master.
      Beowulf 1357–76, 1494–1525, trans. Gavin Bone [Short List no. 70]

The story of *Beowulf* is so simple in its architecture that there could never be any doubt about the necessity of spending time upon the hero's fight with Grendel's mother, and upon the place where it happens; the whole poem turns upon his three great fights, one with Grendel, one with Grendel's mother, the mere-hag, and one with the dragon. The eighth-century poet occupied the rest of his 3,182 lines with preparations for these fights and with the consequences of them: with news, journeys, searches, skirmishes, and rewards, and above all with long speeches in which the characters show their knowledge of past and present events, and their vision of life on this earth. Writers for children have naturally, and rightly, described the fights as fully as the poet did, curtailing the journeys and the speeches.

I A is a novelist's account of what a poet saw. A literal translation (II A) shows how distinctively poetic the original is; it lacks many of the virtues of good prose, or rather does not need them. In comparison with Homer's account of Odysseus' behaviour in a dangerous place (2 II A and B) it is vague and impractical. Each separate detail of 'fire on the flood', 'groves covered with frost' and 'vaulted chamber' is brilliantly clear, but one does not see how the mountain stream feeds the lake, or what causes the storms and the fire, or—any more than Beowulf himself did—why he finds himself in a dry vaulted chamber after being dragged downward through the water. The tusks of the beasts are unforgettable, but why should they be trying to break through his shirt of mail when he is already in the grip of Grendel's mother? They would have to gore her before getting at him. The whole impression is one of sudden flashes and impacts. Even Beowulf's first move in the single combat is unexplained. One does not know how the opponents are positioned; one simply sees the engraved blade of his sword, and hears the 'song' it sings in the air.

Rosemary Sutcliff has rationalized all these uncertainties,[1] and has thus produced a version of the story which is satisfying to the kind of children who demand, at ten or eleven, to understand exactly how things work. The location has been changed from an inland lake to the shore. The unnamed beasts can now become walruses, and in the preceding episodes Hrothgar's followers can be engaged in an orthodox walrus-hunt. The trees are burned with salt, not covered in frost. Storms and rising spray are natural enough here, and even so the 'strange tides' are reported as travellers' tales. The 'hall' of Grendel's mother is placed unambiguously 'above the tide-line', and turned into a cave lit by a fissure in the cliff-top; Beowulf has to rise through the water to reach it. The walruses attack him as he dives down into the sea; Grendel's mother catches him when he reaches the bottom, and then drags him upwards. He is seen to 'tear himself free' before he gives the first stroke with his sword. This retelling of *Beowulf* is not a simplified translation; it is a short novel, in which Rosemary Sutcliff seems to look behind the poem at the historical events and geographical places that may be remembered in it. She fills in gaps that are left by information conveyed piecemeal in speeches; here she takes her description of the lair of Grendel's mother out of the mouth of Hrothgar, and remakes it into straightforward narrative.

A legend is not sacrosanct; it can change its shape like Proteus, or it would not be a legend. The success of the metamorphosis is the only thing that counts. For most of the time Rosemary Sutcliff's *Beowulf* can be read as a lively and perceptive historical novel. But a misshapen

[1] It is possible to attribute them to the oral transmission of the poem and its composition in different stages. On this reading, the episode is not impressionistic but messy, and there is all the more justification for tidying it up. Rosemary Sutcliff is following the criticism of R. W. Chambers.

giant fiend and a water-hag are not historical, and when they appear they upset the carefully preserved realism. One's awareness of discrepancy is only slight, because her writing and plotting are so consistent; nevertheless a Homeric mixture of realism and fantasy does not quite accord with this single-stranded tale.

I A is firmly written, in an entirely modern idiom, but children under ten seem to follow I B more easily if it is read aloud. The diction of I A, like its rational treatment of the story, puts it within the range of slightly older children. The sentences are longer or more complex; slightly abstract or technical phrases like 'driven into the confined space' or 'at the landward end' or 'stroke and lunge' are used where I B has the directly sensuous 'grumbling under-water' and 'the edge of steel slashed home'.

I B is obviously closer than I A to the original poem in its pictures of the place and the fight, and in its flashes of brilliant unrelated detail. There is not much attempt to link the grumbling under-water with the evil lake, or the lake with the trees, or the trees with the fire on the flood. The savage monsters (not walruses) attack Beowulf before Grendel's mother seizes him, but apart from that the combat proceeds much as in the original, in a 'lofty hall' which is *under* the lake. Younger children enjoy the immediate sense-experiences of shivering cold and foggy darkness communicated by I B, and its impressionistic hints of weird and supernatural evil. The flashes of detail come off—or nearly come off—because it is a retelling in verse. In the original poem it is the bounding or clashing verse rhythms that force them to fuse with one another in the imagination of the listener. A translation by Scott Moncrieff gives some idea of the sound, although it almost extinguishes the sense:

Sea-deer many
With worrying tusks his war sark tare,
Chased him the creatures. Then the earl knew
That he was in some or other enemy's hall.

No prose translation of *Beowulf* avoids disjointedness, however dignified the language may be. It is possible to read the Butcher and Lang *Odyssey* for pleasure, but I doubt whether any one ever read the Clark Hall *Beowulf* except as a crib or a reference book. Certainly no one would want to read II A to children of any age, or even to quote from it, except in phrases of three or four words. There is a 'warlike' sound in I B that does carry an audience of children irresistibly through this nightmare sequence: nine-year-olds are usually clutching their desks during

> The dark wave swallowed him, downward he sank.
> Many a savage monster fastened upon him,
> With cruel tusk and talon ripped and slashed
> His mailcoat...

There are two questionable things about the retelling by Ian Serraillier; one is the verse-form he has chosen, and the other is his method of expanding some of the descriptive phrases in the original. His verse is more or less accentual—that is to say, one is more conscious that the line contains a certain number of strong stresses than that it consists of a certain number of syllables. His publisher says that 'the verse follows closely the pattern of the original poem' and one therefore supposes at first that he must be writing in the original poet's metre, in which every line has four stresses. Accentual verse always seems to approximate to the traditional four-stress line, as if the human ear demanded this particular balance, and most of his rhythms do fall into its pattern:

> / He dived into the surge;
>
> The dark wave swallowed him, / downward he sank.
>
> Many a savage / monster fastened upon him.

However there are some lines that can hardly be read without five stresses, and these are lines which are awkward to speak anyway:

> He could not swing his sword, then downward dragged him...
>
> Prince of a thousand fights. The edge of steel...

As he has made a version of a mediaeval accentual poem in what he calls a 'five-stress line' (compare p. 100 below) one wonders whether this *Beowulf* is meant to be in five-stress verse, and whether one is intended to read

> The dark wave swallowed him, downward he sank.
>
> Many a savage monster fastened upon him.

Arguments about prosody always sound pedantic, and of course it does not matter whether a poem for children is in exactly the same verse-form as its source. The vitality and certainty of the verse-rhythms that they hear matter a great deal.

A second question is raised by phrases like 'their branches *feathered* with frost', or 'the *cold* flood on fire *With candles kindling the dark*', or 'Towering high, *like a mountain hiding the sun*'. These are clear, ingenious pictorial images, which attract younger children and help them to concentrate on what is happening; but the personal fancifulness of the italicized words is alien to the anonymity of the legend, and also to the stylized fancifulness of the original poem.

There is bound to be some expansion and contraction of the original in any version that is not strictly literal. II B is a free translation in verse, not a retelling, but Gavin Bone's words do not exactly correspond with Anglo-Saxon ones in phrases like 'where mountain streams go sliding' or 'the horrible dripping weather' or 'the waves of the mingle' or 'bore and blustered him' (compare II A). These additions and rearrangements are not out of keeping with the way in which things are described in the poem, and at some points II B is more literal than II A, and at the same time more arresting. 'Wolf-slopes' is better than 'wolf-haunted slopes'. 'The whelming brim received him brief' catches the sound of *brim wylm onfeng hilde-rince*, although 'brief' is unnecessary and the whole phrase sounds very odd. 'The surging water received the warrior' is conventionally idiomatic, but rather dull. 'Battleflash 'is a more literal translation of the 'epic phrase' for a sword than 'shining weapon', and much more interesting. It must have been more interesting than 'shining weapon' in the eighth century, however often one heard it.

II B does suggest 'the noble brevity' of *Beowulf*, as the translator intended, and its 'picturesque equivalents for ordinary things'. Gavin Bone made a readable poem, which is probably the best translation for the storyteller who wants to produce fragments of 'the real thing' as the crowning glories of his tale (compare p. 77 above). The lines that will irritate children are those in which devotion to Anglo–Saxon 'picturesqueness' has produced queer or obscure archaisms like 'the welkin smurrs' or 'windy nesses'.[1] A translation by Charles Kennedy into the original metre [Short List no. 72] is never annoying in this way; the language is more idiomatic, but somewhat neutrally correct.

II B can sound impressive read aloud, but the reader has to take some trouble to discover its rhythms. It is written in a kind of rhymed free verse; the lines have no fixed length or fixed number of stresses, but the line-endings are clearly marked by the rhymes, which are arranged alternately in quatrains. Most rhymed verse is syllabic and has to be read without any deliberately heavy stressing, but these irregular lines seem to be irregularly accentual, and to need a formal three-, four- or five-stress reading to make any effect. Treated in this fashion, they can suggest the energy of the original poem:

[1] A new verse translation by Kevin Crossley-Holland [Short List no. 71] excludes archaisms, and may prove useful for the same purpose.

4   The waves of the mingle beat up together
4   Wan to the clouds, when the wind stirs
3   The horrible dripping weather...

4   As she came to bottom, bore and blustered him
5   To her courts, that he, though strong, could not drag clear
4   His weapons; but many horrors clustered at him...

5. GAWAIN'S WINTER JOURNEY, AND HIS FIRST SIGHT OF
THE GREEN KNIGHT'S CASTLE ON CHRISTMAS EVE

I. *Versions for children*

A. And the winter came upon him as he travelled, with icy wind and snow, but never a word did he hear of his quest.

At last, on Christmas Eve, he came upon a castle...

— Barbara Leonie Picard, *Stories of King Arthur and his Knights*
[Short List no. 87]

B. Gawain endured all—foes to overcome, and the bitter weather of mid-winter.

On Christmas Eve he rode upon Gringalet through marsh and mire, and prayed that he might find shelter. And on a sudden he came through open parkland to a fine castle set on a little hill above a deep valley where flowed a wide stream. A fair lawn lay in front of it, and many great oak trees on either side; there was a moat before the castle, and a low palisade of wood.

'Now God be thanked,' said Sir Gawain, 'that I have come to this fair dwelling for Christmas'...

— Roger Lancelyn Green, *King Arthur and his Knights of the Round Table*
[Short List no. 83]

C. But his fights wearied him less than the winter weather, when the cold clear rain fell from the clouds and froze into hail before it reached the faded ground below. More nights than he cared for he slept in his armour among the bare rocks, half dead with the cold and the sleet, while the cold beck came rattling down from the crest high above him, and hung over his head in icicles...he rode gaily along a hillside into a deep forest that was wonder-fully wild, with high hills rising on each hand and woods below of huge grey oaks, hundreds together, and a tangle of hazel and hawthorn, with rough shaggy moss hanging over them. Many birds sat shivering on the bare twigs, piping a pitiful little song as the cold nipped them.

The knight on Gringolet passed on his way beneath them, through swamp and mire, all by himself, and troubled about how he was to keep Christmas, if he could not manage to see the due service of the Lord, who on that same night was born of a maiden to heal all our sorrows. And so with a sigh he said,

'I beseech you, Lord Christ, and Mary, gentlest mother so dear, to bring me to some shelter where I may devoutly hear the Mass and matins tomorrow. Humbly I ask it, and say straightway my Paternoster and Ave and Credo.' He rode on, praying as he rode, and confessed his sins, and crossed himself, saying, 'The Cross of Christ be my good speed.'

He had crossed himself but three times when he was aware through the trees of a dwelling circled by a moat, standing on a mound that rose from a piece of meadowland, shut in under the boughs of many great trees that closed in round the moat. It was a castle, the fairest that ever a knight owned, built in a clearing with a park all round it, and round the park a stout palisade of spikes that took in more than two miles of forest land. Gawain looked at the stronghold from that side, and saw it shimmering and shining through the fair oaks, and then he reverently took off his helmet and gave devout thanks to Jesus and Saint Julian, gentle Lord and gentle saint, who had thus shown him kindness and heard his prayer...

On the tower roofs his eye picked out many white chimneys that gleamed like chalk cliffs in the sunlight. And there were so many pinnacles, gaily painted, scattered about everywhere and climbing one above another among the embrasures of the castle, that it looked as though it were cut out of paper, like a model. — M. R. Ridley, *Sir Gawain and the Green Knight* [Short List no. 88]

D. But worse than all warring was the winter rain
That hurtled from the cloud and froze before it fell.
Night after night, by sleet and snow half-slain,
Among the naked rocks he slept his spell
Under canopy of icicles, in his iron bed
Of armour, while the cold streams clattered overhead...
He laughed and smiled
As he rode through the frozen hills to a wondrous wild
Oakwood, with hazel and hawthorn intertwined,
Shaggy with moss; where birds, in the frosty air
And cruel piercing cold, on branches bare
And leafless, piteously piped and pined.

Suddenly he saw—as he passed by marsh and mire—
Set on a hillock in tree-lapped lawn
A moated castle (God above be praised!)
Shimmering and shining in the winter dawn...
loop-holed turrets high
Traced like papercuts against the sky;
With hall and barbican and spires and painted
Pinnacles cunningly wrought and ornamented,
And tall chimneys that twinkled chalk-white
On cloth of blue.
— Ian Serraillier, *The Challenge of the Green Knight* [Short List no. 89]

II. *Original source in translation*

Yet the warring little worried him; worse was the winter,
When the cold clear water cascaded from the clouds
And froze before it could fall to the fallow earth.
Half-slain by the sleet, he slept in his armour
Night after night among the naked rocks,
Where the cold streams ran clattering from the crests above
And hung high over his head in hard icicles. . .

Merrily in the morning by a mountain he rode
Into a wondrously wild wood in a valley,
With high hills on each side overpeering a forest
Of huge heavy oaks, a hundred together.
The hazel and the hawthorn were intertwined,
And all was overgrown with hoar-frosted moss,
And on the bleak branches birds in misery
Piteously piped away, pinched with cold.
The gallant knight on Gringolet galloped under them
Through many a swamp and marsh, a man all alone,
Afraid of missing the functions of the feast day to come,
And not seeing the service of Him who that same night
Of a virgin was verily born to be victor over our strife.
And so, sighing, he said, 'I beseech thee, Lord,
And thee, Mary, mildest mother so dear,
That I may happen on some haven and there hear High Mass
And Matins tomorrow morning: meekly I ask it,
And promptly thereto I pray my Pater and Ave
          And Creed.'
          He crossed himself and cried
          For his sins, and said, 'Christ speed
          My cause, His cross my guide!'
          So prayed he, spurring his steed.

Thrice the sign of the Saviour on himself he had made,
When in the wood he was aware of a dwelling with a moat
On a promontory above a plateau, penned in by the
     boughs
And tremendous trunks of trees, and trench about.
The comeliest castle ever acquired by a knight,
It was placed in an impregnable palisade
Of pointed stakes, on a plain with a park all round,
Containing many trees in its two-mile circumference.
The courteous knight contemplated the castle from one side
As it shimmered and shone through the shining oaks.

Then he heaved off his helmet and heartily thanked
Jesus and Saint Julian, two gentle patrons
Who had given him grace and gratified his wish...

Many chalk-white chimneys the chevalier saw
On the tops of towers twinkling whitely—
And so many painted pinnacles disposed everywhere,
Congregated in clusters beyond the castle embrasures,
That it appeared like a prospect of paper patterning.
    — *Sir Gawain and the Green Knight*, trans. Brian Stone
                                                    [Short List no. 94]

The quest of Gawain takes him through northern terrors of ice and
water and darkness, but light shines more brightly in the fourteenth
century than in the eighth. The sunlit castle of the Green Knight is
larger and more brilliant and more cunningly adorned than the gleaming hall of Hrothgar, and it is suddenly there as if by miracle as soon
as Gawain has finished his confession: 'he was aware of a dwelling in
the wood...' In much the same way the narrative style of II is clear-
sighted and intricate in comparison with the impressionistic, obscurely
powerful language of *Beowulf* (4 IIA and B). The symbolism of the
whole tale makes it too subtle for most children under eleven (see pp.
37–8 above), and the poet's description of Gawain's journey and first
sight of the Green Knight's castle show how much of its meaning is
contained in word-painting as exquisitely fine as the brushwork of
contemporary miniatures. Reducing the scale in order to work it into
a sequence of other Arthurian stories is bound to cause some loss. Of
the two short versions represented here, IB loses less than IA; throughout his Arthurian stories Roger Lancelyn Green is careful to suggest
their inner patterning and latent imagery.

It is perhaps wrong to classify IC as a 'version for children'. It
appeared in a Ward series of legends, some of which seem to be retold for children rather than for grown-ups; it can certainly be read
to children of twelve, and some children of thirteen or fourteen would
read it on their own. On the other hand, M. R. Ridley said that he was
not rewriting the poem, but translating it for 'the ordinary reader' who
could not be persuaded to take any interest in the fourteenth-century
technique of cutting up a hunted deer. Two technical descriptions have
been omitted, and words which exist less for the sense than for the
verse-form are sometimes ignored. The preface to this version shows
that it was made with much the same purpose as Gavin Bone's translation of *Beowulf*, and should be judged in the same way:

Others...will admit that there are two stools on either of which one can, with very precarious safety, sit. One can make a full translation, which omits nothing...or one can go to the other extreme and offer to the reader an 'adaptation' of the story, with such omissions and modifications and additions as the taste of the adapter suggests. Anyone, they think, who attempts anything else will fall sprawling between two stools. I have an idea that there is a sort of humble cushion on the floor between the two stools which may be occupied without grave disaster or falsification, so long as one makes it clear what the cushion is.

This declaration of intent should please any teacher, because it is always hard to sacrifice communicability to the truth of the matter as one sees it, or truth to ease of communication.

The storyteller's choice for eleven-year-olds therefore lies between an adaptation of the poem made especially for children, in verse but not in the original metre (ID), a not quite complete prose translation which is meant to be imaginatively rather than literally exact (IC), and a full verse translation in the original metre in a style 'somewhat more embellished than that of good modern prose' (II). In the business of making the story the right length, and dividing it into instalments, Ian Serraillier's adaptation will make his task much easier; it is short enough to be read to children with hardly any cutting. Long passages have rightly been devoted to highly visual episodes, and ceremonies and speeches have been abridged. Anyone who uses the translations will have to pick and choose for himself; but there are advantages in picking and choosing (see p. 77 above), and once the right passages have been found, the translations are often more imaginative than the adaptation, and not much more difficult.

ID is shorter than IC or II, and occasionally easier because the ideas are more common, or because technical detail has been simplified. 'In the cruel piercing cold' is a more ordinary way of thinking about birds in winter than 'pinched with cold' or 'as the cold nipped them'. From all three passages I have omitted some of the lines in which the complicated architecture of the castle is described, because I think that anyone reading to children would have to omit them. I have kept those that include the poet's sharp-eyed glimpses of 'chalk-white chimneys that twinkled' and 'painted pinnacles powdered everywhere'.[1] In giving

---

[1] I have quoted a few phrases of the original poem in a modernized form or spelling. It should be stressed that this can never be managed with complete passages, rarely with complete sentences. The poem is written in a north-western dialect of Middle English which is to all intents and purposes a foreign language. The storyteller has to find a translation.

the substance of these lines, I D makes an impressionistic list of the different parts of the building, and a fairy tale castle of some sort easily comes to mind:

> loop-holed turrets high
> Traced like papercuts against the sky;
> With hall and barbican and spires and painted
> Pinnacles cunningly wrought and ornamented...

I c is less carefree and shows how the pinnacles were placed—as soon as one has discovered that an *embrasure* is an *opening widening from within made in a parapet*:

And there were so many pinnacles, gaily painted, scattered about everywhere and climbing one above another among the embrasures of the castle, that it looked as though it were cut out of paper, like a model.

M. R. Ridley helps the reader with 'climbing above one another' (for the original 'clambered so thick') because it shows what the construction was, both in fact and as it struck the eye. II is not so helpful, with its 'congregated in clusters beyond the castle embrasures'.

Some of the additional imagery of I D is distracting, and does nothing to make the picture easier to see. 'Canopy of icicles' is weaker than 'hung over his head in icicles', and 'in his iron bed of armour' is fanciful by the side of 'he slept in his armour among the bare rocks'— even if it does not call up an unwanted memory of iron bedsteads. The ironic understatement 'more nights than he cared for', omitted in I D, is much more telling than the added 'iron bed'. There is a similar muddle in 'set on a hillock in tree-lapped lawn'. It is much clearer and simpler to say 'on a mound that rose from a piece of meadowland, shut in under the boughs of many great trees' (I c). Unless the language of the whole tale were a little archaic, a child would think that the lawn was something like the usual small oblong of grass in our gardens. Roger Lancelyn Green gets away with the word in 'a fair lawn lay in front of it, and many great oak trees on either side', because of the Malorian, antiquated ring of his whole sentence. 'Lapped' is certainly perplexing. A child associates the word primarily with a *lap* to sit on, which is unfortunate here; even if the word is understood as 'folding over, like a pleat in fabric', the visual image is still blurred.

These objections to the language of I D are perhaps quibbling. It preserves most of the original poet's pictures, and there is a certain brightness about it that gives children some idea of the visible world as it was seen through late mediaeval eyes. Some of the expansions are justifiable. The shimmering and gleaming and twinkling which are so important to the fourteenth-century poet show that it must have been a winter dawn and that the sky must have been a deep blue, although he does not use the words *dawn* and *blue*. In a version for children it seems right to use them. 'Cut out of paper it seemed' has been slightly elaborated into 'traced like a papercut against the sky'. The two translations also elaborate this phrase, into 'cut out of paper, like a model', and 'appeared like a prospect of paper patterning'. The image shows the incisive, intricate line which the pinnacles make against the sky; it seems to have been suggested by the intricate cut-paper decorations and models that were used at feasts. The 'papercuts' made in many classrooms today are simple specimens of the same craft; in this instance the modern associations of a word are appropriate and happy.

One of Ian Serraillier's methods of telescoping the story has done real damage in this episode. I D does not represent his narrative fairly, because it makes it look as if he left out Gawain's *Pater* and *Ave* altogether. In the original poem Gawain's prayers are described at two points; on the morning of Christmas Eve he prays to the Virgin to guide him to shelter; then a little later, as he passes through the forest, he thinks of his need to find some place where Mass will be said that night, and confesses his sins. Ian Serraillier does include the first prayer briefly, but he leaves out the second one. Consequently the castle just happens to come into sight as the horse plods through marsh and mire; there is none of the amazement created by the original poet when Gawain crosses himself at the end of his prayers and immediately sees the bright castle in front of him, instead of the dark forest that he expected.

Any more or less accentual verse should help to communicate the magic of the legend, but the rhythms of I D are a hindrance rather than a help to grown-up readers. It is only fair to record that children do like this version as a poem, and listen to it more attentively than they listen to prose; but it is not easy to read it to them. In his preface Ian Serraillier says that he chose to write 'basically' in a five-stress line instead of the four-stress line of the original poem. Anyone who has not looked at the preface may well be puzzled to know what the metre is, and how he is supposed to speak the lines which look clumsy. He will sometimes hesitate between a four-, a five-, a six- or even a seven-stress pattern. To my ears the five-stress line is not a satisfactory form, for this poem or for any other; it is bound to seem ungainly, even if the poet is strict in his versification. In practice the voice looks after itself to some extent, and will fall into the traditional and natural four-stress pattern whenever it can, so that the lines will 'go' like this:

loop-holed turrets high
Traced like papercuts against the sky;
With hall and barbican and spires and painted
Pinnacles cunningly wrought and ornamented
And tall chimneys that twinkled chalk-white
On cloth of blue.

II is written in the original metre and probably gives as much idea of the delicate or aggressive rhythms of the original as a translation can. 'Where the cold streams ran clattering from the crests above' is onomatopoeic, although not as startling in sound as the original

Thereas clatterande from the crest the cold burn renneth

Sometimes the turn of phrase has been sacrificed to the sound, as it must be in any verse translation; for instance

Piteously piped away, pinched with cold

catches the thin, bleak sound of the original, but 'away' is unnecessary, and it is not as natural as 'piping a pitiful little song as the cold nipped them'. The most awkward line of II is

Afraid of missing the functions of the feast day to come.

The word 'functions' is a bad equivalent for 'the service of that sire', and I c's prose 'due service of the Lord' is much better: 'functions' suggests bureaucratic formalities, and it is used only to provide the alliteration with 'feast' that the verse-form requires. Similarly 'heaved off his helmet' is unfortunate. The poet tells us that he took it off gently (or conveniently or for convenience); fourteenth-century armour was lighter than most people think and Gawain was too courteous to make a clumsy movement just before uttering his thanksgiving.

It looks as if I B is the best version for younger children, and as if I D is for the library or the older child's bookcase—the pictures are attractive although historically inaccurate, and in a coloured picture-book a child of eleven or twelve will accept a longer text than usual. The teacher or storyteller who is prepared to take some trouble for twelve-year-olds would probably be happier with either I c or II, which have the characteristic virtues of prose and verse translation; II gives more opportunities than I D to the reader who enjoys speaking verse.

6. CINDERELLA'S SISTERS GET READY FOR A BALL

A. Our young misses were also invited; for they cut a very grand figure among the quality. They were mightily delighted at this invitation, and wonderfully busy in chusing out such gowns, petticoats and head clothes as might best become them. This was a new trouble to Cinderilla; for it was she who ironed her sisters' linen, and plaited their ruffles. They talked all day long of nothing but how they should be dressed. 'For my part (said the eldest) I will wear my red velvet suit, with French trimming.'

'And I (said the youngest) shall only have my usual petticoat; but then, to make amends for that, I will put on my gold-flowered mantua, and my diamond stomacher, which is far from being the most ordinary one in the world.'

They sent for the best tire-woman they could get, to make up their head-dresses, and adjust their double pinners, and they had their red brushes and patches from Mademoiselle de la Poché. Cinderilla was likewise called up to them to be consulted in all these matters, for she had excellent notions, and advised them always for the best; nay, and offered her service to dress their heads, which they were very willing she should do. As she was doing this, they said to her, 'Cinderilla, would you not be glad to go to the ball?'

'Ah! (said she) you only jeer at me; it is not for such as I am to go thither.'

'Thou art in the right of it (replied they) it would make the people laugh to see a Cinderbreech at a ball.' Anyone but Cinderilla would have dressed their heads awry; but she was very good, and dressed them perfectly well. They were almost two days without eating, so much they were transported with joy. They broke above a dozen of laces in trying to be laced up close, that they might have a fine slender shape, and they were continually at their looking-glass. At last the happy day came; they went to court, and Cinderilla followed them with her eyes as long as she could, and when she had lost sight of them, she fell a crying.

— Charles Perrault, *Cendrillon*, trans. Guy Miège at some date between 1697 and 1719: text exactly reproduced in *Histories or Tales of Past Times*, Nonesuch 1925 (lim. ed.) and Fortune Press 1928 (lim. ed.), and reproduced with a few very slight alterations in Lang's *Blue Fairy Book* [Short List nos. 150–2]

B. Our two young ladies received invitations, for they cut quite a figure in the country. So there they were, both feeling very pleased and very busy choosing the clothes and the hair-styles which would suit them best. More work for Cinderella, for it was she who ironed her sisters' underwear and goffered their linen cuffs. Their only talk was of what they would wear.

'I' said the elder, 'shall wear my red velvet dress and my collar of English lace.'

'I', said the younger, 'shall wear just my ordinary skirt; but, to make up,

I shall put on my gold-embroidered cape and my diamond clasp, which is quite out of the common.'

The right hairdresser was sent for to supply double-frilled coifs, and patches were bought from the right patch-maker. They called Cinderella to ask her opinion, for she had excellent taste. She made useful suggestions and even offered to do their hair for them. They accepted willingly.

While she was doing it, they said to her:

'Cinderella, how would you like to go to the ball?'

'Oh dear, you are making fun of me. It wouldn't do for me.'

'You are quite right. It would be a joke. People would laugh if they saw a Cinderbottom at the ball.'

Anyone else would have done their hair in knots for them, but she had a sweet nature, and she finished it perfectly. For two days they were so excited that they ate almost nothing. They broke a good dozen laces trying to tighten their stays to make their waists slimmer, and they were never away from their mirrors.

At last the great day arrived. They set off, and Cinderella watched them until they were out of sight. When she could no longer see them, she began to cry.

— Charles Perrault, *Cendrillon*, trans. Geoffrey Brereton [Short List no. 117]

c. Ashputtel's two sisters were asked to come. So they called her up, and said, 'Now, comb our hair, brush our shoes, and tie our sashes for us, for we are going to dance at the King's feast.' Then she did as she was told, but when all was done she could not help crying, for she thought to herself she should have liked to go to the dance too; and at last she begged her mother very hard to let her go. 'You, Ashputtel?' said she. 'You have nothing to wear, no clothes at all, and who cannot even dance—you want to go to the ball?'

— Jacob and Wilhelm Grimm, *Aschenputtel*, trans. Edgar Taylor, 1823
[Short List no. 127]

d. They thought of nothing but dances and parties. So, when they got an invitation to the grand ball at the castle, they could not eat for two days, they were so excited.

'You must come and do our hair,' they told Cinderella. 'You must make it look beautiful because the Prince himself will be there.'

'I wish—Oh, how I wish that I, too, might go to the ball,' Cinderella said, as her clever fingers shaped their curls.

'What, you!' exclaimed the Ugly Sisters, and they laughed so unkindly, that anyone else but Cinderella would have tugged at their hair. But Cinderella was Cinderella—as good as she was pretty. And so she did her very best to make the Sisters look handsome. She pressed their fine dresses, and she fetched and carried all day long, until at last they were ready to leave for the wonderful ball.

'Now I am really all alone,' Cinderella told her white cat, as she sat down by the fire. 'You are the only one who loves me...'

But Cinderella did have someone else to love her besides her little white cat.

— *My Book of Cinderella*, Odhams All Colour Book Series, 1960 (name of writer not given)

E. The younger sister who was short and dumpy chose a cloak of emerald green. Cinderella thought it was quite the wrong colour, and made her less graceful than ever. It hurt her not to be able to tell her stepsister so, and to see the soft flower-like colours which she loved cast aside.

At last the night of the ball came. Poor Cinderella! Her stepmother and sisters were so bad-tempered, and scolded and ordered her about so much that she did not know who to obey first.

'That curl is not right. Brush it out and do it again,' said the younger sister when Cinderella was trying hard to make her hair look nice. Anyone could see that both sisters were angry at having to have their hair curled with hot irons, while Cinderella stood there with lovely, naturally curly golden ringlets glinting in the candlelight.

Cinderella tried again to make the stiff curls lie neatly, but it was no use trying to please. 'You are brushing too hard, you clumsy girl', shouted the younger sister. 'You'll spoil the whole effect'...

Cinderella imagined what the ball would be like. She thought of the glittering lights, the lovely dresses, sparkling jewels, and of the handsome Prince dancing in the minuets. In fact, Cinderella almost imagined she really was at the ball!

'Oh, how I wish I could go with you!' she said.

'Don't be such a foolish girl,' said her stepmother. 'You know quite well that you cannot come. Just look at you now! Wouldn't the Prince laugh if he were to see you!'

Cinderella was thoughtful for a moment then screwed up her courage to say:

'Couldn't you let me have one of the dresses you have in that big chest? There are so many that surely one would fit me. I promise you would not be ashamed of me if you let me go with you.'

'Don't say any more, child! You can't go, and that's the end of it', answered her stepmother angrily.

— *Cinderella*, Nelson, ?1956 (undated: name of writer not given)

F. Invitations to the ball were sent to all the Princesses, Duchesses and great ladies, and among others to Cinderella's two proud sisters.

No one even thought of inviting poor Cinderella, but the proud sisters were very much excited. Cinderella was so kind that she didn't say a word about being disappointed, but sewed and ironed for her proud sisters, helping them to get their dresses ready. When the day of the ball came she helped them to dress, and brushed and arranged their hair for them, and they just called and shouted for anything they wanted. At last they were ready, and Cinderella went to the door and saw them go off in a grand coach drawn by four horses.

Then at last poor little Cinderella began to cry.

— Amabel Williams-Ellis, *Cinderella*, in *Princesses and Trolls*
[Short List no. 195]

G. At last the first day of the festival arrived and the two sisters began dressing for the big ball. It took them all afternoon, and when they had finished, they were worth looking at.

They were dressed in satin and silk. Their bustles were puffed, their bodices stuffed, their skirts were ruffled and tufted with bows; their sleeves were muffled with furbelows. They wore bells that tinkled, and glittering rings; and rubies and pearls and little birds' wings! They plastered their pimples and covered their scars with moons and stars and hearts. They powdered their hair, and piled it high with plumes and jewelled darts.

At the last minute Cinderella was called in to curl their hair, lace up their bodices and dust off their shoes. When the poor little girl heard they were going to a party at the King's palace, her eyes sparkled and she asked her stepmother whether she might not go too.

'You?' cried the stepmother. 'You, all dusty and cindery, want to go to a party? You haven't even a dress to wear and you can't dance.'

— Wanda Gàg, *Cinderella*, freely adapted from the Grimms'
Aschenputtel [Short List no. 129]

The tale of Cinderella deserves its fame, but does not deserve the cheapening and distortion that so often follow fame in the nineteenth and twentieth centuries. It is a folk tale which was 'retold' at the turn of the seventeenth century (see p. 41 above), so sensitively that for ever afterwards it has been remembered as an aristocratic children's story. It is not a story about Wishes Come True, although people are always saying so, even in forewords written for children; it is a story about Trial, Recognition and Judgement. In traditional stories people who wish always come to a bad end (compare p. 84 above). Cinderella is her father's true heir, and is born to be a queen. Her place in the family is usurped by the Proud Sisters, and they try to prevent her from entering the contest by which the right to the kingdom is to be decided. Her situation is the same as that of the untried Theseus, or Sigurd, or Arthur, or Beaumains, or La Cote Male Tale; the glass (or fur) slipper has the same place in her story as the Sword in the Stone has in the story of Arthur's kingship. The knights have no weapons or tourna-

5   CAO

ment armour; she has no ball-dress. She differs only in being a woman instead of a man,[1] and in suffering more from her foster-parent and foster-sisters, since one of the usurpers has married her real father. In stepmother stories representation of the heroine's true house and lineage is divided between the Father and the Prince, just as in exposed-baby stories the role of usurper is divided between the upstart king and the unknowing foster-father.

As soon as one sees that Cinderella is 'really 'a princess, and that her cindery rags are a disguise which is stripped away by magic, the story can never be told as the story of a little waif, without name or inheritance, who dreams of an unnatural transformation of herself and finds that magic makes it 'come true'. The imagery latent in the tale does not shadow adolescent wish-fulfilment. It suggests the stripping away of the disguise that conceals the soul from the eyes of others— even the shedding of the ragged personalities that prevent it from manifesting itself as it should by nature or by grace.[2] Cinderella must be a virtuous maiden, and she must suffer at the hands of the usurpers, but she must suffer like a princess, and not like an ignorant and repining little girl.

Perrault (A and B) makes his Cinderella a girl whom we can accept as a candidate for the throne, when she comes to the test; she will be a good queen, for she is getting through the present initiation with dignity. She is intelligent and has good taste; she performs the appointed tasks thoroughly, but without servility. She is not making a martyr of herself. She does more than is required, but Perrault's short record of it in 'even offered to do their hair for them' does not suggest self-righteousness. 'She had a sweet nature' is originally *elle estoit bonne*, which is quite simple and undemonstrative. When the usurping Sisters taunt her, she replies with 'Oh dear, you are making fun of me', which

---

[1] The position of women as heroines in folklore might have something to do with memories of a matriarchal society, or with the transmission of the stories by successive generations of old wives and nurses.

[2] Of course these interpretations are heads and tails of the same penny; it is quite possible to say that we like to think we are princesses when we are 'really' scullery-maids by origin. I am concerned only to point out the likeness between *Cinderella* and legends which are not commonly seen as images of wish-fulfilment. In *The Myth of the Birth of the Hero* Otto Rank gives the same wish-fulfilment interpretation to all of them.

In an early version of *Cinderella*, and in the related *Donkey-Skin*, the heroine is understandably disgraced; either she herself has murdered a previous stepmother, or else her father has contracted, or tried to contract, an incestuous union with her. In these variants her exile among the cinders is an expiation or a cleansing from pollution, and the ring or shoe by which the Prince knows her is even more clearly a token of restoration to an original state from which she has fallen.

is natural, and unruffled, and also shows a certain urbanity; she knows quite well what they are up to, and is not going to be drawn. There is no pleading, and no self-pity, *and no wishing*. She follows them with her eyes as long as she can, and only then begins to cry. The nearest she gets to a wish is the 'If only I could...', in the midst of her tears, in her later reply to her godmother's point-blank question as to why she is crying. It takes only a few seconds for her to recover her wits enough to make useful suggestions about raw material, such as rat-traps, for her godmother to use in her magic.

The Grimms' early nineteenth-century Cinderella (c and g) is not quite as self-controlled. She does plead with the Stepmother, and she does burst into tears before the Sisters have left. Nevertheless the passage is so short in the original, closely translated in c, that there is no time for Cinderella to explore her own emotions. In g Wanda Gàg sensibly leaves this part alone, expanding only the description of the Sisters' toilette. It is natural that there should be more dialogue between Cinderella and her stepmother in the Grimm variant of the story: the contrast between stepmother and real mother is more important throughout, and later it is a magic bird and a magic tree on the real mother's grave that throw down the gold and silver clothes which are Cinderella's birthright.

D and E have been included to show how much the figure of Cinderella has been diminished in the popular storytelling of the present time. It is not just a matter of vulgar language or sentimental trimming. The heroine herself has been turned into a cry-baby, a child rather than a young woman, and a very unpleasantly sugary and self-satisfied child at that. She has to be 'as good as she was pretty'. She is given 'lovely, naturally curly golden ringlets glinting in the candlelight' (after doing the rough housework and sitting in the ashes?) and seems to feel some complacency in watching the Sisters' annoyance when their straight hair will not curl like hers. She is plentifully endowed with a capacity for day-dreaming, and we are asked to consider it a virtue, as if it were a kind of artistic genius:

She thought of the glittering lights, the lovely dresses, sparkling jewels, and of the handsome Prince dancing in the minuets. In fact, Cinderella almost imagined she really was at the ball!

She tries to make the Stepmother 'feel awful' by pleading that she has plenty of dresses of her own in the chest; no wonder the Stepmother loses her temper. She is 'hurt' by the taste of the Sisters; she did not tell them, but one cannot help feeling that she made it very apparent. She catches up the white kitten when she is feeling passionately sorry for herself. 'You are the only one who loves me', she says, and the kitten must have hated it.

In Perrault Cinderella is a girl undergoing the tests that will show whether she is a queen or not; in this respect she is a heroine comparable with the heroes of legend. But A and B are quite different in temper from any of the other original sources that I have reproduced in this section. This original source is already a children's story, and one that shows a shrewd knowledge of children's tastes. Perrault knew that very young children like humour, and repetition, and conversations, and little touches of detail from the daily life of their own families. He also knew that they are frightened if they see grown-ups displaying strong personal emotion. Consequently his *Cinderella* is more light-hearted, familiar and everyday than the folk tales incorporated by poets in Greek legends, or taken down from peasant storytellers in the nineteenth century. It is not put back in time into some heroic or golden age; it is given a definite contemporary setting in the court of Louis XIV. Cinderella's family belongs, or almost belongs, to 'the quality'. The Sisters talk for days about the various garments that make up a fashionable *toilette* in 1700: a 'petticoat' (*jupe*) or underskirt, quilted and flowered, and nearly all revealed in front by the 'mantua' (*manteau*), a silk overgown cut somewhat loosely, open to the waist, with the skirt looped back into a bustle; a *barrière*, which A equates with the English 'stomacher', or embroidered cover for the front of the laced corset, seen between the edges of the 'mantua' bodice; and the 'double pinner' (*cornettes à deux rangs*), a headdress of two upstanding stiffened lace frills, which is almost a uniform in polite society. All this must have been tremendously entertaining to the Perrault children, who no doubt overheard young women gossiping about clothes, and giggled at exclamations over broken corset laces.

A *Cinderella* as easy and amusing as this could now be produced only by stripping the folk tale down again to its bare plot, and setting it in a modern house, with modern clothes, and dishwashers, and motorcars, and sherry parties.[1] To a writer this would mean his own house, and his wife's clothes. In addition to unavoidable national overtones there would be the unmistakeable class characteristics about which we now feel so embarrassed. The resulting tale might be entertaining to

---

[1] It has been done by Osbert Sitwell, but only as a grown-up satire on the self-pitying Cinderella depicted in D and E.

children of five or six, but only to the writer's own children, and to others like them (compare p. 8 above and note on Short List no. 120). And there is nothing much like kingship in modern society. As tradition has canonized Perrault's coach and footmen, and even his corset laces, it seems better to agree that he has fixed the action of *Cinderella* in 1700 for all successive generations, and take advantage of the fact that none of us, however we live, know what the court of Louis XIV was like, without having pictures to look at. If the story-teller exploits the period charm of the tale, it will raise the age at which it can first be told, perhaps to eight or nine or even ten. At this age children can listen to Perrault himself; nothing could be more fresh and crisp and even than his narrative. However the period detail begins to worry the storyteller when it comes to choosing a translation.

A is very nearly contemporary with Perrault's book, and it delights the grown-up reader by giving him the flavour of life and literature at the turn of the seventeenth century. 'Our young misses' is just the right term for the Sisters. They are not exactly ladies of the court; they are on the fringe of it, being members of the 'ever-rising rising middle class', then making new pretensions to leisure and culture. The Stepmother is a 'madam', like the London 'City Madams'. 'Mightily delighted with the invitation, and wonderfully busy in choosing out such gowns...as might become them' is written in the fashionable colloquial English that we hear in Restoration comedy, and it suits the tale. The articles of attire discussed by the Sisters present no problem to Guy Miège, because they are still being worn, and he can use the ordinary English names for them.

I do not think that much of this pleasure will be shared by children of eight. They may notice an indefinitely old-fashioned effect, but nothing more. Some of them will be put off by the un-English use of 'thou' and 'you', where Perrault's *tu* and *vous* show that the Sisters are addressing Cinderella as a servant, and that she is replying to them as her mistresses. Yet Lang, who was a good judge, thought that Miège's translation would be attractive to children; in 1889 he used it for all the Perrault stories in his *Blue Fairy Book*, although he had more recent versions to choose from. The few alterations he made were very slight; the rude nickname 'Cinderbreech' was changed into the less improper 'Cinderwench', and some of the fashion-vocabulary was modified. Oddly enough, Miège's fashion-vocabulary may now be a help rather than a hindrance to the storyteller who brings plenty of pictures with him. 'Double pinner' has no previous associations for children, and they can attach the word to their picture at once. 'Coif' may already be associated with other things, for instance with a nun's headdress, which is as unlike the 'double pinners' as anything could be. Some of the dialogue of the Sisters may have to be cut, even though it expresses their snobbery so well; it is interesting to come across two or three new names for clothes, but six or seven would be tedious.

These two translations are probably of equal value for reading to children; one group may be happier with the old, and another with the new. B is lively, and manages to imitate Perrault's neat, brisk manner in modern English. A class of children who had not heard many old stories would probably prefer it to A.

Some teachers and storytellers feel that the less well-known variant of *Cinderella* collected by the Grimm brothers is more interesting than Perrault's story. c does not give a fair impression of it, because in this variant the Sisters are less important than the Stepmother, and none of the usurpers are given as much prominence as the magic bird and the magic tree. In preparing his Proud Sisters for the king's three-day feast—a much more heroic or mediaeval affair than Perrault's ball— Grimm may be influenced by Perrault; literary fairy tales can turn back into folk tales transmitted by word of mouth.

The Grimm brothers never try to follow Perrault's method of adapting a peasant tale by putting in details from their own children's everyday life. There is no description at all of contemporary fashion. The phase translated in 1823 as 'tie our sashes for us' (c), which does suggest Regency ball-dresses, is *schnalle uns die schnallen*, and probably means 'buckle our shoes, do up our shoe-buckles, or shoe-straps'. The tale is timeless, and the sadness of Cinderella's ordeal is not relieved by any wit or humour. It was never a story for children under eight, and it never will be.

If one chooses this variant of the story, there will be no temptation to make it brisk in the Perrault manner; but in telling it to children one may have to go beyond the original words. Edgar Taylor's fairly literal contemporary translation (c) shows that the Grimm narrative is fluent but bleak. There is no word-painting, and no impersonation. The spoken word is not at all vivid; no one would ever say

'You, Ashputtel? You have nothing to wear, no clothes at all, and who cannot even dance—you want to go to the ball?'

A little rearrangement and spontaneous development produces the audibly shrill protest of Wanda Gàg's outraged Stepmother (G):

'You? You, all dusty and cindery, want to go to a party? You haven't even a dress to wear and you can't dance.'

The character is created in the words. Wanda Gàg's description of the scene in which the sisters are dressing is exuberant, and lightens the tone of the story. She puts them into the clothes of about 1700, without using any of the technical terms of the period; she is probably remembering Perrault here. This mixture of sources does not matter much, since the Grimm tale has no period of its own. The mixture that is deadly to its spirit is Walt Disney's ugly patchwork in which magic worked by a godmother is stitched on to magic worked by a bird and a tree. The 'book of the film' is still available.

G is probably the best version of the Grimm story to read to eight- and nine-year-olds. Wanda Gàg's Cinderella is a practical, high-spirited person who 'does not mope or cry' and washes the cinders out of her hair herself. There is honest homeliness, as well as serious magic, in this writer's storytelling. It is a pity that she calls Cinderella a 'little girl 'throughout the story, because although Cinderella may have been 'little' when she planted the magic hazel twig that grew into the magic tree, she cannot be 'little' when she rides off as the Prince's bride, even allowing for the mediaeval custom of child marriage; but this only means remembering to leave out one word.

In a preface of 1947 Wanda Gàg explains how she first came to 'retell' the Grimm stories. She made a literal translation, and found that some of them, especially those in dialect, sounded clear and lively as they were.

Others, which were smooth, warm and colourful in the original, came out thin, lifeless and clumsy. It seemed evident that in the case of the latter, only a free translation could convey the true flavour of the originals.

Not all her alterations and developments were determined by the kind of German written by the Grimm brothers. Some were made on purpose to interest modern children in stories that were first written down for an audience that included adults, because although she herself was 'avidly reading fairy tales' at fourteen, she thought in the mid-1930's that 'the fairy-tale age limit' had dropped by about two years, and therefore envisaged an audience of four- to twelve-year-olds. Her account of the language that she was compelled to use is so good that it should be quoted in full.

It seemed advisable to simplify some sections in order that a four-to-twelve age group might be assured of getting the full value of the stories.

By simplification I mean:

(*a*) freeing hybrid stories of confusing passages;

(*b*) using repetition for clarity where a mature style does not include it;

(*c*) employing actual dialogue to sustain or revive interest in places where the narrative is too condensed for children.

However, I do not mean writing in words of one or two syllables. True, the *careless* use of large words is confusing to children; but long, even unfamiliar words are relished and easily absorbed by them, provided they have enough colour and sound-value.

The quality of Amabel Williams-Ellis's work for children is not well represented by F: it is flat in comparison with the free and lively writing in her collection of Grimm stories [Short List no. 128], which does not include *Cinderella*. F is given here as an example of a very short and simple *Cinderella* which is inoffensive, and could be read by a teacher who had some particular reason for telling the story to a class of five- or six-year-olds. At least it would be better to use F than to use D or E.

I do not believe that reading from D or E could be justified in any situation. The language in which these passages are written is as objectionable as their portrait of Cinderella. Yet whereas one can argue about Cinderella herself, it is almost impossible to produce reasons for saying that the language of D and E is sentimental and vulgar. Any attempt to dispute the question with someone who wants to defend D and E will look like a display of snobbery instead of an exercise in logic.

Those who dislike D and E will probably fasten upon phrases like 'as her clever fingers shaped their curls', 'to see the soft flower-like colours which she loved cast aside', 'lovely, naturally curly golden ringlets glinting in the candlelight', 'the glittering lights, the lovely dresses, sparkling jewels, and the handsome Prince dancing in the minuets'. Talking among themselves, they will probably say, 'It's like a woman's magazine'.

This is an opinion, not an argument. What can be said in reply to the defendant who claims either that women's magazines are good, or that, since they are the only publications that many children see at home, a teacher might as well make use of their language in order to make good stories seem natural to them? Not very much, but something may be better than nothing.

The words I have just quoted from D and E are words that cheat, and if children are used to cheating language there is all the more reason for introducing them to honest writing. They cheat because, like a gushing man or woman, they gush with feeling that is not stirred by anything in particular, and is always the same; never fear, or admiration, or awe, or hunger, but a comfortable brooding satisfaction that prevents the reader from seeing what the story would otherwise put in front of his eyes. If he *saw* Cinderella the reader would feel respect for her skill or self-control, excitement by, or admiration for her beauty, and contempt or amusement when the Sisters chose the wrong clothes. '*Clever fingers shaped*' and 'lovely, naturally curly' and 'flower-like colours cast aside' obliterate these distinctions in a single response: 'Oh, how sweet!' A common cosiness silvers everything.

One observation drawn from experience might be allowed to qualify as an argument. Many readers who once knew and liked the stories in women's magazines have changed their minds and now like the novels of Jane Austen much better. I have yet to meet a reader who once knew and liked the novels of Jane Austen and then rejected them for the stories in women's magazines. By the same token, a reader who really knows Perrault and Wanda Gàg's Grimm is most unlikely to go back to the anonymous modern versions I have been castigating.

7. THE COURTIERS OF THE EMPEROR OF CHINA LOOK FOR THE REAL NIGHTINGALE, AND THE ARTIFICIAL NIGHTINGALE TAKES HER PLACE

A. Whilst on their way, a cow began to low.

'Oh!' cried the court pages, 'now we have her! It is certainly an extraordinary voice for so small an animal; surely I have heard it somewhere before.'

'No, those are cows you hear lowing,' said the little kitchen-maid; 'we are still far from the place.'

The frogs were now croaking in the pond.

'That is famous!' said the chief court preacher, 'now I hear her; it sounds just like little church-bells.'

'No, those are frogs,' said the little kitchen-maid, 'but now I think we shall soon hear her.'

Then began the nightingale to sing.

'There she is!' said the little girl, 'listen! listen! there she sits'; and she pointed to a little grey bird up in the branches.

'Is it possible?' said the Gentleman Usher, 'I should not have thought it. How simple she looks! she must certainly have changed colour at the sight of so many distinguished personages.'

'Little nightingale!' called out the kitchen-maid, 'our gracious Emperor wishes you to sing something to him.'

'With the greatest pleasure,' replied the nightingale, and she sang in such a manner that it was delightful to hear her.

'It sounds like glass bells,' said the Gentleman Usher. 'And look at her little throat, how it moves! It is singular that we should never have heard her before; she will have a great success at court.'

'Shall I sing again to the Emperor?' asked the nightingale, for she thought the Emperor was among them.

'Most excellent nightingale!' said the Gentleman Usher, 'I have the honour to invite you to a court-festival, which is to take place this evening, when His Imperial Majesty will doubtless be enchanted with your delightful song.'

'My song would sound far better among the green trees,' said the nightingale: however she followed willingly . . .

So the artificial bird must now sing alone; he was quite as successful as the real nightingale; and then he was so much prettier to look at; his plumage sparkled with jewels.

Three and thirty times he sang one and the same tune, and yet he was not weary; every one would willingly have heard him again; however, the Emperor now wished the real nightingale to sing something—but where was she? No one had remarked that she had flown out of the open window; flown away to her own green wood.

'What is the meaning of this?' said the Emperor; and all the courtiers abused the nightingale, and called her a most ungrateful creature. 'We have the best bird, at all events,' said they, and for the four and thirtieth time, they hear the same tune, but still they did not quite know it, because it was so difficult. The artist praised the bird inordinately; indeed he declared it was superior to the real nightingale, not only in its exterior, all sparkling with diamonds, but also intrinsically.

'For see, my noble lords, his Imperial Majesty especially, with the real nightingale one could never reckon on what was coming: but everything is settled with the artificial bird! he will sing in this one way, and no other: this can be proved, he can be taken to pieces, and the works be shown, where the wheels lie, how they move, and how one follows from another.'

— Hans Christian Andersen, *The Nightingale*, trans. Caroline Peachey, 1852 [text reproduced with a few very slight alterations in Short List no. 137]; also (without ascription to translator) in *Hans Christian Andersen's Fairy Tales*, illustrated Jiri Trnka, Paul Hamlyn, 1959, and (with ascription) in *Hans Christian Andersen's Fairy Tales*, illustrated Grabianski, Jonathan Cape, 1963

B. As they were going along, a cow began to moo. 'Ah, there she is!' said the courtiers. 'What remarkable strength in such a small creature! Yes, it's certainly not the first time we've heard her.'

'No, but that's a cow mooing,' said the little kitchen-maid. 'We've still got a long way to go.'

Then some frogs started croaking in the pond. 'Delightful!' said the Emperor's chaplain. 'Now I can hear her: just like little church-bells.'

'No, those are frogs,' said the little kitchen-maid. 'But I expect we shall soon hear her now.' And then the nightingale began to sing.

'There she is!' said the little girl. 'Listen, listen! There she is, up there'— and she pointed to a little grey bird up in the branches.

'Is it possible?' said the gentleman-in-waiting. 'Why, I never pictured her like that. How ordinary she looks! I expect she's off colour through having so many distinguished visitors.'

'Little nightingale,' called out the small kitchen-maid quite boldly, 'our gracious Emperor would like you to sing to him.'

'With the greatest of pleasure,' said the nightingale, and at once began to sing most deliciously.

'Just like glass bells,' observed the gentleman-in-waiting. 'And look at the way her little throat keeps working. I can't make out why we've never heard her before. She'll make a great hit at Court.'

'Shall I sing once more to the Emperor?' asked the nightingale, for she thought the Emperor was there.

'My excellent little nightingale,' replied the gentleman-in-waiting, 'it is my very pleasant duty to summon you to a concert this evening at the palace, where you will enchant His Imperial Majesty with your delightful singing.'

'It sounds best out in the open,' said the nightingale. Still, she went along readily enough...

After that, the artificial bird had to sing by itself. It was just as popular as the real one, and of course it was also much prettier to look at, glittering there like a cluster of brooches and bracelets.

Over and over again it sang its one and only song—thirty-three times without tiring—and the listeners would have liked to hear it all once more, but the Emperor thought that now it was time for the real nightingale to do some singing...But wherever was she? No one had noticed her fly out of the open window, away to her own green woods.

'Bless my soul, what's the meaning of this?' said the Emperor; and all the courtiers were highly indignant and said what an ungrateful creature the nightingale was. 'Still, we've got the best one,' they added; and then the artificial bird was obliged to sing once more. That was the thirty-fourth time they were hearing the same song; but they didn't quite know it even yet, for it was so difficult. And the Master of Music gave the bird extraordinary praise; in fact, he declared that it was better than the real nightingale, not merely because of its outward appearance and all the wonderful diamonds, but also for the works inside.

'You see, ladies and gentleman and, above all, Your Imperial Majesty, with the real nightingale there's no telling what's going to happen. But with the artificial bird everything is fixed beforehand. Such-and-such will be heard and no other. One can account for it all: one can open it up and show the human mind at work, the position of the cylinders, how they go round, and the way in which one thing follows from another!'

— Hans Christian Andersen, *The Nightingale*, trans. R. P. Keigwin

[Short List no. 138]

c. 'Moo-ooo-oooo,' came a call from the forest.

'Ping pong, ping pong, that is the nightingale. Such melody!' exclaimed the Chief Minister, rubbing his hands together delightedly. But Cherry Blossom only laughed.

'That is no nightingale, but the call of a cow ready for milking,' she said.

'Ping?' asked the Chief Minister. 'Ping *pong*,' he added unhappily.

Time and again one of the courtiers thought that he could hear the nightingale, but when the party stopped to listen, it was only the twitter of an ordinary forest bird or the high hum of the bees. Everyone grew despondent, except Cherry Blossom, who began to chant in a high little voice:

Nightingale, sweet nightingale, sing me your song.
In my dreams I hear you all the night long.'

And as she sang, from the depths of the forest a glorious voice rose, becoming louder and louder. Enraptured, the searchers knew that the nightingale was approaching. A little grey bird flew into sight and settled on the branch of a tree above their heads, still singing beautifully. It was hard to believe that such a small bird could have so grand a voice, but there was no doubt that here was the wonderful nightingale at last.

With a great many pings and pongs, the Chief Minister tried to persuade the nightingale to accompany them to the Emperor, and in a while the bird agreed, for she realized the honour of being asked to give a Command Performance...

There seemed no doubt that the Japanese clockwork nightingale was indeed superior, and the Emperor ordered that it should remain in his presence. The real nightingale was forgotten, and nobody noticed when she flew quietly out of the window and back to the precious freedom of her forest. When they did discover that the bird had flown, there were few regrets, for the clockwork nightingale was now quite the centre of attraction. The Emperor himself never grew tired of having the bird wound up so that he could hear its song; and the courtiers never grew tired of hearing the same song over and over again either, for they were obliged to enjoy whatever pleased the Emperor. Besides, the mechanical nightingale was certainly beautiful to behold, whatever other qualities it lacked; and it could be made to sing for the Emperor whenever he wished, unlike the real nightingale, who was not a machine.

The Chief Minister was loudest in his praise of the new clockwork nightingale, for it kept the Emperor from wanting to have anyone walked on.

'Ping pong, ping *pong*,' he said. 'What a miracle of creation is this handsome clockwork bird. Indeed, your Imperial Majesty possesses the finest nightingale in the Orient.'

— Shirley Goulden, *More Tales from Hans Andersen*, W. H. Allen, 1958

The Nightingale is a fantastic, symbolic tale growing around a core of elemental opposites: freedom and imprisonment, simplicity and elaboration, the organic and the mechanical. The fact that it is an 'invented' tale makes it vulnerable to depredation by unthinking adapters, but does not confer immutability upon it as a right; after all, it is itself an adaptation of traditional things—the wisdom of the humblest and weakest character, the foolish choice of a monarch given a miraculous gift, the magic power of a talking animal or bird, and the crowned skeleton king of the Dance of Death. Anyone who *can* steal from Andersen's tale is free to do so; but the thief must be able to make off with his loot without dropping and damaging it. Adaptation will be a failure if it splits Andersen's symbolic core, and does not create a new one.

Since the Second World War the prettifying of Andersen's tales to suit 'the youngest reader' seems to have stopped, and it is hard to believe that in 1910 a series of children's books graded *The Snow Queen* as a 'story for five-year-olds'. Modern adaptations are modish rather than sentimental. The 'ping-pong' language given to the courtiers in c is probably meant to be funny and clever; the birds and bees in the forest through which the searchers walk are probably meant to give local colour and 'human interest'. In fact, both changes weaken the story. Andersen's courtiers (A and B) are much funnier, with their culture-snobbery—the pages cannot believe that they have never heard any singer supposed to be famous—and their habit of thinking inside their own artificial professional limits—the court-preacher can think of nothing but church-bells as a simile for the song of the supposed nightingale. The absurd repetition of their mistake, first when they hear a cow and then when they hear the frogs, is exactly the sort of repetition that children enjoy, and much too good to be dismissed as 'time and again one of the courtiers thought that he could hear the nightingale'. The 'ordinary forest bird' is dull, and 'the high hum of the bees' is silly, apart from the use of a hackneyed phrase; bees do not hum in forests.

The worst damage is done by the conversion of the little kitchen-maid into Cherry Blossom, the daughter of one of the palace guards. It is essential to the theme of the tale that the one human being who knows where the real nightingale lives should be the lowliest servant in the whole court, who goes away from it often to visit her parents on the sea-shore; and it is important that she should speak naturally, 'boldly' and even humorously, as the little kitchen-maid does. It is ridiculous to let her 'chant' something like a pop-song 'in a little high voice'.

Throughout c Andersen's romantic love of freedom and simplicity is flouted, in the manner as well as in the substance of the writing. The only thing about the forest that matters to Andersen is that it is alive, and green, and free. The phrase he uses when the nightingale flies away from the palace, 'away to her own green woods' (Danish, *til sine grønne Skove*) echoes her own warning to the courtiers, 'it sounds best out in the open' (*i det Grønne*). This echo is lost in c, and so is the dramatic effect of the 'open window' by which the nightingale escapes from her jewelled cage. Andersen shows us the Emperor beguiled by the false charm of the clockwork bird's song, which seems beautiful because it is difficult, and then, even after hearing it thirty-three times, thinking of the real nightingale only as a rival in a competition; it is precisely at this moment that he breaks off with 'Bless my soul!', and we feel that the court is blind and airless, and that we must somehow follow the nightingale through those

magic casements, opening on the foam.[1]

A real adaptation of *The Nightingale* is a very different thing from c; it takes place in Oscar Wilde's *The Happy Prince*, where the nightingale singing unknown truths about the Emperor's subjects becomes the swallow that brings the penitent prince messages about the misery in his kingdom. A theme and an image is reborn in another writer's mind; in the same way Andersen's Snow Queen is reborn as the White Witch of C. S. Lewis's Narnia.

If children are ready to listen to the story of *The Nightingale*, they are ready to listen to Andersen's words, which are as simple as any words could be in relation to the ideas that they have to express. Cutting may be necessary at the end of the story, in the dialogue of the Emperor and Death, with its weighted religious emotion; but in read-

[1] Andersen could read English although he could not speak it fluently. By *c.* 1843 when *The Nightingale* (published 1845) was written, he might have read Keats' *Ode to a Nightingale* (published 1820). I do not know of any record that he did so.

ing these passages in which the two nightingales make their first court appearances, nothing need be added and nothing need be taken away. The only choice that a storyteller has to make is a choice between different translations.

A is the most popular nineteenth-century translation, which has often been attacked by Danish scholars on account of its inaccuracies and redundancies. An English reader knowing no Danish cannot judge accuracy, but can hardly help noticing that A sounds stiff and ungainly, especially in dialogue. As so much of the story is conducted by letting all the characters speak for themselves, the whole effect is diminished by remarks like

'I should not have thought it. How simple she looks! She must certainly have changed colour at the sight of so many distinguished personages.'

R. P. Keigwin's recent translation (B) is much fresher at this point, and the gentleman-in-waiting talks as a rather heavily benevolent official might be expected to talk:

'Why, I never pictured her like that! How ordinary she looks! I expect she's off colour through having so many distinguished visitors'.

'Off colour' is a more likely attempt at wit on this gentleman's part than 'changed her colour', which suggests blushing; the nightingale is grey and drab. In the words given to the Master of the Music, B is conspicuously easier and funnier than A. The idea behind his speech could easily be considered difficult and unsuitable for children: the Master of the Music is a proper nineteenth-century Utilitarian (or twentieth-century sociologist) who thinks that consciousness is mechanical, and that the human mind works like a musical box. Caroline Peachey's version does perhaps suggest that Andersen has forgotten his Chinese character in a moment of philosophical earnestness:

'But everything is settled with the artificial bird! He will sing in this one way, and no other; this can be proved, he can be taken to pieces, and the works be shown, where the wheels lie, how they move, and how one follows from another.'

R. P. Keigwin makes us so vividly aware of a talkative, fussy little expert, flustered by anything unexpected and only happy when everything is under his control according to his rules, that the essential theme is quite clear and real to a ten- or eleven-year-old listener:

'But with the artificial bird everything is fixed beforehand. Such-and-such will be heard, and no other. One can account for it all; one can open it up and show the human mind at work, the position of the cylinders, how they go round, and the way in which one thing follows from another!'

Andersen is not just sugaring a pill; he is thinking in the concrete.

R. P. Keigwin's is probably the best translation of all. There are other good ones by M. R. James and L. W. Kingsland [Short List nos. 136 and 139. Berating a poor Victorian translation usually amounts to flogging a dead donkey, since it is usually only the good ones that survive; but Caroline Peachey's is still being reproduced in new picture-books, often unacknowledged, with few changes except for the correction of obvious grammatical howlers like the 'Whilst on their way, a cow began to low' at the beginning of A. The lapse of copyright probably accounts for its undeserved longevity.

Short List of Books

This is a *short* list, not a complete one. I have given greatest prominence to the four main European traditions I have considered in this book; in this revised edition I have also included sections on the myth and legend of the Old Testament, and on the traditional stories of the Third World and Eastern Europe, because the former badly need to be sought out, and the latter are already being sought out with growing interest. There is now a huge mass of Third World legend and folk tale in print in English versions for children, and my lists are necessarily brief and cursorily annotated, but teachers whose purposes or 'projects' require these stories may find it useful to see them classified geographically. I have given comparatively little space to the humorous folk tales and animal fables that are not 'of faërye' and often make good nursery stories, because they do not have the strong poetic or symbolic significance that has been the burden of my argument; they are slightly represented in the sub-section on anthologies of fairy tales for younger children. I still believe that many of the best fairy tales are not stories for very young children, and have therefore disregarded most attempts to present them in nursery form, but in this edition I have included a selection of the fairy-tale picture-books that have appeared in recent years; some of them are scrupulously edited as well as being beautiful to look at and attractive to a mixed age-group, and altogether they are an auspicious innovation in modern publishing. In listing children's books, I have included only those that I know to be generally useful, and a few (such as Victorian retellings) that may be useful on rare occasions. I have tried to include a warning in my notes on the latter. I have not included any books that seem to me to be bad, but I have doubtless omitted many good ones. In my choice of modern invented legends, tales of magic and 'young novels' with legendary characters in them I have obviously had to be arbitrary; there is no general consensus of taste in recently produced fiction, and moreover these *genres* have no accepted names or established boundaries. 'Modern Hybrid Myth, Legend and Fantasy' and 'Modern Hybrid Fairy Tales' are my own hybrid titles, invented merely for convenience in classification.

Books that provide the pictures and information discussed in chapter III under the subheading 'The Visual Image and the Historical Setting', are here grouped under the stories to which they relate. In

each of my main sections on the Greek, Northern and Arthurian traditions, there are three sub-sections within which the arrangement is
alphabetical: children's books come first, followed by translations of
original sources, and then by books giving historical and visual
material. A short section on the Old Testament relates to my chapter II
section 4. In the main section devoted to the fourth tradition—Fairy
Tale—the sub-sections are as follows: collectors and writers of fairy
tales, including modern editions of translations, retellings, and original
texts in English, come first, *in chronological order*, since in this one sub-
section (unlike the others) a chronological arrangement by author
seemed more useful than alphabetical order; recent anthologies of
fairy tales for eight- to eleven-year-olds come next; then recent
anthologies for children under seven. This main section (like the
others) ends with books giving historical and visual material. It is
followed by sections on Modern Hybrid Myth, Legend and Fantasy,
and Modern Hybrid Fairy Tales, which include the kind of writing
I have mentioned in the preface to this edition, pp. xiv–xviii. Then
come the sections on Myth, Legend and Fairy Tale from the Third
World and Eastern Europe, which include books referred to in the
preface p. viii.

Following these main sections, I have given brief lists of historical
surveys of children's literature, and of some books that discuss the
use of myth and fairy tale in teaching art, drama, dance and 'creative
writing'. At the end I have made a very selective and probably ill-
balanced list of the books that I have myself found interesting in their
conflicting estimates of the meaning and importance of myth and
folklore. This list is intended to provide a beginning for anyone who
becomes interested in these tales as they have been written for children,
and would like to pursue some of the questions raised in the section
of chapter I subheaded 'Significances and Values'. The bibliographies
attached to most of these studies will show how enormous the subject
is. Here, and in the earlier sub-sections on historical material, I have
tried to distinguish between the books that make sense to someone who is starting from scratch, and the ones that would be hard
going for any reader, however intelligent, who had not already
picked up a little elementary knowledge. This has been done not
in any spirit of condescension, but out of personal experience of mis-
understandings caused by starting in the wrong place. I have briefly
annotated some of the beginner's books, but usually I have not
attempted to comment on the more specialized studies; the reader

whose interest is already awakened will get some idea of the character of these books from their titles, and once he is inside a bookshop or a library, a glance at their tables of contents will tell him what he wants to know.

Since the list is intended for beginners and not for bibliographers, I have concentrated my attention upon editions which are still in print, reprinting, or only recently out of print—that is, books which can be bought, or else found easily in public libraries; and I have not described early first editions. I have given the publisher and the date of the *first* printing of English books published later than 1945, ignoring reprintings or fresh issues by the same publisher unless they contain important changes and are really 'revised editions' from the ordinary reader's point of view. When a book first came out before 1945, and has been given a new dress by a new publisher since then, I have given the date of its first appearance in brackets, followed by details of more recent editions. For the sake of practical convenience, I have also mentioned paperback editions when they exist, and American editions of books first published in England. My evidence for American publication is taken from what is conveniently accessible to the ordinary English reader in the *Cumulative Book Index* and the American *Books in Print*—I have not held these books in my hands—and therefore the dates given for these American editions do not conform to my usual rule; sometimes there is no date, and sometimes the date must represent a date of reprinting. The regular order of listed editions of any one work is as follows: 1. English hardback edition(s); 2. English paperback edition(s); 3. American hardback edition(s); 4. American paperback edition(s). In the case of books first published in America, of course, the American hardback and paperback editions come first. The place of publication is given *if other than London*; London is occasionally mentioned when certain books, which the reader might expect to be published by the same firm in England and America, are not, in fact, obtainable from the American branches of certain English publishers.

THE GREEK MYTHS AND LEGENDS
Children's books

1 BAKER, GEORGE. *The Realms of Gold*. Illustrated by Geoffrey Fraser. University of London Press, 1954.

> Not really a book for children under eleven, but useful to a sixth-former or grown-up wanting to revive and integrate memories of

half-forgotten stories: an imaginatively interwoven continuous saga of the heroic stories and minor tales of the Bronze Age royal houses. Indexed: a more readable reference book than nos. 50–3. Language crisp and very compact. Includes Pelops, Perseus, Theseus, Jason, Heracles, the Trojan War, Odysseus.

2 CAVANDER, KENNETH. *The Iliad and Odyssey of Homer.* B.B.C. publications no. 8535, 1969, o.p.; part of the *Odyssey* printed in *Living Language*, B.B.C. publications, Autumn 1973.

A dramatic retelling in four- and five-stress verse written for a series of successful school broadcasts. Vigorous, perhaps more Northern than Homeric in effect; useful basis for acting and other kinds of performance.

3 CHURCH, ALFRED J. *The Children's Iliad* (1908) and *The Children's Odyssey* (1907). Reprinted together as *The Iliad and the Odyssey of Homer.* Illustrated by Eugene Karlin. Collier-Macmillan, London and New York, 1964.

A clear version in almost Homeric detail, in a plain, dignified, rhythmic style not quite as romantic as no. 16 or as Homeric as nos. 23 and 24. Like nos. 26 and 27, right in tone and language for children of ten to eleven, but more difficult in that it does not sound modern. Good for reading aloud: events arranged in chronological order. A beautifully printed book, with delicate line illustrations. Uses Latin names.

4 FARMER, PENELOPE. *Daedalus and Icarus.* Illustrated by Chris Connor. Collins, 1971: Harcourt Brace, New York, 1971.

A picture-book for children over eight; the text suggests an audience of about ten. An expanded, detailed narrative in short-story form, not attempting to create the austerity of poetic legend, and supplying personal imagery and interpretation. Effective pictures which give a sense of Cretan background. Some non-classical but not inconsistent narrative invention.

5 —— *The Serpent's Teeth: The Story of Cadmus.* Illustrated by Chris Connor. Collins, 1971: Harcourt Brace, New York, 1972.

Similar in treatment to no. 4; not a very exciting or self-contained story for children.

6 —— *The Story of Persephone.* Illustrated by Graham McCallum. Collins, 1972: Morrow, New York, 1973.

Text similar in treatment to no. 4; pictures romantic, richly coloured, perhaps over-dramatic, might attract a ten-year-old unfamiliar with myth.

7 GARFIELD, LEON and BLISHEN, EDWARD. *The God Beneath the Sea.* Illustrated by Charles Keeping. Longman, 1970: Pantheon, New York, 1971.

Nos. 7 and 8 are the most unusual and highly wrought retellings of Greek stories to appear after 1970: very beautiful illustrations which do not represent narrative scenes but carry running themes almost symbolically. It is difficult to sense what audience the writers had in mind: the complexity of intertwined events and psychological patterns, and of descriptive language, suggest that they were thinking of intelligent teenagers or adults.

Closely based on the work of Robert Graves, no. 50, as the writers claim, these books are structured around metaphysical patterns not necessarily present in their sources, elaborate the personal motivation of the chief characters, and elaborate in imagery or description the acts of sex and violence basic to Greek creation and evolution stories, but treated sparely by early poets. They concentrate upon stories not usually told in collections for children: the castration of Uranus, the begetting of the Olympian family of Twelve, the double fall of Hephaestus, the Promethean creation of Man, Sisyphus, the labours of Heracles.

Virtually an original coherent symbolic romance woven out of the material of myth. Extracts of creation stories might be useful in primary school.

8 —— *The Golden Shadow.* Illustrated by Charles Keeping. Longman, 1973: Pantheon, New York, 1973.

9 GRAVES, ROBERT. *The Siege and Fall of Troy.* Illustrated by Walter Hodges. Cassell, 1958: Doubleday, New York, 1963; Dell, New York.

10 —— *Myths of Ancient Greece.* Illustrated by Joan Kiddell-Monroe. Cassell, 1960: Doubleday, New York, 1960.

Nos. 9 and 10 are short, snappy stories, almost cheeky in tone, reflecting the historical explanation of myth given in no. 50 below. Too bare to be effective read aloud: could serve as a child's reference book. Joan Kiddell-Monroe's illustrations possibly the best black-and-white pictures for under-elevens.

11 GREEN, ROGER LANCELYN. *A Book of Myths.* Illustrated by Joan Kiddell-Monroe. Dent (Illustrated Children's Classics), 1965: Dutton, New York, 1965.

Includes Greek creation myths, Demeter and Persephone, Prometheus, Pandora. Also Northern creation myths, the death of Balder, Ragnarok. Full and strictly classical retelling, more austere than some of this writer's work: stresses religious themes.

12 ——— *Jason and the Golden Fleece.* Illustrated by Janet and Anne Grahame Johnstone. Purnell, 1968.

A large picture-book in the style of no. 18, but comparatively flashy—both in the drawing of faces and bodies, and in the layout of text (unnecessary subheadings and captions). Not nearly such a good version of the Jason story as no. 33, but may be useful if large coloured pictures are needed.

13 ——— *Old Greek Fairy Tales.* Illustrated by E. H. Shepard. Bell, 1958. Includes Eros and Psyche (as *The Invisible Prince*), Bellerophon (as *The Prince and the Flying Horse*), Perseus (as *The Terrible Head*), Midas (as *The Golden Touch*), Orpheus and Eurydice (as *The Wonderful Musician*).

A fairly simple but free retelling, drawing upon a variety of poetic sources. Especially useful for reading to eight-year-olds, as it leaves the unimportant characters anonymous.

14 ——— *Stories of Ancient Greece.* Illustrated by Doreen Roberts. Paul Hamlyn, 1967.

Includes Epimetheus and Pandora, Phaethon, the Muses, Bellerophon and Pegasus, Daedalus and Icarus, Pygmalion, Atalanta, Phrixus and Helle, Jason, Polyphemus and Galatea. A large picture-book, very useful for good eight- to eleven-year-old versions of some shorter myths and fables otherwise available only in the more adult nos. 1 and 36. The pictures are eye-catching, too bright and impressionistic, but they might lure a tough child unaccustomed to fantasy.

15 ——— *Tales of the Greek Heroes.* Illustrated by Betty Middleton-Sandford. Penguin (Puffin), London and Baltimore, 1958.

16 ——— *The Tale of Troy.* Illustrated by Betty Middleton-Sandford. Penguin (Puffin), London and Baltimore, 1958.

Nos. 15 and 16 are good to read aloud, and easier for children to read themselves than nos. 31 to 34. Simple, flowing, rather romantic storytelling; taken coherently from a range of sources. No. 16 the best first account of the Trojan War, but too brief on the Wanderings of Odysseus. No. 15 contains Prometheus, Jason, Perseus, Theseus. Very bad illustrations.

17 ——— Text of nos. 15 and 16 as *Heroes of Greece and Troy.* Illustrated by Heather Copley and Christopher Chamberlain. Bodley Head, 1960: British Book Service, Toronto, 1960: revised edition, Bodley Head, 1973.

Better line illustrations: still rather sketchy.

18 —— *Tales of the Greeks and Trojans*. Illustrated by Janet and Anne Grahame Johnstone. Purnell, 1963: Ginn, New York, 1965.

A large picture-book. Illustrations rather bright, but clear and historically justifiable. Text more brief than nos. 15 and 16, but an adequate commentary on the pictures.

19 HOLLINGHURST, HUGH. *Gods and Heroes of Ancient Greece*. Illustrated by Raymond Pitt. Heinemann Educational, 1973.

An anthology for teaching which gives full descriptions of crucial scenes and episodes from a variety of translations and versions for children, linked by brief narrative summary: also suggestions for 'things to do' in composition, drama, art and use of reference books. Produced as a class text; very useful to primary teachers wanting a step-by-step guide to selecting, cutting and 'following up'. Includes the Trojan War, Odysseus, Heracles, Jason, Perseus and Theseus.

20 KINGSLEY, CHARLES. *The Heroes* (1856). Illustrated by Joan Kiddell-Monroe. Dent (Illustrated Children's Classics), 1963: Dutton, New York, 1963.

Perseus, Jason and the Argonauts, Theseus. Not suitable for most children today, but an imaginative and well-read child may like it. The best of all the Victorian retellings of Greek stories, in romantic poetic prose, drawing on a range of classical sources.

The illustrations to this edition are less restrained than those of no. 10; colour plates rather crude. An edition with better illustrations by Charles Keeping is published in Hutchinson Junior Classics (1961), but with text mutilated by abridgement.

21 LANG, ANDREW. *Tales of Troy and Greece* (1907). Illustrated by Edward Bawden. Faber, 1968; Faber paperback, 1971. In part, reprinted as *The Adventures of Odysseus*. Illustrated by Joan Kiddell-Monroe. Dent (Children's Illustrated Classics), 1962: Dutton, New York, 1962.

A lucid, poetic prose retelling of the Trojan legends; a good example of Victorian romantic style, free from sentimentality. Children of nine to eleven will usually find nos. 26 or 27 more lively, but an imaginative and well-read child would find this version attractive.

22 LINES, KATHLEEN (selected, edited and in part written by). *The Faber Book of Greek Legends*. Illustrated by Faith Jaques. Faber, 1973.

Anthology of versions by different writers ranging in date from Lamb to Rosemary Sutcliff; despite this range keeping throughout a fairly simple, formal prose style appropriate to legend: attempts a kind of comprehensiveness from the creation and begetting of the gods to the founding of Rome, omitting the legends of Perseus, Theseus and Heracles, but including the Trojan War and the home-coming of the Greeks and wanderings of Aeneas. Useful source of some less available stories: Phrixus and Helle, Melampus, Antigone, the marriage of Peleus and Thetis, the Golden Ass of Apuleius.

Well indexed so that nine-year-olds could use it themselves as a reference book. Some stories good for reading aloud, notably Perse-phone, Antigone, and Phrixus and Helle: some, notably the creation stories, too compressed and stuffed with fact for this use. Straight-forward, sometimes felicitous illustrations.

23 MARVIN, F. S.; MAYOR, R. J. G.; and STAWELL, F. M. *The Story of the Iliad* (1909). Dent (King's Treasuries), 1921.

24 —— *The Adventures of Odysseus* (1905). Dent (King's Treasuries), 1920. Nos. 23 and 24 useful to read aloud to children over ten; epic in language—almost an abbreviated translation of Homer. Not attrac-tive for children to handle; illustrations too small. Homer's flashback order is retained.

25 MURPHY, MARTIN. *Stories from Ovid*. Illustrated by June Barber. Oxford University Press, 1971.

Somewhat abridged translations of the better known stories of the *Metamorphoses* in a clear but rather flat style. Not as good as nos. 36 or 46 for reading aloud, but preface and headnotes useful to teachers or older children. Designed as a class text for secondary courses; line illustrations dull, some nice photographs which shew continuity in visual art.

26 PICARD, BARBARA LEONIE. *The Odyssey of Homer*. Illustrated by Joan Kiddell-Monroe. Oxford University Press, 1952: Walck, New York, 1952.

Order rearranged into chronological sequence: language restrained and dignified, but not conspicuously archaic. Very good for reading aloud: children over ten will read it themselves. Illustrations good, but more difficult than those of no. 10, and difficult for ten-year-olds.

27 —— *The Iliad of Homer*. Illustrated by Joan Kiddell-Monroe. Oxford University Press, London, 1960: Walck, New York, 1960.

Like no. 26 in style, but as the story is more difficult it is most useful for occasional quotations: see note prefaced to nos. 40 to 48 below.

28 RAVEN, DAVID. *Stories from Homer*. Oxford University Press, 1973.

Similar in presentation and appearance to no. 25. Useful for giving an impression of which stories come distinctively from Homer if that is the teacher's purpose, and prefatory material is useful. Nevertheless nos. 23, 24, 26, 27, give a much better sense of the colouring of Homer's poetry than this bare version. Good collection of illustrations from vase-painting and reliefs for children over eleven.

29 REEVES, JAMES. *Heroes and Monsters*. Illustrated by Sarah Nechamkin. Blackie, 1969.

A simple but dignified and lively version of the most important heroic tales and some others not readily available to children except in the more sophisticated no. 36. Language has no poetic formality, but is plain enough to avoid obtrusive colloquialism. The number of *dramatis personae* and difficult names is cleverly kept small. Very useful for putting into the hands of children from eight onwards: it is a pity that illustrations are sketchy and unevocative. Includes Prometheus, Demeter and Persephone, Daedalus and Icarus, Phaeton, Midas, Heracles, Perseus, Baucis and Philemon, Eros and Psyche, Orpheus, Theseus, Arion.

30 —— *The Voyage of Odysseus*. Illustrated by Eric Fraser. Blackie, 1973.

Similar in presentation to no. 29 except that the illustrations are more informative and more imaginative. Distinctly easier than no. 26 and can be given to children of eight to read on their own.

31 SERRAILLIER, IAN. *The Gorgon's Head, The Story of Perseus*. Illustrated by William Stobbs. Oxford University Press, 1961; with text of no. 32, Heinemann (New Windmill), 1965: Walck, New York, 1962.

32 —— *The Way of Danger, The Story of Theseus*. Illustrated by William Stobbs. Oxford University Press, 1962: Walck, New York, 1963.

33 —— *The Clashing Rocks* [story of Jason and the *Argo*]. Illustrated by William Stobbs. Oxford University Press, 1963; Heinemann (New Windmill), 1970: Walck, New York, 1964.

34 —— *A Fall from the Sky: The Story of Daedalus and Icarus*. Illustrated by William Stobbs. Nelson, 1966: Walck, New York, 1966.

Nos. 31 to 34 are original modern versions: sometimes a little forced. More detailed and more consciously modern in language than nos. 15 and 16 above. Very good illustrations, reminiscent of Greek drawing but showing how things are made. Effective for reading aloud.

35 WARNER, REX. *Greeks and Trojans*. Illustrated by Edward Bawden. MacGibbon and Kee, 1951; Heinemann (New Windmill), 1952 [no illustrations]: Michigan State University Press, 1953.

Close to Homer but more concise than no. 27 above: continues story to sack of Troy and gives Judgement of Paris at beginning. Very well written, but difficult for children under fourteen. Imaginative drawings for adults only.

36 —— *Men and Gods*. Illustrated by Elizabeth Corselis. MacGibbon and Kee, 1950; Heinemann (New Windmill), 1951 [no illustrations]: Random, New York, 1959.

Detailed, accomplished, sophisticated version of the shorter myths and legends: closer to Ovid than any other. Uses Latin names. With appropriate cutting, good for reading the simpler stories to ten-year-olds—Demeter and Persephone, Orpheus, Phaethon, Prometheus, Midas, Eros and Psyche.

37 —— *The Vengeance of the Gods*. MacGibbon and Kee, 1954; Heinemann Educational (New Windmill), 1969.

Includes Prometheus and the tragic stories of Alcestis, Iphigeneia, Agamemnon, Orestes.

38 —— *The Stories of the Greeks*. MacGibbon and Kee, 1967: Farrar, Straus and Giroux, New York, 1967.

Nos. 35 to 37 published together with a good critical preface and evocative rather than illustrative photographs of archaic and classical sculpture. A finely printed book for adults, not a children's book in appearance: for the storyteller's own exhibition shelf, and for reading aloud.

39 WATSON, JANE WERNER. *The Iliad and the Odyssey*. Illustrated by Alice and Martin Provensen. Paul Hamlyn, 1956: Golden Press, New York, 1964.

A large picture-book. Aesthetically more pleasurable but less helpful than no. 18 above to ordinary children. Lovely colouring, more archaic dress (650 B.C.), drawing closer to vases, less realistic. Text merely adequate.

Original sources in translation

Nos. 40 to 48 are of no use for reading to children consecutively, but they may give the storyteller ideas, and evocative fragments of a few lines can be quoted verbatim to give children the feeling of hearing something from the distant past—for method, see quotations from Homer by the Quennells in no. 60, and p. 77 above. References to the sources of any particular story are given in nos. 50, 52–3 and 56. Only poetically interesting ones are listed here.

40 APOLLONIUS OF RHODES. *The Voyage of Argo* [the *Argonautica*]. Translated by E. V. Rieu. Penguin, London and Baltimore, 1959.

41 HOMER. *The Odyssey*. Translated by S. H. Butcher and Andrew Lang. Macmillan, London, 1879; Macmillan (Globe edition), London and New York.

42 —— *The Iliad*. Translated by Andrew Lang, Walter Leaf and Ernest Myers. Macmillan, London, 1882; Macmillan (Globe edition), London and New York.

Nos. 41 and 42 are the 'authorized version', very literal, obviously archaic: preferred by many historians and critics because of absence of misleading modernisms, and suggestion of the artificiality of original epic language.

43 —— *The Odyssey*. Translated by E. V. Rieu. Penguin, London and Baltimore, 1946.

44 —— *The Iliad*. Translated by E. V. Rieu. Penguin, London and Baltimore, 1950.

Nos. 43 and 44 are idiomatic modern versions, rather colloquial: easy to read as stories. No line numbers.

45 OVID. *Metamorphoses*. With a translation by F. J. Miller. 2 vols. Heinemann (Loeb Series), 1916: Harvard University Press.

Nos. 45 and 47 give the Latin text and a fairly literal English translation on opposite pages.

46 —— *Metamorphoses*. Translated and introduced by Mary M. Innes. Penguin, London and Baltimore, 1955.

Idiomatic modern prose. No line numbers.

47 VERGIL. *Eclogues, Georgics and Aeneid*. With a translation by H. R. Fairclough. 2 vols. Heinemann (Loeb Series), 1916: Harvard University Press.

48 —— *The Eclogues, Georgics and Aeneid of Virgil*. Translated by C. Day Lewis. (First published separately: *Georgics*, Cape, 1940; *Aeneid*, Hogarth, 1952; *Eclogues*, Cape, 1963.) Oxford Paperback, London and New York, 1966: Doubleday (Anchor Books), New York, 1964.

A fine modern verse translation, quite widely 'received'.

The historical setting: origins and transmission of stories

Nos. 49 to 56 are all addressed to the non-specialist. Nos. 50 and 52–3 and 56 give references to the source of each story and summaries of variant forms; prefaces summarize the writers' methods of interpretation.

49 FINLEY, M. I. *The World of Odysseus*. Chatto and Windus, 1954; Penguin, 1962: (Compass) Viking Press, New York, 1965.

Examines Homeric social life as representative of conditions in 1000–800 B.C.: chapters 1 and 2 give an easy account of the composition of epic poetry.

50 GRAVES, ROBERT. *The Greek Myths*. 2 vols. Penguin, London and Baltimore, 1955.

51 HARVEY, SIR PAUL. *The Oxford Companion to Classical Literature*. Oxford University Press, Oxford and New York, 1937.

52 KERENYI, C. *The Gods of the Greeks*. Translated by Norman Cameron. Thames and Hudson, 1951; Penguin, 1958: Vanguard Press, New York.

53 —— *The Heroes of the Greeks*. Translated by H. J. Rose. Thames and Hudson, 1959: Grove Press, New York, 1952.

No. 53 also gives a large, useful series of photographic reproductions.

54 RENAULT, MARY. *The King Must Die*. Longmans, 1958; Four Square, 1961: Pantheon Books, New York, 1958; Random House (Vintage Books), New York; Pocket Books, New York.

55 —— *The Bull from the Sea*. Longmans, 1962; Four Square, 1964: Pantheon Books, New York, 1962; Pocket Books, New York, 1963.

Nos. 54 and 55 are realistic historical novels which recreate events in the early Aegean world which may be partially remembered in heroic legends. Painless history for adults. Some intelligent children begin them at ten, but they should never be confused with the legends in teaching.

56 ROSE, H. J. *A Handbook of Greek Mythology*. Methuen, 1928, revised edition, 1958: Dutton, New York, 1959.

The historical setting: the visual image

See also nos. 10, 18, 31–4, 39. Nos. 57 and 61 useful for photographs and drawings—for classroom display, and for use as a touchstone in judging illustrations in children's books, and in making illustrations. No. 60 can be read by children, provided that history is not confused with mythology. See p. 55 above.

57 BOARDMAN, JOHN. *Greek Art*. Thames and Hudson, 1964: Praeger, New York, 1964.

58 *Greek Mythology*, Paul Hamlyn, 1963.

Useful for reproductions only.

59 LAVER, JAMES. *Costume in Antiquity.* Illustrated by Erhart Klepper. Thames and Hudson, 1964: C. N. Potter, New York.

Valuable method of illustration: taken from original paintings and reliefs, but showing make of clothes more clearly than photographs.

60 QUENNELL, MARJORIE and C. H. *Everyday Things in Ancient Greece.* Batsford, 1929–32, brought up to date and abbreviated by Kathleen Freeman, 1954: Putnam, New York, 1954.

61 SCHEFOLD, KARL. *Myth and Legend in Early Greek Art.* Translated by Audrey Hicks. Thames and Hudson, 1966: Abrams, New York, 1966.

THE NORTHERN MYTHS AND LEGENDS

Children's books

See also no. 11 for creation myths, the death of Balder, Ragnarok.

62 CROSSLEY-HOLLAND, KEVIN. *Havelok the Dane.* Illustrated by Brian Wildsmith. Macmillan, 1964: Dutton, New York, 1965.

Almost a short historical novel for ten- to twelve-year-olds, giving the story of *The Lay of Havelok the Dane*, a mediaeval romance preserving a legend of Saxon and Viking wars; mediaeval setting emphasized. Suitable illustrations.

63 GREEN, ROGER LANCELYN. *Myths of the Norsemen.* Illustrated by Brian Wildsmith. Bodley Head, 1962: Dufour, Chester Springs, 1964 [originally published as *The Saga of Asgard*, Penguin, 1960]. Illustrations too sketchy.

64 PICARD, BARBARA LEONIE. *Tales of the Norse Gods and Heroes.* Illustrated by Joan Kiddell-Monroe. Oxford University Press, London and New York, 1953.

Good illustrations.

Nos. 63 and 64 both give good versions of the important stories, and better versions of the saga of the Volsungs than those by Dorothy Hosford and E. M. Almedingen in the Ward Golden Legend Series. No. 63 cuts the Signy-Sinfiolti episodes and rearranges the ending. No. 64 is more severe in style: no. 63 is more modern and lyrical and gives more interpretation.

65 SERRAILLIER, IAN. *Beowulf the Warrior.* Illustrated by Severin. Oxford University Press, 1954: Walck, New York, 1961. Included in *The Windmill Book of Ballads*, Heinemann, 1962.

Retelling in his own accentual verse, not the original metre but vigorous enough to be appropriate. Closer than no. 67 to order and descriptive phrases of original. Good illustrations.

66 —— *Havelok the Warrior.* Illustrated by Gareth Floyd. Hamilton, 1967: Walck, New York, 1967.

An effective retelling of *Havelok*, shorter and easier than no. 62; some stress on magic and simple psychological realism, no introduction of mediaeval local colour.

67 SUTCLIFF, ROSEMARY. *Beowulf.* Illustrated by Charles Keeping. Bodley Head, 1961: Dutton, New York. As *Dragon Slayer*, Penguin, 1966.

Prose version, like a good short historical novel. More realistic, less episodic than no. 65. Good illustrations.

Both no. 65 and no. 67 give a better idea of the timeless quality of the Beowulf legend than is given by Robert Nye's *Bee Hunter: The Adventures of Beowulf* (Faber, 1968). This is an inventive, often imaginative experiment in remaking the story with material from other sources in order to stress the supernatural and the symbolism of good and evil; but the modern Jungian philosophy explicitly imposed upon the tale clashes with both its pagan and its Christian traditions, and some innovations are marked by the grotesque fantasy of Celtic legendary tradition rather than by the gravity of Anglo-Saxon poetry. In nos. 65 and 67 the evil of Grendel and his mother is allowed to speak for itself.

68 SYNGE, URSULA. *Weland: Smith of the Gods.* Illustrated by Charles Keeping. Bodley Head, 1972: S. G. Phillips, New York, 1973.

A vigorous, detailed, imaginative version of one of the most tragic, violent but also romantic legends; based on the Lay of Volund and beautifully structured; too subtle and too harsh for children under ten, it is a stimulating book for eleven- to fifteen-year-olds and even for sixth form work.

Original sources in translation

See note prefaced to nos. 40–48 above.

69 *Beowulf.* Translated by J. R. Clark Hall (1911). Revised and with preface [on language of translation] by J. R. R. Tolkien, Allen and Unwin, 1940; revised and with introduction by C. L. Wrenn, 1950: Barnes and Noble, New York.

The 'authorized version'. See note on no. 42, and pp. 77–9 above.

70 ——— Translated, illustrated and introduced by Gavin Bone. Blackwell, 1945.

A free-verse translation, not in the original metre, intended to get the pleasure of reading Anglo-Saxon poetry 'through to the general reader', concentrating on its 'impressionistic' quality. Useful for reading to children over eleven; a well-printed book that looks more aesthetic than academic and could be put straight into their hands if a copy could be found.

71 ——— Translated by Kevin Crossley-Holland and introduced by Bruce Mitchell, with drawings by Brigitte Hanf. Macmillan, London and New York, 1968.

A free, predominantly four-stress verse translation made with much the same purpose as no. 70, but avoiding archaisms; 'by and large faithful to the letter of the original, but it is the mood' that came first; intended to be read aloud, and with a few exceptions the lines fall into natural rhythmic patterns; may prove effective for quoting and for teenagers to read. Useful, readable introduction, and appendix giving specimens of original with literal gloss and critical commentary.

72 ——— Translated and introduced by Charles W. Kennedy. Oxford University Press, London and New York, 1940.

A translation into the original alliterative four-stress metre, preserving 'picturesque epic' phrases and synonyms, but not awkwardly archaic; could be read to children over eleven.

73 ——— Translated and introduced by David Wright. Penguin, London and Baltimore, 1957.

An idiomatic modern prose version: the style does not suit this poem.

74 *Saga of the Volsungs (The)*. Edited, translated and introduced by R. G. Finch. Nelson, 1965.

The historical setting: origins and transmission of stories

Nos. 75 to 77 and 79 are all written for the non-specialist. No. 78 is humane and interesting, but more difficult. See also no. 348, which is the best introduction to Northern stories.

75 BRØNSTED, JOHANNES. *The Vikings*. Translated by E. Bannister-Good. Penguin, London and Baltimore, 1960.

Also gives photographs of weapons and treasure.

76 DAVIDSON, H. R. ELLIS. *Gods and Myths of Northern Europe*. Penguin, London and Baltimore, 1964.

77 SYKES, EGERTON. *Everyman's Dictionary of Non-Classical Mythology*. Dent, 1952, revised edition 1961: Dutton, New York, 1961.

78 WHITELOCK, DOROTHY. *The Audience of Beowulf*. Oxford University Press, London and New York, 1951.

79 —— *The Beginnings of English Society*. Penguin, London and Baltimore, 1952.

The historical setting: the visual image

Nos. 80 to 82 for illustrations: nos. 80 and 81 also for children's reading. See note prefaced to nos. 57 to 61 above.

80 QUENNELL, MARJORIE and C. H. *Everyday Life in Roman and Anglo-Saxon Times*. Batsford, 1926, revised edition 1959: Putnam, New York, 1960.

81 SORRELL, JOHN HAMILTON and ALAN. *Saxon England*. Lutterworth, 1964.

82 *Sutton Hoo ship burial (The)* (1947). Revised edition, British Museum, 1964.

For photographs of treasure. Text for historians only.

THE ARTHURIAN ROMANCES

Children's books

83 GREEN, ROGER LANCELYN. *King Arthur and his Knights of the Round Table*. Illustrated by Lotte Reiniger. Penguin, London and Baltimore, 1953.

Appropriate and original scissor-cut illustrations. The differences between this retelling and Barbara Leonie Picard's (no. 87) are characteristic of the two writers. See note on no. 64 above.

84 —— *Sir Lancelot of the Lake*. Illustrated by Janet and Anne Grahame Johnstone. Purnell, 1966.

A large picture-book; text much better than that of no. 91 below: includes lesser-known French stories. Illustrations clear and appropriate: style better suited to this subject than to that of no. 18 above.

85 LE CAIN, ERROL. *King Arthur's Sword*. Faber, 1968.

Picture-book for children of six to nine: fantastic pictures richly coloured suggest something of mediaeval miniatures: text emphasizes far-fetched magic.

86 MALORY, SIR THOMAS. Abridged and slightly modernized by Brian Kennedy Cook, illustrated by John G. Galsworthy. *King Arthur of Britain*, 1946; *Sir Lancelot*, 1951; *The Holy Grail*, 1953; Ward (Golden Legend Series).

Very useful for reading aloud to children of eleven; and to put into the hands of children over thirteen who are capable of enjoying Malory's language but likely to be put off by the size of his book and his interweaving of stories. Clear and suitable illustrations: periods of clothes and armour mixed.

87 PICARD, BARBARA LEONIE. *Stories of King Arthur and his Knights*. Illustrated by Roy Morgan. Oxford University Press, 1955: Walck, New York, 1955.

See note on no. 83 above. Good woodcut illustrations.

88 RIDLEY, M. R. *Sir Gawain and the Green Knight*. Illustrated by John G. Galsworthy. Ward (Gold Legend Series), 1945.

A free and abridged translation rather than a retelling: gives a very good idea of the original, as far as any prose can. Less immediately exciting than no. 89 below, but more sensitive. Good, historically accurate line illustrations.

89 SERRAILLIER, IAN. *The Challenge of the Green Knight*. Illustrated by V. Ambrus. Oxford University Press, 1966: Walck, New York, 1967.

In the same style as no. 65 above, but less successful: a retelling in a metre that does not suit the original. Lively, inventive, but sometimes rumbustious and over-modern. Illustrations attractive in line and colour, but the lady's clothes are out of date.

90 SUTCLIFF, ROSEMARY. *Tristan and Iseult*. Illustrated by Victor Ambrus. Bodley Head, 1971; Penguin (Puffin), 1974.

'I have tried to get back to the Celtic original as much as possible, and in doing this I have made one big change in the story': the magic potion is omitted. More earthy in setting and dialogue than retellings based on French romance and Malory, but still a legend in character, not a historical novel (compare no. 102) Firm, rhythmic prose.

91 WILSON, BARBARA KER. *Legends of the Round Table*. Illustrated by Maria Calati. Paul Hamlyn, 1966.

A large picture-book. A poor text, starting with some dull Joseph of Arimathea and Merlin stories. Imaginative colouring and mediaeval backgrounds.

Original sources, in translation if necessary

See note prefaced to nos. 40 to 48 above.

92 CHRETIEN DE TROYES. *Arthurian Romances* [Erec et Enide, Cliges, Yvain, Lancelot]. Translated by W. W. Comfort. Dent (Everyman) 1914; reprinted 1967.

93 —— *The Story of the Grail.* Translated by W. R. Linker. University of North Carolina Press, Chapel Hill, 1960.

94 *Gawain (Sir) and the Green Knight.* Translated and introduced by Brian Stone. Penguin, London and Baltimore, 1959.

A good translation in the original metre, in a 'style somewhat more embellished than that of good modern prose'.

95 MALORY, SIR THOMAS. *The Works.* Edited and introduced by E. Vinaver. Oxford University Press (Standard Authors), London and New York, 1954.

96 —— *Le Morte D'Arthur.* Edited by Janet Cowan, with introduction by John Lawlor. 2 vols. Penguin, 1969.

Caxton's text unmodified by Winchester MS: modern spelling, punctuation and paragraphing, original syntax and most major archaic forms retained. Introduction touches on originality in 'matter of love'.

97 WOLFRAM VON ESCHENBACH. *Parʒival.* Translated into English verse by Jessie L. Weston. 2 vols. David Nutt, 1894.

The historical setting: origin and transmission of stories

98 ASHE, GEOFFREY. *All about King Arthur.* W. H. Allen, 1969.

Intended for children, and within the grasp of able nine- to eleven-year-olds. Covers much of the same historical and archaeological ground as no. 100 but more simply with little quotation and reference: less on legendary tradition. Partisan in treatment of Camelot and Avalon: no. 100 is more helpful as teaching material.

99 BRADBROOK, M. C. *Sir Thomas Malory.* Longmans (Writers and their Work Series), 1958: British Book Centre, New York.

100 CLANCY, JOSEPH P. *Pendragon: Arthur and his Britain.* Macmillan, 1971: Praeger, New York, 1971.

Written 'primarily for young people', in fact very accessible to the general reader, sixth-formers and clever secondary or primary

children interested in the evolution of the historical into the legendary
Arthur: deals in detail but readably with literary and archaeological
sources and gives a reconstruction of Dark Age Britain, acknowledg-
ing conjecture for what it is. Easier than no. 101 and more cautious
than no. 98. Very useful primary teaching background material.

101 LOOMIS, R. S. *The Development of Arthurian Romance.* Hutchinson
(H. University Library), 1963: Hillary House, New York, 1963;
Harper and Row (Torchbooks), New York.

102 SUTCLIFF, ROSEMARY. *Sword at Sunset.* Hodder and Stoughton, 1963;
Coronet Books, 1971.

An adult historical novel, reconstructing the legendary acts of
Arthur and his knights as part of Romano-British resistance to the
Saxons.

103 VINAVER, E. *Malory.* Oxford University Press, Oxford, 1929.

104 WILLIAMS, CHARLES. *Arthurian Torso, containing the posthumous
fragment of the Figure of Arthur . . . and a commentary on the Arthurian
poems of Charles Williams by C. S. Lewis.* Oxford University Press,
1948.

The historical setting: the visual image

See note prefaced to nos. 57 to 61 above. See also nos. 84, 85, 88, 91.

105 BROOKE, IRIS. *English Costume of the early Middle Ages.* Black, 1936:
Barnes and Noble, New York, 1956. *English Costume of the later
Middle Ages,* Black, 1935: Barnes and Noble, New York, 1956.

106 *Duc de Berry's Book of Hours.* Berne-Hallwag (Orbis Pictus Series).

107 EVANS, JOAN. *The Flowering of the Middle Ages.* Thames and Hudson,
1966: McGraw-Hill, New York, 1966.

A large picture-book for display: good coloured reproductions of
scenes from secular life from miniatures, fresco and sculpture.

108 OAKESHOTT, R. EWART. *A Knight and his Armour.* Illustrated by the
author. Lutterworth, 1961: Dufour, Chester Springs, 1963.

109 QUENNELL, MARJORIE and C. H. *Everyday Things in England 1066–
1499.* Batsford, 1918, revised edition 1950: Putnam, New York,
1956.

110 RICKERT, E. *Chaucer's World.* Columbia University Press, New York
and London, 1948; Columbia paperback, 1962.

THE MYTH AND LEGEND OF THE OLD TESTAMENT

111 *Bible Stories for Children*. Text adapted from the Jerusalem Bible. Illustrated by Brother Eric of Taizé. Darton, Longman and Todd, 1968.

One of the most useful recent books for reading to children from seven to fourteen or putting into their hands; based on the purest and plainest modern translation, sensitively abridged, with minimum of interpolated explanation. The language is thus very clear and the stories make their own effect. Imaginative neo-archaic pictures in stained glass colours.

112 DE LA MARE, WALTER. *Stories from the Bible*. Illustrated by John Farleigh, Faber, 1929; illustrated by Irene Hawkins, Faber, 1947; illustrated by Edward Ardizzone, Faber, 1961: Knopf, New York, 1961.

A lyrical and subtle retelling of stories from the first nine books of the Old Testament which will catch the imagination of some older children who enjoy the language of Tolkien or Le Guin (nos. 237, 239, 229 to 231); they expand and interpret as well as summarizing and simplifying. Fragments can be used in telling stories to younger children. The Farleigh engravings are classics in the history of English book-illustration and suit this text; they also suit the taste of the present better than either the 1947 or 1961 illustrations, although Ardizzone's drawing is lively and unsentimental.

113 GREEN, ROGER LANCELYN. *The Tale of Ancient Israel*. Illustrated by Charles Keeping. Dent, 1969: Dutton, New York, 1969.

A very good version of Old Testament narrative for children from nine to fourteen; making use of non-biblical Rabbinical material to complete stories and bring out their folk-tale and legendary shape, it attaches them to present Jewish and Christian customs and to their setting in Israel and Egypt. The only version for children that attempts to establish the tone and diction of saga and does not require the reader to be Christian.

114 KOSSOFF, DAVID. *Bible Stories*. Collins, 1968; Fontana, 1971: Warner Paperback, New York, 1973.

If a storyteller wants an individual, free-and-easy retelling of these stories without the dignity and archaism of heroic legend, these versions which are frankly personal, speculative and anecdotal are much better than the popular *Bible Story Book* of K. N. Taylor which is based on *The Living Bible*, which in turn purports to give a straightforward translation in impossibly colloquial and often limp English. Kossoff's control of his bluff, meandering manner shews a performer's ear for spoken rhythm, and his speculations provide talking-points. Good for mixed age-groups from seven to fourteen.

115 REEVES, JAMES. *The Road to a Kingdom: Stories from the Old and New Testaments.* Illustrated by Richard Kennedy. Heinemann, 1965.

Generally dignified, uncluttered outlines of the Genesis and patri-archal stories and the beginning of kingship under Saul and David; then the life of Christ, with a linking chapter 'Isaiah' on exile and prophecy. Usually very plain in style, with echoes of A.V.: not much imposed interpretation, although the idea of the Kingdom is a running thread. Some non-biblical embroidery in the Flood and the Nativity. The unqualified use of 'God' throughout may make some difficulties. Can be read by eight- to eleven-year-olds, and to younger children.

116 TURNER, PHILIP. *Bible Story.* Illustrated by Brian Wildsmith. Oxford University Press, London, 1968: Watts, New York, 1969.

Very expressive illustrations and a good plainly written text for children from eight to eleven; it gives coherence and direction to the series of stories chosen but not as much sense of myth and heroic legend as no. 113. A traditional Christian sense of the structure of the whole cycle is implicit but not imposed on the reader.

FAIRY TALES

Chronological list of collectors and writers of fairy tales, including modern editions of translations, retellings, and original texts in English

Most of these stories are not suitable for children under eight, and many are better heard at nine or ten.

117 PERRAULT, CHARLES [1628–1703]. *The Fairy Tales of Charles Perrault.* Translated and introduced by Geoffrey Brereton, with original woodcuts. Penguin, London and Baltimore, 1957.

The best translation to read to children: lively and idiomatic. Not attractive for them to handle themselves.

118 —— *The Fairy Tales of Charles Perrault.* Translated by Norman Denny, illustrated by Philippe Jullian. Bodley Head, 1951.

Readable version, attractive page: drawings too impressionistic.

119 —— *Perrault's Complete Fairy Tales.* Translated by A. E. Johnson and others, illustrated by W. Heath Robinson. Constable, 1962: Dodd, New York, 1961.

Good edition for children to read themselves. The *art nouveau*, Beardsley-ish line illustrations almost suit the text, when they are not too much like caricature.

120 ——— *The Sleeping Beauty and Other Tales* [*Cinderella and Puss-in-Boots*]. Retold by Roger Lancelyn Green, illustrated by René Cloke. Ward, 1947.

Full, humorous word-of-mouth retelling, *not* a translation; adapted to an upper middle-class five- to seven-year-old; would not suit a class of mixed social background. Illustrations clear, but spoilt by Tarrant fairies.

121 ——— *Cinderella*. Translation and adaptation unascribed; illustrated by Errol le Cain. Faber, 1972.

A free version of Perrault which is often quite good, except for the touch of mercy at the end. The highly wrought pictures in the manner of Beardsley catch the courtly sophistication of the tale, and would attract children over eight, not a nursery group.

See also nos. 150 to 152, *The Blue Fairy Book*, for early eighteenth-century translations of Perrault by Guy Miège, and nos. 181 and 182.

122 D'AULNOY, MARIE CATHERINE LA MOTTE, COMTESSE [1650–1705]. *Princess Rosette* and *The Friendly Frog* included in no. 119 above.

123 ——— *Goldilocks*, *The White Cat* and *The Yellow Dwarf* included in no. 151 below.

124 ——— *The White Cat*. Retold and illustrated by Errol le Cain. Faber, 1973.

An elegant delicately coloured picture-book for children from six to nine.

125 LEPRINCE DE BEAUMONT, JEANNE MARIE, MME [1711–81]. *Beauty and the Beast* included in nos. 119 and 211.

Story previously written by Mme Gabrielle de Gallon de Villeneuve [d. 1755] but not so well, and not for children.

126 ——— *Beauty and the Beast*. Retold by Philippa Pearce, illustrated by Alan Barrett. Longman Young Books, 1972: T. Y. Crowell, New York, 1972.

A retelling, not a close translation: dignified, fresh and evocative, it succeeds in presenting the tale as a 'powerful fable on the meaning of love'. A romantically beautiful picture-book in which the background of the pages is part of the printed design. Accessible to seven-year-olds, and might convince an older child that it was a serious work of art. Good note on sources.

127 GRIMM, JACOB [1785–1863], and WILHELM [1786–1859]. *Grimms'*
Fairy Tales. [Translated by Edgar Taylor, 1823.] Illustrated by
George Cruikshank. Penguin (Puffin) 1948, reissued 1971. Also
reprinted with illustrations by Ulrick Schramm. Oxford University
Press, 1962: Walck, New York, 1962.

A dignified, rather stiff translation—but any direct translation of
Grimm sounds stiff. Cruikshank's illustrations of 1823 are much more
sympathetic than those of Ulrick Schramm.

128 —— *Grimm's Fairy Tales.* Retold by Amabel Williams-Ellis, illustrated
by Fritz Wegner. Blackie, 1959.

Between a free translation and an adaptation; the stories are enlarged
and given more dialogue and incidental comment and description,
but not altered in shape or interpretation. Some horrors softened
a little, but this is not a nursery version. Lively and idiomatic in
style: sympathetic illustrations. The best version for reading any
stories not included in nos. 129 and 130; the style of the book suggests
a slightly higher age-range. Notes for storytellers on sources and
interpretation.

129 —— *Tales from Grimm.* Freely translated and illustrated by Wanda
Gàg. Coward–McCann, New York, 1936: Faber, 1937.

Includes *Rapunzel, The Fisherman and his Wife, Snow White and
Rose Red, Hansel and Gretel, Aschenputtel* [Cinderella].

130 —— *More tales from Grimm.* Freely translated and illustrated by
Wanda Gàg. Coward–McCann, New York, 1947: Faber, 1962.

Includes *Mother Holle, Jorinda and Joringel, The Shoemaker and the
Elves, Rose-Bud, The Six Swans, The Wolf and the Seven Little Kids.*
Nos. 129 and 130 are lively versions which suggest oral story-telling;
good for reading to younger children. Sympathetic, detailed illustrations, spoilt by occasional sentimentality or caricature.

131 —— *Snow White and the Seven Dwarfs.* Retold and illustrated by
Wanda Gàg. Coward–McCann, New York, 1938: Faber, 1938.

Illustrations more crude and sentimental than those of nos. 129 and
130.

132 —— *The Secret Shoemakers and other stories.* Freely adapted by James
Reeves, illustrated by Edward Ardizzone. Abelard-Schuman, New
York and London, 1966: Penguin (Puffin), 1969.

Very good imaginative, word-of-mouth versions for eight-year-olds:
also includes the Grimm *Jorinda and Joringel,* as *The Witch's Castle.*
Lovely illustrations, in the right tradition.

133 —— *The Blue Light*. Story used as the base of *The Cold Flame*, by James Reeves, illustrated by Charles Keeping. Hamilton, 1967.

Development of the Grimm plot into an adolescent long short story. An interesting experiment in making the substance of fairy tale available to sophisticated teenagers. Symbolic meaning in keeping with folklore, but sometimes fits this story awkwardly.

134 —— *The Water of Life*. Story used as the base of *The Path of Gold*, by James Reeves, illustrated by Krystyna Turska. Hamilton, 1972.

A short-story treatment not unlike no. 133 in giving more detail of character and behaviour, but the original is a more sprawling tale combining several motifs. Less symbolism; it could be read to eleven-year-olds.

135 —— *The Juniper Tree and Other Tales from Grimm*. Translated by Lore Segal and Randall Jarell. Illustrated by Maurice Sendak. Farrar, Straus and Giroux, New York, 1973: Bodley Head, 1974.

Useful source of some lesser known stories, and also includes *The Fisherman and his Wife*, *The Golden Bird*, *Rapunzel*, *Snow White*. Original and appropriate illustrations.

136 ANDERSEN, HANS CHRISTIAN [1805–75]. *Forty-two Stories*. Translated and introduced by M. R. James (1930). Illustrated by Robin Jaques. Faber, 1968.

Good translation and sympathetic illustrations.

137 —— *Fairy Tales and Legends*. [Translated by Caroline Peachey, 1852.] Illustrated by Rex Whistler. Bodley Head, 1935: Dufour, Chester Springs, 1935.

Valuable for wood-engraved illustrations, perhaps the best apart from Pedersen's in no. 138; in delicate vignette style, very magical, perhaps not quite domestic enough. Inferior translation.

138 —— *Fairy Tales*. Edited and introduced by Svend Larson, translated by R. P. Keigwin, illustrated by Vilhelm Pedersen. 4 vols. Flensted, Odense, 1951–60.

Pencil drawings by the illustrator chosen by Andersen, and some of the engravings made from them: very delicate and beautiful. Small books which children over ten like to handle: too small for young children. Sensitive, idiomatic translation; the best to read aloud.

139 —— *Fairy Tales*. Translated by L. W. Kingsland, illustrated by E. H. Shepard. Oxford University Press, London, 1962: Walck, New York, 1962.

Good illustrations in the Pedersen tradition, although less magical and delicate. Good idiomatic translation.

140 —— *The Nightingale*. Translated by Eva le Gallienne, illustrated by Nancy Ekholm Burkert. Harper and Row, New York, 1965: Collins, London, 1967.

A large picture-book; delicate in colour and design, concentrating on elegant *chinoiseries* but sometimes catching the romantic spirit of the tale. Readable translation, not as close to the original as no. 138.

141 —— *Seven Tales*. Translated by Eva Le Gallienne, illustrated by Maurice Sendak. Harper and Row, New York, 1959: World's Work, 1972.

Readable, rhythmic translation, not as close to the original as no. 138; thoughtful and imaginative illuminations and pictures give the tales a mediaeval setting. Prefaces by both translator and illustrator contain good criticism.

142 —— *Stories from Hans Christian Andersen*. Selected and prefaced by Philippa Pearce; illustrated by Pauline Baynes. Collins, 1972.

Translation substantially that of Caroline Peachey (see no. 137) with minor verbal alterations; no ascription. Illustrations suitable, but not up to Pauline Baynes' best work, and much poorer than nos. 238 and 240. Includes the most important stories.

143 —— *The Complete Fairy Tales and Stories*. Translated by Erik Christian Haugaard. Gollancz, 1974.

An idiomatic, faithful translation of the whole body of Andersen's work in this *genre*, including his own notes. 156 stories, many previously untranslated into English. In appearance a scholar's edition, not a children's book. Useful introduction.

144 MACDONALD, GEORGE [1824–1905]. *The Princess and the Goblin* (1872). With original illustrations by Arthur Hughes. Penguin (Puffin), London and Baltimore, 1964.

145 —— *The Princess and Curdie* (1882). Illustrated by Helen Stratton. Penguin (Puffin), London and Baltimore, 1966.

146 —— *At the Back of the North Wind* (1871). Illustrated by Harvey Dinnerstein, Collier–Macmillan, New York and London, 1964.

The fantasy of nos. 144 and 145 is poetic, exciting, and attractive to modern children. No. 146 is Macdonald's most famous story, but the sentiment of the realistic passages makes it harder to adapt for a modern audience.

147 —— *The Light Princess* (1867). Illustrated by Maurice Sendak. Farrar, Straus and Giroux, New York, 1969: Bodley Head, 1972.

Witty, comic tale, sophisticated enough for children over nine.

148 —— *The Golden Key* (1867). With afterword by W. H. Auden, illustrated by Maurice Sendak. Farrar, Straus and Giroux, New York, 1967: Bodley Head, 1972.

149 —— *Phantastes* (1858). Pan/Ballantyne, 1971.

Nos. 147 to 149 are adult fantasies, the first witty, the other two romantic and lyrical. No use for younger children but readers over eleven who like the books listed under *Modern Hybrid Myth* may find a new interest in them.

150 LANG, ANDREW [1844–1912]. *The Blue Fairy Book*. Illustrated by H. J. Ford and G. P. Jacomb Hood. Longmans, 1889. *The Yellow Fairy Book*. Illustrated by H. J. Ford. Longmans, 1894.

Valuable for original illustrations, especially of *The Yellow Fairy Book*, if a second-hand copy can be found that has not been read to pieces. The series of twelve 'coloured' books ended in 1910. Many of the better known stories have been more accurately or idiomatically translated elsewhere.

151 —— Facsimile editions of *The Blue Fairy Book*, and the eleven other 'coloured' books. Dover, New York, 1965–8.

152 —— New editions of *The Blue Fairy Book* and seven other 'coloured' books. Illustrated by Ben Kutcher and others. Longmans, 1949–50. To be avoided if possible: commonplace illustrations, and an unattractive page.

153 JACOBS, JOSEPH [1854–1916]. *English Fairy Tales* (1890). *More English Fairy Tales* (1894). Both illustrated by John Batten. Both vols. reprinted in one as *English Fairy Tales*, with original prefaces and notes but with illustrations by Margery Gill. Bodley Head, 1968. Selected tales, also with illustrations by Margery Gill, Penguin (Puffin), 1970. Facsimiles of original editions, 2 vols. separately, Dover Publications Inc., New York, 1968.

Mostly in the rustic colloquial language of the tellers from whom the tales were collected, with an earthy agricultural-labouring class background: these native variants of European tales are often less exciting and comprehensible to modern, urban English children than the variants in Perrault and Grimm. Some of the simplest and funniest stories included in more readable nursery form in no. 199. Useful to the storyteller for *The Three Sillies*, *The Three Bears*, *Jack the Giant-Killer*, *Whittington and his Cat*; also for two Cinderella variants, *Cap o' Rushes and Tattercoats*.

Batten's bold yet delicate romantic *art nouveau* illustrations make a facsimile or second-hand copy of the original edition desirable.

Margery Gill's line drawings are suitable but comparatively characterless.

154 WILDE, OSCAR [1856–1900]. *The Happy Prince and Other Stories* (1888). Illustrated by Lars Bo. Penguin (Puffin), London and Baltimore, 1962.

Includes *The Selfish Giant* and *The Star Child*. Romantic, symbolic tales in stylized poetic prose: attractive to many children of nine and ten.

155 THURBER, JAMES [1894–1963]. *The White Deer*. Harcourt, New York, 1945: Penguin, 1963.

156 —— *The Thirteen Clocks*. Simon and Schuster, New York, 1950. *The Wonderful O*. Simon and Schuster, New York, 1957. Reprinted together, illustrated by Ronald Searle. Penguin (Puffin), 1962.

Nos. 155 and 156 are on the fringe of the humorous Andersen tradition. Almost, but not quite parody.

157 GALLICO, PAUL [1897–]. *Snowflake*. Michael Joseph, 1952.

In the Romantic Andersen tradition.

158 PEARCE, PHILIPPA. *The Squirrel Wife*. Illustrated by Derek Collard. Longman Young Books, 1971: Crowell, New York, 1972.

A very delicately imaginative invented fairy tale, making use of many traditional motifs of choice and metamorphosis: printed with borders and initials in a proliferating *art nouveau* style which helps to create the magic of the forest.

159 LE CAIN, ERROL. *The Cabbage Princess*. Faber, 1969.

Witty and sophisticated, with a shrewd moral. The 'foolish wishes' *motif* told in the Perrault–Wilde tradition. A picture-book for children over eight.

Recent picture-books of single fairy tales for children under seven

Since 1968 the fairy-tale picture-book has been taken up by reputable publishers and illustrators and nos. 160 to 182 bear no relation to the sentimental cheap versions of earlier years (compare pp. 40, 114–115). The choice of stories is generally well suited to the mode of presentation and to an audience of five to seven, although a few might be better left for more sophisticated treatment. Nos. 162, 169, 175, 176, 178 are real nursery books for children under five. See no. 187 for a useful series of betwixt-and-between books which balance pictures and text. The publishing history of picture-books is complicated: most of them are printed in Europe and appear in several languages. I have given only the London imprint.

160 ANDERSEN, HANS CHRISTIAN. *The Steadfast Tin Soldier.* [Text simplified from translation by Caroline Peachey, unascribed]; illustrated by Monika Laimgruber. Hamish Hamilton, 1970.

Imaginative pictures deserve a better text. One of the stories that is right for younger children.

161 —— *The Emperor's New Clothes.* [Translation unascribed]; illustrated by Monika Laimgruber. Hamish Hamilton, 1973.

Fairly close translation and good pictures for five- to seven-year-olds. Sensible choice of tale for this age-group.

162 GRIMM, JACOB. *The Elves and the Shoemaker.* [Retelling unascribed], illustrated by Katrin Brandt. Bodley Head, 1968; Penguin (Picture Puffins) 1970.

For beginning readers of about five, or for nursery telling.

163 —— *Jorinda and Jorindel.* Translation by Edgar Taylor abridged and slightly modified by Bernadette Watts; illustrated by Bernadette Watts. Oxford University Press, 1970.

Pictures in the Wildsmith tradition of colouring which suits this story.

164 —— *King Thrushbeard.* [Free translation unascribed]; illustrated by Felix Hoffman. Oxford University Press, 1970.

A rather savage Taming of the Shrew for this age-range: good text and pictures.

165 —— *The Golden Bird.* Translated by Richard Sadler, illustrated by Lilo Fromm. Sadler, 1970.

One of the best moral and magical tales: text good and good illustrations in the Wildsmith tradition.

166 —— *The Fisherman and His Wife.* Translation by Margaret Hunt (1884) somewhat modified; illustrated by Katrin Brandt. Bodley Head, 1970.

A shapely moral fable, the humour well caught in the pictures. Good for six- to eight-year-olds to read on their own.

167 —— *The Brave Little Tailor.* [Abridged retelling unascribed]; illustrated by Gerhard Oberländer. Hamish Hamilton, 1971.

Text adequate, attractive pictures.

168 —— *How the Moon Began.* Retold by James Reeves, illustrated by Edward Ardizzone. Abelard Schuman, 1971.

One of the comic tall stories of the Grimm brothers; rustic humour well caught by the illustrator.

169 —— *The Hedgehog and the Hare.* Retold and illustrated by Wendy Watson. Longman, 1971.

One of the widespread folk beast fables collected by the brothers Grimm (compare Aesop's 'Hare and the Tortoise'); makes a good nursery story: beautiful wood-engravings, good text.

170 —— *Briar Rose; the story of the Sleeping Beauty.* Translation by Lucy Crane (1882) slightly adapted by Kathleen Lines; illustrated by Margery Gill. Bodley Head, 1972.

One of a series of 'Bodley Head Fairy Tale Picture Books' which are all excellent in text and design, using either slightly modified classical translations or good modern retellings, and giving full notes on sources. In appearance they would suit readers of five to seven, and could be shown to younger children: this and some of the other stories in the series are perhaps better kept for older children, but the books are a very welcome alternative to chain-store versions.

171 —— *Mother Holly.* [Free abridged retelling unascribed]; illustrated by Bernadette Watts. Oxford University Press, 1972.

Text disappointing, with an added happy ending: Richard Sadler's 'Mother Carey' is less misleading than 'Holly'. Pictures make the contrasted daughters into small children, but the German town setting is nicely suggested.

172 —— *Snow-White and the Seven Dwarfs.* Retelling by Kathleen Lines based on translation by Herta Ryder; illustrated by Fritz Wegner. Bodley Head, 1973.

See note on no. 170.

173 —— *Tom Thumb.* [Abridged version of translation by Edgar Taylor, unascribed]; illustrated by Felix Hoffman. Oxford University Press, 1973.

Text adequate, pictures imaginative in texture and colour.

174 —— *The Six Swans.* Illustrated by Adrie Hospes. Bodley Head, 1973. See note on no. 170.

175 —— *The Wolf and the Seven Little Kids.* [Fairly close translation, unascribed]; illustrated by Felix Hoffman. Oxford University Press, 1958.

A good nursery tale: sympathetic pictures.

176 —— *The Wolf and the Seven Little Kids.* Translated by Richard Sadler. Illustrated by Regine Grube-Heinecke. Sadler, 1967.

177 —— *Mother Carey* [*Frau Hollë*]. Translated by Richard Sadler, illustrated by Regine Grube-Heinecke. Sadler, 1969.

One of the shapely, imaginative magic fables that suit five- to seven-year-olds: good text, beautifully coloured but rather coyly drawn illustrations.

178 —— *How the Willow Wren became King.* Retold and illustrated by Uta Glauber; [English translator unnamed]. Abelard-Schuman, 1970.

Admirable nursery fable: lovely pictures, good text for under-fives.

179 —— *Rumpelstiltskin.* Retold by Kathleen Lines with reference to nineteenth-century translations; illustrated by William Stobbs. Bodley Head, 1970.

See note on no. 170.

180 —— *The Poor Woodcutter and the Dove.* Retold and illustrated by Max Velthuijs; [English translator unnamed]. Abelard-Schuman, 1970.

Sympathetically presented as a nursery tale; the *motif* is the same as that of 'The Fisherman and his Wife' which is a better story.

181 PERRAULT, CHARLES. *Cinderella.* Translation of Robert Samber (1729) modified by Kathleen Lines: illustrated by Shirley Hughes. Bodley Head, 1970.

See note on no. 170. Very thoughtful illustrations which put the story into Perrault's time.

182 —— *The Little Red Riding Hood.* Translated by Robert Samber (1729) and slightly adapted by Kathleen Lines, illustrated by William Stobbs. Bodley Head, 1972.

See note on no. 170.

Recent anthologies of fairy tales and traditional stories for eight- to eleven-year-olds

Nos. 183 to 197 are the modern equivalents of Lang's 'coloured' Fairy Books (nos. 150–2). The traditional stories in them are mostly those collected from other countries and continents in the later nineteenth and twentieth centuries, and therefore not as familiar (or as important) as the stories of Perrault, Grimm and Andersen. They have the advantage of freshness and might (nos. 188 and 190 especially) convert a child put off fairy tales by bad nursery versions of Perrault. Nos. 183, 184, 196 and 197 give sources of stories, and helpful notes on origins and artistic character.

183 COLWELL, EILEEN (selected by). *A Storyteller's Choice, a selection of*

stories, with notes on how to tell them. Illustrated by Carol Barker. Bodley Head, 1963: Walck, New York, 1964.

Includes *The Magic Tea-Kettle* (Japanese, told by Rhoda Power) and good versions of Mme D'Aulnoy's *The White Cat* and Andersen's *The Nightingale.*

184 —— *A Second Storyteller's Choice, a selection of stories with notes on how to tell them.* Illustrated by Prudence Seward. Bodley Head, 1965: Walck, New York, 1965.

Includes *Brother Johannick and his Silver Bell* (Breton) and Eleanor Farjeon's *Bertha Goldfoot.*

Nos. 183 and 184 are varied, well-balanced collections of stories for telling, or reading aloud: they avoid the usual anthology pieces, and contain more humour than many fairy-tale collections. A mixture of 'invented' and traditional stories from various countries, all of a more or less fabulous or romantic kind. Good beginner's books for anyone who wants to supplement the more central traditions of legend and fairy tale, with imaginative and practical notes on the technique of storytelling.

185 CORRIN, SARA and STEPHEN. *Stories for Eight-Year-Olds.* Faber, 1971. Includes stories from heroic legends of various cultures and some romantic fairy-tale.

186 GREEN, ROGER LANCELYN (selected by). *Modern Fairy Stories.* Illustrated by E. H. Shepard. Dent (Illustrated Children's Classics), 1955: Dutton, New York, 1956.

Useful collection of sixteen nineteenth-century 'invented' fairy tales. Includes Ruskin's *King of the Golden River* (1851), Lewis Carroll's *Bruno's Revenge* (1867) and Kenneth Grahame's *The Reluctant Dragon* (1890).

187 HAVILAND, VIRGINIA (retold by). *Favourite Fairy Tales Told in . . . : England,* Boston 1959, London 1969; *France,* Boston 1959, London 1967; *Germany,* Boston 1959, London 1969; *Ireland,* Boston 1961; *Italy,* Boston 1965, London 1966; *Norway,* Boston 1961, London 1967; *Poland,* Boston 1963, London 1966; *Russia,* Boston 1961, London 1967; *Scotland,* Boston 1963, London 1966; *Spain,* Boston 1963, London 1966; *Sweden,* Boston 1966, London 1969; *Japan,* London 1969, Boston 1967; *Greece,* Boston 1970, London 1971; *India,* Boston 1973. Illustrated by various artists; Little Brown & Co., Boston: Bodley Head, London.

A useful series intended for the 'age when picture-books are left behind and many other fairy-tale versions are too difficult'; well

adapted to it in choice of tales, page design and pictures. Good for
seven- to nine-year-olds to read on their own; moral fable and folk
magic rather than myth or poetic symbolism.

188 HARRIS, ROSEMARY. *The Lotus and the Grail: Legends from East to
West.* Illustrated by Errol le Cain. Faber, 1974.

Very individual, shrewd and evocative versions in romance or long-
short-story form; for children from nine to fourteen and grown-ups.
Unfortunately no notes on sources.

189 LINES, KATHLEEN (selected by). *Tales of Magic and Enchantment.*
Illustrated by Alan Howard. Faber, 1966: Transatlantic Arts, New
York.

A discriminating anthology of heroic legends and longer, more
romantic fairy tales for children of about ten. Includes Andersen's
The Little Mermaid and *The Wild Swans*, a shortened version of
Helen Waddell's dignified retelling of the story of Joseph, and Lang's
brief but poetic abridgement of Morris's version of the story of
Sigurd. Illustrations decorative and fantastic, perhaps better on
grotesque subjects than on lyrical ones. Gives references to sources.

190 MANNING-SANDERS, RUTH. *A Book of Giants*, 1962; *A Book of
Dwarfs*, 1963; *A Book of Dragons*, 1964; *A Book of Witches*, 1965; *A
Book of Wizards*, 1966; *A Book of Mermaids*, 1967; *A Book of
Ghosts and Goblins*, 1968; *A Book of Princes and Princesses*, 1969; *A
Book of Devils and Demons*, 1970; *A Book of Charms and Changelings*,
1971; *A Book of Ogres and Trolls*, 1972; *A Book of Sorcerers and
Spells*, 1973; *A Book of Magic Animals*, 1974; all illustrated by
Robin Jacques, Methuen; Pan: Dutton, New York.

A series of anthologies of fairy tales, not trespassing beyond the line
dividing fairy tale from heroic legend. On the whole the stories are
among the more light-hearted, humorous or inventive of popular
tales. Good, clean-cut, idiomatic and rhythmical prose; the stories
are retold, not translated, with the same kind of freedom as nos. 129
to 134 by Wanda Gàg and James Reeves. Very good, meticulously
detailed illustrations in exactly the right convention. No references
to the sources of the tales.

191 *Myths and Legends*: English (James Reeves), 1954; Irish (Eileen
O'Faolain), 1954; Scottish (Barbara Ker Wilson), 1954; Scandi-
navian (Gwyn Jones), 1955; Russian (C. Downing), 1956; Yugoslav
(Nada Curcija-Prodanovic), 1957; German (Barbara Leonie Picard),
1958; Swiss-Alpine (Fritz Müller, translated by K. Potts), 1958;
Japanese (H. and W. McAlpine), 1958; Red Indian (R. Manning-

Sanders), 1960; Chinese (C. Birch), 1961; Indian (J. E. B. Gray), 1961; African (K. Arnott), 1962; West Indian (P. M. Sherlock), 1966; all illustrated by Joan Kiddell-Monroe. Oxford University Press, London: Walck, New York.

A mixture of fable, fairy tale, saga and legend, varying in interest according to the teller and the particular story. A good quarry for the teacher prepared to pick and choose. James Reeves's *English Fables and Fairy Stories* is valuable for our native tales (often not the best, as stories); simpler to read than no. 153.

192 PIGGOTT, JULIET (selected by). *Famous Fairy Tales of the World.* Frederick Muller, 1965.

193 —— *Myth and Moonshine: A Collection of Magical Tales.* Illustrated by Sara Silcock. Frederick Muller, 1973.

Nos. 192 and 193 are anthologies of stories from the country-by-country series published by Muller, which varies in interest according to tale and teller.

194 PROVENSEN, ALICE and MARTIN (selected and illustrated by). *The Provensen Book of Fairy Tales.* Random, New York, 1971: Collins, 1972.

Good collection of late nineteenth- and twentieth-century invented fairy tales, mostly in the traditional style and setting. A large picture-book, attractive in colouring although too crude in drawing. Includes Elinor Mordaunt's gay and witty 'The Prince and the Goose Girl', a *Taming of the Shrew* in reverse, Wilde's 'Happy Prince', Andersen's 'The Nightingale', and Rackham's version of 'Beauty and the Beast'.

195 WILLIAMS-ELLIS, AMABEL. *Princesses and Trolls, Twelve traditional stories retold.* Illustrated by Judith Brook. Barrie, 1950.

196 —— *Round the World Fairy Tales.* Illustrated by William Stobbs. Blackie, 1963: Ryerson Press, New York, 1963: Warne, New York, 1966. Reissued in 2 vols. without original notes, as *Dragons and Princes* and *Princesses and Witches.* Blackie, 1966.

197 —— *Old World and New World Fairy Tales.* Illustrated by William Stobbs. Blackie, 1966: Warne, New York, 1967.

Recent anthologies of fairy tales and traditional stories
for children under seven

198 AINSWORTH, RUTH. *Fairy Gold: Favourite fairy tales retold for the
very young*. Illustrated by Barbara Hope Steinberg. Heinemann, 1972.

Fairly dignified simplifications although rather too easy-going in
prose style, and beautiful line and silhouette illustrations in the
Beardsley manner. The best known tales of Andersen and the Grimm
brothers.

199 COLWELL, EILEEN. *Tell me a Story, a Collection for Under Fives*.
Illustrated by Judith Bledsoe. Penguin (Young Puffin), London and
Baltimore, 1962.

The Three Bears, The Three Little Pigs, The Three Billy-goats Gruff,
and others. Not all fairy tales.

200 ——— *Tell me another Story, a Collection for the Fours to Sixes*. Illustrated by Gunvor Edwards. Penguin (Young Puffin), London and
Baltimore, 1964.

Includes simple versions of poetic Grimm and Perrault stories which
are better left until children can hear the real thing.

201 CORRIN, SARA and STEPHEN (selected by). *Stories for Seven-Year-
Olds*. Illustrated by Shirley Hughes. Faber, 1964: Transatlantic Arts,
New York, 1964.

Includes a good translation of the Scandinavian *East of the Sun and
West of the Moon*: some of the most approachable Grimm and
Andersen stories, in versions by Wanda Gàg and M. R. James.
Good illustrations.

202 ——— (edited by). *Stories for Six-Year-Olds and other young readers*.
Illustrated by Shirley Hughes. Faber, 1967: Watts, New York, 1969.
A collection that includes some real nursery stories of a fairy-tale
kind, both traditional (*The Three Bears, The Gingerbread Boy*) and
modern (*The Enormous Apple Pie, The Laughing Dragon*) together
with some of the powerful and lyrical French stories (*The Sleeping
Beauty, Beauty and the Beast*) which suffer by being simplified. See
note on no. 200 above. Useful, but not so well chosen as no. 201,
especially for a theoretically lower age-range.

203 ——— *A Time to Laugh; Thirty Stories for Young Children*. Faber, 1972.

Includes several comic European and African beast-fables.

204 HAVILAND, VIRGINIA (selected by). *The Fairy Tale Treasury*. Illustrated by Raymond Briggs. Hamish Hamilton, 1972.

205 LINES, KATHLEEN (selected by). *A Ring of Tales*. Illustrated by Harold Jones. Oxford University Press, London, 1958: Watts, New York, 1959.

Includes Alison Uttley's *The Spice Woman's Basket*. Very good, meticulous, unsentimental illustrations.

206 —— (selected and sometimes adapted by). *The Ten-Minute Story-Book*. Illustrated by Winifred Marks. Oxford University Press, London, 1943.

Some real nursery tales and some which perhaps should not be simplified for under-sevens.

207 MONTGOMERIE, NORAH. *To Read and to Tell*. Illustrated by Margery Gill. Bodley Head, 1962: Arco Publishing Co., New York, 1964.

Includes many good traditional nursery stories and animal fables; also some myths and poetic fairy tales which should not be simplified.

The historical setting: origins and transmission of stories

See also nos. 117, 143 and 347. J. R. R. Tolkien gives a readable account of the mixing of tales in 'the cauldron of story', and Geoffrey Brereton's preface is an easy introduction to theories about the history of folk-lore.

208 BAIN, R. NISBET. *Hans Christian Andersen, a Biography*. Lawrence and Bullen, 1895.

209 *Grimm's Household Tales. With the Author's Notes...* Translated by Margaret Hunt, with a preface by Andrew Lang. 2 vols. Bell, 1884.

210 LARSEN, SVEND; BOMHOLT, JULIUS; RUBOW, PAUL V.; DAL, ERIK; and WOEL, CAI M. *A Book on the Danish Writer Hans Christian Andersen, his Life and Work*. Samvirkerådet for dansk kulturarbejde i udlandet, Copenhagen, 1956.

211 OPIE, IONA and PETER. *The Classic Fairy Tales*. Book Club Associates and Oxford University Press, 1974.

Twenty-four of the most influential tales of the European tradition printed from the earliest or most important early literary sources; good historical introduction, notes on sources and variants prefixed to each tale, and bibliography. A reference book rather than a book for children to handle, although some historically-minded children might be attracted to it. Valuable for reproductions of nineteenth-century illustrations in various styles.

The historical setting: the visual image

See the work of illustrators who understand fairy tale, especially nos. 135, 138, 141, 151, 190.

MODERN HYBRID MYTH, LEGEND AND FANTASY

Nos. 212 to 240 differ from the invented stories in my list of *Fairy Tales* in drawing upon the heroic legends of various cultures and in being treated with more personal freedom. They are usually long and often cyclic, and most are written for an audience of adults or teenage children. No. 232 however is read by children under eleven. Since 1968 the *genre* known as 'fantasy' in the book trade has proliferated, and it overlaps science fiction, historical fiction, invented fairy stories, family stories with magic in them, and stories of travelling in time. I have included only those in which the inheritance from traditional myth, legend and folklore is unmistakable.

Nos. 213, 229 to 231 and 237 to 240 take place in the heroic past and are written with varying degrees of heroic dignity: nos. 214 to 218, 220 to 225, 233 and 234 are novels in which children interact with legendary beings; nos. 212 and 226 to 228 are unlike anything else. The first writers in this kind (after E. Nesbit) were C. S. Lewis, Tolkien and Alan Garner. The 'young novels' of this school help to fill what used to be a gap in stories that would attract children between eleven and fourteen, especially boys.

212 ADAMS, RICHARD. *Watership Down.* Rex Collings, 1972; Penguin, 1973.

> Heroic saga of rabbits establishing a new warren: quite individual in kind, realistic in natural history but an invented legend in its debt to Tolkien's kind of narrative and the inclusion of invented rabbit mythology. Written as a long novel for older children.

213 AIKEN, JOAN. *The Whispering Mountain.* Cape, 1969: Doubleday, New York, 1969.

> Elements of Celtic tradition (the sacred magic harp), romantic imagery of creative inspiration, historical fiction and serious fantasy (the mountain itself). The touch is light and the pace brisk. This writer's work always has an original colouring which results from the successful mixture of ordinarily incompatible material.

214 BEACHCROFT, NINA. *Well Met by Witchlight.* Heinemann, 1972.

> Black and white magic; a story about and for children of seven to ten, with faint fairy-tale echoes but closer to family fiction. Lively.

215 COOPER, SUSAN. *Over Sea, Under Stone.* Cape, 1965; Penguin, 1968: Harcourt Brace, New York, 1966.

216 —— *The Dark is Rising*. Chatto and Windus, 1973: Atheneum, New York, 1973.

217 —— *Greenwitch*. Chatto and Windus, 1974.

Three books of an intended five-book cycle of black and white magic in which modern children move in time and see re-enacted patterns: for children over ten. Sensitive creation of character and setting.

218 CLARKE, PAULINE. *The Two Faces of Silenus*. Faber, 1972: Coward, New York, 1972.

Older children in Italy bringing Silenus to life and seeing their lives altered by him: after the Garner pattern.

219 DRUCE, ROBERT. *Firefang*. Bell, 1972.

A past and present dragon story: witchcraft and rural comedy.

220 FARMER, PENELOPE. *A Castle of Bone*. Chatto and Windus, 1972; Penguin (Puffin), 1970: Atheneum, New York, 1972.

Experience of legend in dream and magic, with suggestions of allegory.

221 GARNER, ALAN. *The Weirdstone of Brisingamen*. Collins, 1960; Penguin, 1963: Walck, New York, 1969.

222 —— *The Moon of Gomrath*. Collins, 1963; Penguin, 1965: Walck, New York, 1967.

223 —— *Elidor*. Collins, 1965; Penguin, 1967: Walck, New York, 1967.
Nos. 220 to 223 are tales in which modern children encounter legendary beings through magic: 'young novels' that attract children from ten to fourteen.

224 —— *The Owl Service*. Collins, 1967: Walck, New York, 1968.

225 —— *Red Shift*. Collins, 1973: Macmillan, New York, 1973.

Nos. 224 and 225 seem to be written for an older adolescent and adult audience: myth is re-enacted in modern life and adolescence is treated with almost aggressive realism. In no. 225 the young people have become brutalized and the language bludgeoning.

226 HARRIS, ROSEMARY. *The Moon in the Cloud*. Faber, 1968, (paper) 1972: Macmillan, New York, 1970.

227 —— *The Shadow on the Sun*. Faber, 1970: Macmillan, New York, 1970.

228 —— *The Bright and Morning Star*. Faber, 1972: Macmillan, New York, 1972.

Nos. 226 to 228 are a trilogy wholly original in material, manner and language: not in the Tolkien tradition, they are invented legend in that they start from the Flood story, include talking beasts and suggest universal themes. Delicate comedy and a Jane-Austenish eye for behaviour; probably the best new writing for children of nine and over in the decade 1964–74; handling of language recalls Kipling's stories.

229 LE GUIN, URSULA. *A wizard of Earthsea.* Parnassus Press, New York, 1968; Ace Books, New York, 1970: Penguin, 1971.

230 —— *The Tombs of Atuan.* 'Worlds of Fantasy', New York, 1970–1971; Atheneum, New York, 1971: Gollancz, 1972.

231 —— *The Farthest Shore.* Gollancz, 1973; Penguin, 1974.

Nos. 229 to 231 are invented legend rather in the Tolkien manner, with more sorcery and more explicit psychological interpretation; less austere, more modern in language; for children over twelve.

232 LEWIS, C. S. *The Chronicles of Narnia.* Illustrated by Pauline Baynes. Consisting of:

The Lion, the Witch and the Wardrobe. Bles, 1950; Penguin (Puffin), 1959: Macmillan, New York, 1951.

Prince Caspian. Bles, 1951; Penguin (Puffin), 1962: Macmillan, New York, 1951.

The Voyage of the Dawn Treader. Bles, 1952; Penguin (Puffin), 1965: Macmillan, New York, 1952.

The Silver Chair. Bles, 1953; Penguin (Puffin), 1965: Macmillan, New York, 1953.

The Horse and his Boy. Bles, 1954; Penguin (Puffin), 1965: Macmillan, New York, 1954.

The Magician's Nephew. Bodley Head, 1955; Penguin (Puffin), 1964: Macmillan, New York, 1955.

The Last Battle. Bodley Head, 1956; Penguin (Puffin), 1964: Macmillan, New York, 1956.

Like nos. 237 and 239, a cycle of 'invented 'myth, legend and fairy tale, but written for younger children (eight to ten). The stories begin with modern children taken by magic into Narnia.

233 LIVELY, PENELOPE. *The Whispering Knights.* Heinemann, 1971. Modern children and Arthurian echoes.

234 —— *The Wild Hunt of Hagworthy.* Heinemann, 1971: Dutton, New York, 1972.

Modern children and trooping-fairy echoes. All the 'young novels'
by this writer depend in some measure upon magic and exchanges
between present and past: this and no. 233 have stronger connections
with legend than the rest.

235 NYE, ROBERT. *Taliesin.* Illustrated by Sheila Hawkins. Faber, 1966:
Hill and Wang, New York, 1967.

The pre-Arthurian exploits and marvels of Merlin or Taliesin:
legendary material from the Mabinogion woven into an original
long short story. Similar to nos. 246 and 247 in tone—often comic,
far-fetched, off-hand—but with more lyricism, interest in character
and suggestion of symbolism. A 'young novel' for nine- to fourteen-
year-olds.

236 STEWART, MARY. *Ludo and the Star Horse.* Illustrated by Gino
d'Achille. Brockhampton, 1974.

Journey through the Houses of the Zodiac peopled by classical heroes
and supernatural beings.

237 TOLKIEN, J. R. R. *The Hobbit.* Allen and Unwin, 1937; Allen and
Unwin paperback, 1966: Houghton Mifflin, New York, 1938; Ballantine Books, New York.

238 —— *Farmer Giles of Ham.* Illustrated by Pauline Baynes. Allen and
Unwin, 1949: Houghton Mifflin, New York.

239 —— *The Lord of the Rings.* 3 vols. Allen and Unwin, 1954–5, revised
edition, 1966; Allen and Unwin paperback, 1968: Houghton
Mifflin, New York, 1954–6; Ballantine Books, New York.

240 —— *Smith of Wootton Major.* Illustrated by Pauline Baynes. Allen
and Unwin, 1967.

No. 237 is an 'invented' magical heroic legend written for children,
the prologue to no. 239, which is a cycle of grown-up 'invented'
myth, legend and fairy tale, also read by some children of twelve.
Nos. 238 and 240 are simpler, lighter fairy tales in a domesticated
Dark Ages-to-mediaeval setting, rather like that of the Arthurian
stories. See no. 347 for the short grown-up fantasy, *Leaf by Niggle.*

MODERN HYBRID FAIRY TALES

Nos. 241 to 248 differ from most of the invented stories in my list of *Fairy
Tales* (including some modern ones) because they mix elements of a realistic
modern family story with magic and fairy tale themes. Unlike nos. 212 to
240 in my list of *Modern Hybrid Myth* they are mostly short stories; nos. 243

to 246 can be read to very young children and nos. 241, 242, 246 and 247 may provide a way into fantasy for children over eight who scorn traditional fairy tales.

241 AIKEN, JOAN. *A Harp of Fishbones and other stories*. Illustrated by Pat Marriott. Cape, 1972.

Invented fairy stories, making some use of traditional *motifs*; the title story has a long-ago setting, but most of the others are set in clearly particularized modern town or country neighbourhoods. Imaginative and witty interweaving of magic and shrewd comedy; would serve as a bridge between science fiction and fantasy for some older children and teenagers.

242 HUGHES, TED. *The Iron Man*. Illustrated by George Adamson. Faber, 1968; paper 1971: as *The Iron Giant*, Harper and Row, New York, 1968.

An original short fable containing a science-fiction giant robot and a fairy-tale dragon out of space: the touch is light but the symbolic pattern rich. Good for very mixed age-groups.

243 MAHY, MARGARET. *A Lion in the Meadow*. Illustrated by Jenny Williams. Dent, 1969; Penguin (Picture Puffin), 1972: Franklin Watts, 1969.

244 —— *The Dragon of an Ordinary Family*. Illustrated by Helen Oxenburg. Heinemann, 1969.

245 —— *The Boy with Two Shadows*. Illustrated by Jenny Williams. Dent, 1971: Franklin Watts, 1971.

Nos. 243 to 245 are for beginning readers or nursery telling and shewing: magic events in 'ordinary families'. Crisp, shapely and funny.

246 NYE, ROBERT. *Wishing Gold*. Illustrated by Helen Craig. Macmillan, 1970: Hill and Wang, New York, 1971.

Cast in a long short-story form, a fairy tale of legendary Ireland and nowhere: the structure is the writer's, the *motifs* largely taken from folklore and Celtic legend: the narrative style an odd, individual and successful hybrid of traditional repetitive formula and modern raciness. The impertinent wit and the briskness of the prose suit the grotesqueness of much Celtic legend and make it seem acceptable to present ears: could be read to eight- to ten-year-olds who might find the original material silly.

247 —— *Poor Pumpkin.* Illustrated by Derek Collard, Macmillan, 1971.

Invented fairy tales in various distinct traditions, using the worlds of Grimm, English folklore and Chinese fantasy. Often comic and far-fetched: written in a natural, somewhat casual-seeming, entirely unromantic prose: the treatment is almost that of a realistic short story. Good introduction to fantasy for hard-headed eight- to ten-year-olds.

248 STEWART, MARY. *The Little Broomstick.* Illustrated by Shirley Hughes. Brockhampton. 1971.

Witchcraft in a modern setting: some humour.

MYTH, LEGEND AND FAIRY TALE FROM THE
THIRD WORLD AND EASTERN EUROPE

Stories from Eastern Europe

249 AIKEN, JOAN. *The Kingdom under the Sea and other stories.* Illustrated by Jan Pienkowski. Cape, 1971.

East European fairy tales freely and very imaginatively retold. The tradition contains a mixture of archetypal symbolism, worldly wisdom, comic fantasy and grotesques: this version gives coherence and avoids silliness. Original illustrations and page illumination in colour and silhouette in the *art nouveau* manner; almost a picture-book for older children from nine into the teens; some stories could be read and shewn to younger listeners. 'The Reed Girl' is an interesting variant of the Orpheus and Eurydice tale.

250 ALMEDINGEN, E. M. (retold by). *Russian Fairy Tales.* Illustrated by Hazel Cook. Frederick Muller, 1957.

251 BUDBERG, MOURA and WILLIAMS-ELLIS, AMABEL (retold by). *Russian Fairy Tales.* Illustrated by Sarah Nechamkin. Blackie, 1965.

Romances, folk tales of magic, comic and animal fables.

252 DOWNING, CHARLES (retold by). *Russian Tales and Legends.* Illustrated by Joan Kiddell-Monroe. Oxford University Press, London, 1956.

Legends from epic and short heroic poems: many romantic and some comic folk tales. For distinctly older children than nos. 250, 251 and 256—probably over twelve.

253 *The Fire Bird: A Russian Folk Tale* [English text unascribed]. Illustrated by Toma Bogdanovic. Blackie, 1973.

A picture-book for children over seven. Lyrical tale, rich illustrations in the Wildsmith style.

254 GINSBURG, MIRRA (retold by). *Three Rolls and One Doughnut: Fables from Russia*. Illustrated by Anita Lobel. Longman Young Books, 1973.

Short comic tales of peasant life: pen-and-ink drawing in the tradition of the Lang Fairy Books.

255 HAVILAND, VIRGINIA (retold by). *Favourite Fairy Tales Told in Greece*. Illustrated by Nonny Hogrogian. Little, Brown & Co., Boston, 1970: Bodley Head, 1971.

See note on no. 187.

256 —— *Favourite Fairy Tales Told in Russia*. Illustrated by Herbert Danska. Little, Brown & Co., Boston, 1961: Bodley Head, 1967.

See note on no. 187.

257 —— *Favourite Fairy Tales Told in Poland*. Illustrated by Felix Hoffman. Little, Brown & Co., Boston, 1963: Bodley Head, 1966.

See note on no. 187.

258 KAPLAN, IRMA. *Heroes of Kalevala*. Illustrated by Barbara Brown. Frederick Muller, 1973.

Finnish myth and legend of the creation and the early days; a distinct cycle unrelated to Norse stories. For children of nine to fourteen.

259 *The Magic Ring: A Classic Russian Tale*. Translated by Olga Kuthanova, illustrated by Michael Romberg. Hamlyn, 1972.

Fantastic tale of magic and transformed animals. A picture book for children over seven or eight.

260 MANNING-SANDERS, RUTH (retold by). *Damian and the Dragon: Folk and Fairy Tales from Greece*. Illustrated by William Stobbs. Oxford University Press, 1965; Methuen, 1973.

Fables, romances and clever trick stories.

261 MICHAEL, MAURICE and PAMELA (retold by). *Fairy Tales from Bohemia*. Illustrated by John Lathey. Frederick Muller, 1966.

262 OFFER, CHARLES K. (retold by). *Salt above Gold and other Bohemian folk stories*. Illustrated by W. D. Lewis. Oxford University Press, 1968.

263 WILSON, BARBARA KER (retold by). *Greek Fairy Tales*. Illustrated by Harry Toothill. Frederick Muller, 1966.

Animal and magic folklore with Germanic and Eastern affinities: no connection with ancient Greek legend.

264 YEOMAN, JOHN. *The Apple of Youth and other Russian folk stories.* Illustrated by B. Swiderska. Oxford University Press, 1967.

265 ZAJDLER, ZOË (retold by). *Polish Fairy Tales.* Illustrated by Hazel Cook. Frederick Muller, 1959.

Stories from the Near East

266 BROCKETT, ELEANOR (retold by). *Persian Fairy Tales.* Illustrated by Harry Toothill. Frederick Muller, 1962.

Some legends, including the story of Sohrab and Rustum, and romantic or comic tales of magic.

267 PICARD, BARBARA LEONIE. *Three Ancient Kings.* Illustrated by Philip Gough. Kaye and Ward, 1972.

Includes the legend of Gilgamesh (Sumerian-Babylonian).

268 SHAH, AMINA (retold by). *Arabian Fairy Tales.* Illustrated by George Buday. Muller, 1969.

269 TICHY, JAROSLAV. *Persian Fairy Tales.* Freely adapted by Jane Carruth, illustrated by Ludek Manasek. Hamlyn, 1971.

Almost a large picture-book for children over eight. Mostly romantic tales of magic; a few heroic adventures.

270 WESTWOOD, JENNIFER. *Gilgamesh and other Babylonian Tales.* Illustrated by Michael Charlton. Bodley Head, 1968.

Includes the creation story from the 'Enuma etish' which has parallels with the Genesis myth. Good preface and glossary of the gods.

Stories from Africa

271 APPIAH, PEGGY. *Tales of an Ashanti Father.* André Deutsch, 1967.

272 —— *The Pineapple Child and other tales from the Ashanti.* Illustrated by Mora Dickson. André Deutsch, 1969.

Nos. 271 and 272 are folk tales from Ghana narrated from oral tradition in shapely, lively English; mostly animal fables and tall stories of Kwaku Ananse, the rogue-hero who is partly spider and partly man. Good for reading aloud to eight- to twelve-year-olds: many plots in common with European folklore.

273 —— *The Children of Ananse.* Illustrated by Mora Dickson. Evans Bros., 1968.

Story of modern children in an Ashanti village where new customs meet old ones, with folk tales interwoven in the plot.

274 ARNOTT, KATHLEEN (retold by). *African Myths and Legends.* Illustrated by Joan Kiddell-Monroe. Oxford University Press, London, 1962.

Despite the title, does not contain myth or legend; animal fables and just-so-stories presented to somewhat older children than no. 275; bibliography.

275 —— *African Fairy Tales.* Illustrated by Shyam Varma. Frederick Muller, 1967.

Mostly animal fables: some folk tales of magic.

276 —— *Auta the Giant Killer and other Nigerian folk stories.* Illustrated by Uzo Egonu. Oxford University Press, 1971.

Tall stories and beast fables: almost a picture-book in design for the six to eight age range.

277 —— *Tales of Temba: Traditional African Stories.* Illustrated by Victor Ambrus. Blackie, 1967.

Bantu folk tales arranged to shew one hero's growth from infancy to warrior manhood. Animal fables, magic, trickery and men against gods.

278 BERE, RENNIE. *Crocodile's Eggs for Supper.* Illustrated by John Paige. André Deutsch, 1973.

Animal folk tales of the Acholi of Northern Uganda. Told in an appropriately spare, sometimes ironic style: some of the characters identical with those of nos. 271 to 273 (and with those of Uncle Remus). Stories contain shrewd observation of human and animal behaviour: not as rich in practical morality as nos. 280 and 281. Useful note on background of tribal life.

279 BERTOL, ROLAND (retold and introduced by). *Sundiata: the Epic of the Lion King.* Illustrated by Trevor Stubley. Crowell, New York, 1970: Hamish Hamilton, 1972.

Legends of a thirteenth-century emperor of the Islamic African kingdom of Mali and his fight with a demon king.

280 HARMAN, HUMPHREY. *Tales told near a Crocodile: A Collection of Stories from Nyanza.* Illustrated by Grace Huxtable. Hutchinson, 1962.

281 —— *More Tales told near a Crocodile.* Illustrated by Beryl Sanders. Hutchinson, 1973.

From the shores of Lake Victoria (Nyanza) in Kenya and Uganda. Very well told stories collected from oral tradition: the early days of the world, beast fables, human adventures. Shrewd, often comic, quite subtle in practical morality and observation of human and animal behaviour; would suit a mixed audience of seven to twelve.

282 HOLDING, JAMES. *The King's Contest and other North African Tales.* Illustrated by Charles Keeping. Abelard-Schuman, 1964.

Stories from Egypt, Tunisia, the Sahara—Muslim North Africa. Useful to anyone wanting local colour of this particular region: as stories, rather sprawling and inconsistent in *genre*: could be read by children of seven to nine on their own.

283 LUM, PETER (retold by). *Fairy Tales from the Barbary Coast: Algeria, Tunisia and Morocco.* Frederick Muller, 1967.

Mostly magic romance; Islamic African.

284 MCDERMOTT, GERALD (retold and illustrated by). *Anansi the Spider: A Tale from the Ashanti.* Holt, Rinehart and Winston, New York, 1972: Hamish Hamilton, 1973.

A picture-book adapted from an animated film. For beginning readers and telling to under-fives. Original page design.

285 MITCHISON, NAOMI. *African Heroes.* Illustrated by William Stobbs. Bodley Head, 1968.

Kings and warriors of legendary and historical periods: a mixture of tradition and reconstructed history. Linking notes on contemporary contacts with European colonizers.

286 SEED, JENNY. *The Bushman's Dream.* Illustrated by Bernard Brett. Hamish Hamilton, 1974.

Fragments of folklore collected from the Bushmen of South Africa assembled into a continuous tale of the Early Time of the world: a kind of creation myth without a beginning.

Stories from India

287 GRAY, J. E. B. (retold by). *Indian Tales and Legends.* Illustrated by Joan Kiddell-Monroe. Oxford University Press, 1961.

Heroic legend, including short versions of the story of Rama and Sita from the *Ramayana* and the story of Nala and Damayanti from the *Mahabharata*; romantic tales; animal and moral fables. For children over ten.

288 HAVILAND, VIRGINIA (retold by). *Favorite Fairy Tales Told in India.* Illustrated by Blair Lent. Little, Brown and Co., Boston, 1973. See note on no. 187.

289 PICARD, BARBARA LEONIE. *The Story of Rama and Sita.* Illustrated by Charles W. Stewart. Harrap, 1960.

The best retelling for children of ten to fourteen of the story of the *Ramayana*, the epic which underlies most of the narrative art of India, Burma and Thailand; regrettably out of print, and there is no substitute.

290 —— *The Story of the Pandavas retold from the Mahabharata.* Illustrated by Charles Stewart. Denis Dobson, 1968. Tale of Krishna from the other classical Indian epic.

291 STEEL, FLORA ANNIE. *Tales of the Punjab* (1894). With notes by R. C. Temple, illustrated by David Gentleman. Bodley Head, 1973.

Beast fables, tales of magic and trickery, some more courtly romances; intended for a double audience of folklorists and children. Not a child's book in presentation, but readable.

292 THAPAR, ROMILA (retold by). *Indian Tales.* Illustrated by Abu. Bell, 1961.

A mixture of myth, heroic legend and romantic and moral folk tale, including a short version of the story of Rama and Sita. Easier than nos. 289 and 290 for children from nine to twelve.

293 TURNBULL, LUCIA (retold by). *Indian Fairy Tales (Romance, Legend and Fable).* Illustrated by Hazel Cook. Frederick Muller, 1959.

294 ZINKIN, TAYA. *The Faithful Parrot and other Indian folk stories.* Illustrated by S. Varma. Oxford University Press, 1968.

Stories from the Far East

295 BIRCH, CYRIL. *Chinese Myths and Fantasies.* Illustrated by Joan Kiddell-Monroe. Oxford University Press, London 1961.

Includes creation, flood, rebellion and magic stories.

296 BONNET, LESLIE (retold by). *Chinese Fairy Tales.* Illustrated by H. Toothill. Frederick Muller, 1958.

Good tales, but the book is dingy in appearance.

297 BROCKETT, ELEANOR (retold by). *Burmese and Thai Fairy Tales.* Illustrated by Harry and Ilse Toothill. Frederick Muller, 1965.

298 DE LEEUW, ADÈLE (retold by). *Indonesian Fairy Tales.* Illustrated by Harry Toothill. Frederick Muller, 1966.

299 HARRIS, ROSEMARY. *The Child in the Bamboo Grove.* Illustrated by Errol le Cain. Faber, 1971: S. G. Phillips, New York, 1972.

Japanese fairy tale with a motif akin to that of Andersen's Thumbelina: also a just-so-story of Mount Fujiyama. An imaginative, fairly sophisticated picture-book. Beautifully crisp and shapely narrative.

300 —— *The King's White Elephant.* Illustrated by Errol le Cain. Faber, 1973.

A Siamese tale: similar in style and appearance to no. 299.

301 HAVILAND, VIRGINIA (retold by). *Favourite Fairy Tales Told in Japan.* Illustrated by George Suyeoka. Bodley Head, 1967: Little, Brown and Co., Boston, 1969.

See note on no. 187.

302 KEELY, H. H. and PRICE, CHRISTINE (retold by). *The City of the Dagger, and Other Tales from Burma.* Illustrated by Christine Price. F. Warne, 1972.

303 MACALPINE, HELEN and WILLIAM (retold by). *Japanese Tales and Legends.* Illustrated by Joan Kiddell-Monroe. Oxford University Press, London, 1958.

Creation myth, early days of the islands, heroic legend, romantic and magic tales.

304 PIGGOTT, JULIET (retold by). *Japanese Fairy Tales* (1962). Illustrated by Genjiro Mita. Frederick Muller, 1972.

305 SANDERS, TAO TAO. *The Herd Boy and the Ox and other Chinese folk stories.* Illustrated by Europa Chang. Oxford University Press, 1971.

306 STEINBERG, BARBARA HOPE. *The Magic Millstones and other Japanese folk stories.* Illustrated by Esmé Eve. Oxford University Press, 1969.

Stories from the Antipodes and the Pacific

307 BEIER, ULLI (compiled by). *When the Moon was Big and other Legends from New Guinea.* Illustrated by Georgina Beier. William Collins, Sydney and London, 1972.

Stories taken from oral tradition and written down by New Guinea students; the early days of the world, just-so-stories, and heroes and monsters. Useful prefatory note.

308 MOUNTFORD, C. P. *The Dreamtime; Australian Aboriginal Myths.* Paintings by Ainslie Roberts. Angus and Robertson, 1966.

309 —— *The Dawn of Time; Australian Aboriginal Myths.* Paintings by Ainslie Roberts. Angus and Robertson, 1969.

310 —— *The First Sunrise; Australian Aboriginal Myths.* Paintings by Ainslie Roberts. Robert Hale, 1972.

Nos. 308 to 310 are grown-up picture-books with summaries of tales as commentary on an impressive series of narrative paintings which can be shown to children. Creation, the elements, early days of the world and animal just-so-stories.

311 REED, A. W. *Fairy Tales from the Pacific Islands.* Illustrated by Stewart Irwin. Frederick Muller, 1969.

312 —— *Maori Legends.* Illustrated by Roger Hart. David and Charles, Newton Abbot, 1972.

Creation, non-human races of intelligent beings, monsters and journeys. Good text and imaginative pictures. A finely printed book for children over twelve, or for the storyteller to draw from.

313 RUST, DORIS. *Tales from the Australian Bush.* Illustrated by Cecil Elgee. Faber, 1968.

Animal fables and just-so stories told for children under seven: well suited to this age.

American Indian and African Stories from the New World

314 HULPACH, VLADIMIR. *American Indian Tales and Legends.* Translated by George Theiner, illustrated by Miloslav Troup. Paul Hamlyn, 1965.

Creation myth, just-so-stories and animal fables. Large thick picture-book for children over eight. Quite good brief text, glowing pictures.

315 LUM, PETER (retold by). *Folk Tales from North America.* Illustrated by John Spencer. Frederick Muller, 1973.

American Indian and Eskimo tales: creation myth, tales of gods and nature spirits, just-so-stories, animal fables. Good introduction and prefatory note. Much better in page design and pictures than earlier numbers in the Muller series.

316 MANNING-SANDERS, RUTH (retold by). *Red Indian Folk and Fairy Tales.* Illustrated by C. Walter Hodges. Oxford University Press, 1960.

Animal fables, magic tales and tall stories.

317 MEEHAN, JOHN (retold by). *South American Fairy Tales*. Illustrated by José Pradera. Frederick Muller, 1970.

Some stories almost entirely American Indian, some almost entirely Spanish American, some mixed. It is a pity that the writer did not distinguish pre- and post-Conquest settings in arrangement and notes, but the storyteller looking for Indian myth and legend will be able to find it.

318 PIGGOTT, JULIET (retold by). *Mexican Folk Tales*. Illustrated by John Spencer. Frederick Muller, 1973.

Includes an Indian creation myth; up to the new Muller standard of appearance and introduction.

319 SHERLOCK, P. M. *Anansi the Spider Man: Jamaican Folk Tales*. Illustrated by Marcia Brown. Macmillan, 1956

West Indian versions of African fables: lively retelling.

320 —— (retold by). *West Indian Folk-Tales*. Illustrated by Joan Kiddell-Monroe. Oxford University Press, London, 1966.

West African animal and rogue-Anansi tales transplanted to America.

BOOKS ON CHILDREN'S BOOKS

Nos. 322, 323 and 325 are all historical surveys which contain some discussion of twentieth-century fantasy. Nos. 323 and 325 deal with the Victorian revival of myth and folklore, and with the 'invented' fairy tale. No. 325 gives more biographical information than the others, and interesting personal criticism. The literary criticism of no. 324 is relevant to the work of storyteller and teacher.

321 BLISHEN, EDWARD; GARFIELD, LEON and KEEPING, CHARLES. 'Greek Myths and the twentieth century reader'. *Children's Literature in Education* no. 3, November 1970.

Describes the writing of nos. 7 and 8:

322 CROUCH, MARCUS. *Treasure Seekers and Borrowers, Children's Books in Britain 1900–1960*. The Library Association, 1962.

323 DARTON, F. J. HARVEY. *Children's Books in England, Five Centuries of Social Life*. Cambridge University Press, Cambridge and New York, 1932, revised edition 1958.

Contains lists of 'books on books' and of special studies of writers and periods.

324 EGOFF, SHEILA; STUBB, G. T. and ASHLEY, L. F. (edited by). *Only connect: readings on children's literature*. Oxford University Press, Toronto and New York, 1969.

Good critical anthology: the section on 'Fairy Tales, Fantasy, Animals' contains especially penetrating essays by Tolkien, C. S. Lewis and P. L. Travers.

325 GREEN, ROGER LANCELYN. *Tellers of Tales, Children's Books and their authors from 1800 to 1964*. Ward, 1946, revised edition 1965: Watts, New York, 1965.

Contains useful author-bibliographies and a chronological list of children's books.

326 HUGHES, TED. 'Myth and Education'. *Children's Literature in Education* no. 1, March, 1970.

Essay defending the use of myth and describing his own writing of *The Iron Man* (no. 242): in interpretation of dragons anti-idealist.

327 RAY, SHEILA G. *Children's Fiction: a Handbook for Librarians*. Brockhampton, 1970; revised edition 1972.

Useful as a collection of annotated bibliographies.

PRESENTATION AND CREATION IN THE CLASSROOM

328 ADAMS, ANTHONY. *Team teaching and the Teaching of English*. Pergamon Press, 1970.

Inadequate in its understanding of the peculiar nature of imaginative literature, and concerned entirely with secondary teaching, but gives (pp. 112–15) schemes for project work including myth.

329 BAKER, GEORGE. *Exploring Myths and Legends*. Illustrated by Sylvia and Cyril Deakins. Odhams, 1966.

A readable but close-packed account of comparative mythology designed for children: could be put into the hands of fairly able and curious eight- to eleven-year-olds who know some of the stories and want to know how traditions evolved. A small, unalarming book of 96 pages; succeeds without condescension in making an inherently adult subject intelligible, but at the cost of some over-simplification: sometimes suggests that myths are inferior substitutes for science.

330 BOLT, SYDNEY and GARD, ROGER. *The Teaching of Fiction in Schools*. Hutchinson Educational, 1970.

Invaluable methodology for any teacher of stories; studies literary thinking by children in the classroom. Books considered do not include myth, but range from *Paddington* through *Treasure Island* to *Huckleberry Finn*, and the considerations are vital to all imaginative literature. A much-needed critique of 'project' method: first and last chapters especially useful.

331 BRITTON, BARBARA. 'The Shared Book'. *Growing Point*, vol. 2, no. 3, September 1972.

Useful short article coming from the horse's mouth, defining what a parent or teacher can add to a child's experience of stories.

332 HILL, JANET. *Children are People: The Librarian in the Community*. Hamish Hamilton, 1973.

Critical and sometimes contentious: points in chapters on 'Book selection', 'Introducing and Publicising Books' and 'Attitudes to Books' relevant to all storytellers, not just librarians.

333 JONES, ANTHONY and BUTTREY, JUNE. *Children and Stories*. Blackwell, Oxford, 1970.

A practical study of children's responses and original work, giving useful booklists, year reading lists and suggestions for 'follow-up' work-cards. Sensible defence of periods of intensive listening, especially in chapter 5, 'Sharing Stories'.

334 KOHL, HERBERT R. *36 Children*. New American Library, New York, 1968: Gollancz, 1968; Penguin, 1972.

An extreme anarchist critique of structure in teaching, based upon work with eleven- to fourteen-year-old black children in Harlem. Impractical (unless a teacher wants chaos) but contains (pp. 114–17, 131–5 and 151–4) interesting examples of children's work stimulated by myth. The writer's interpretation of myth misleading.

335 MARSHALL, SYBIL MARY. *An Experiment in Education*. Cambridge University Press, Cambridge and New York, 1963; Cambridge paperback, 1966.

The most practical and level-headed book on integrated creative work in a junior school.

336 MELZI, KAY. *Art in the Primary School*. Blackwell, Oxford, 1967. Includes section on literature as a starting-point for painting.

337 *Moving and Growing, Physical Education in the Primary School. Part One*. Ministry of Education Pamphlet no. 24, H.M. Stationery Office, 1952.

Chapter 4 contains sections on movement as an art, dance, and dramatic movement.

338 RUSSELL, JOAN. *Modern Dance in Education.* Macdonald and Evans, 1958.

Chapters on dance-drama, and dance in the Primary School.

339 SANSOM, DAVID. 'Read this: you'll love it'. *Children's Literature in Education* no. 4, March 1971.

Practical suggestions for talking about stories and collecting new readers.

340 SAWYER, RUTH. *The Way of the Storyteller* (1942, revised 1962). Viking Press, New York, 1965. Chapters 7 and 8 useful on technique and preparation for storytelling.

341 SPENCER, MARGARET. 'Stories and Storytelling'. In *Children Using Language,* edited by Anthony Jones and Jeremy Mulford. Oxford University Press, 1971.

Essay giving substantial quotations from children's work and remarks on topics.

342 SUMMERFIELD, GEOFFREY. *Topics in English for the Secondary School.* Batsford, 1965.

Misleading in its confusion of imaginative literature with *reportage,* but lists may suggest ways of introducing stories into topics.

THE INTERPRETATION OF MYTH, LEGEND AND FAIRY TALE

Personal, poetic and general studies

Nos. 343 to 348 are all addressed to the non-specialist. See also no. 117; the preface gives a sane personal estimate of fairy tales.

343 CHESTERTON, G. K. 'The Priest of Spring'. In *A Miscellany of Men* (1912). Included in *Stories, Essays, and Poems,* Dent (Everyman), 1935.

Short essay satirizing 'the Solar Myth': gives pagan mythology idealized human origins and relates it to Christian belief.

344 LEWIS, C. S. *Surprised by Joy.* Bles, 1955; Fontana, 1959: Harvest Books, New York, 1956; Harcourt paperback, New York, 1966.

Autobiography: chapter I describes his experience of fantasy as a child, in reading and writing.

345 MACNEICE, LOUIS. *Varieties of Parable* (1963 Clark Lectures). Cambridge University Press, Cambridge, 1965; New York, 1966.

A practising poet's sane and sensitive criticism of the literature of fantasy and symbol: good pages on his childhood reading of myth, on Andeᵣsen, and on Victorian 'invented' fairy tales.

346 RAINE, KATHLEEN. *Defending Ancient Springs.* Oxford University Press, London and New York, 1967.

Illuminating essays 'On the Symbol' (p. 105) and 'On the mythological' (p. 123).

347 TOLKIEN, J. R. R. 'On Fairy Stories'. In *Leaf by Niggle.* Allen and Unwin, 1964.

The best criticism of fantasy in print: sane and imaginative discussion of 'the cauldron of story', as well as the ingredients that went into the stew. Sheds light on myth and legend as well as fairy tale, and on children.

348 —— *Beowulf: The Monsters and the Critics* (British Academy Lecture). Oxford University Press, 1936.

Helpful to a proper understanding of all dragons, not only the one in *Beowulf*: also on the whole of Greek and Northern mythology.

Historical and anthropological criticism

Nos. 350 and 351 are thorough, but compact and interesting to the general reader; nos. 349 and 353 to 357 are large, detailed, specialized studies, but the account of ritual and folklore in no. 353 is readable.

349 AARNE, ANTTI. *The Types of the Folktale: A Classification and Bibliography* (1910). Translated and enlarged by Stith Thompson. FF Communications no. 184, Helsinki, 1961.

350 BRIGGS, KATHARINE M. *The Anatomy of Puck: An Examination of Fairy Beliefs among Shakespeare's Contemporaries and Successors.* Routledge and Kegan Paul, 1959: Hillary, New York.

Chapters 1 and 2 give evidence for English traditions of tall 'heroic' fairies and dwarfish domestic ones; also fairy godmothers.

351 —— *The Fairies in Tradition and Literature.* Routledge and Kegan Paul, 1967.

352 DOUGLAS, MARY. *Natural Symbols: Explorations in Cosmology.* Barrie and Rockliff, 1970; Penguin, 1973: Random, New York; Pantheon, New York, 1970.

353 FRAZER, SIR JAMES GEORGE. *The Golden Bough* (2 vols, 1890; 12 vols. 1911–15). Abridged edition (1922) in 1 vol., Macmillan, London and New York, 1962.

Primitive religion, especially Dying God myth and ritual. The largest collection easily available: conclusions dated.

354 GRAVES, ROBERT. *The White Goddess, A Historical Grammar of Poetic Myth.* Faber, 1947; Faber paperback, 1959: Farrar, Strauss and Giroux, New York, 1966; Noonday paperback, New York.

355 MALINOWSKI, BRONISLAW. *Myth in Primitive Psychology.* Kegan Paul, 1926. Included in *Magic, Science and Religion and Other Essays,* introduced by Robert Redfield. Doubleday Anchor Books, New York, 1955.

356 THOMPSON, STITH. *Motif-Index of Folk-Literature: A Classification of Narrative Elements in Folktales, Ballads, Myths, Fables, Mediaeval Romances, Exempla, Fabliaux, Jest Books and Local Legends* (1932–6). Revised edition, 6 vols. Rosenkilde and Bagger, Copenhagen, 1955–8.

357 WESTON, JESSIE. *From Ritual to Romance.* Cambridge University Press, Cambridge, 1920.

Origin of Grail stories: theory contested in no. 101.

Psychological criticism

Nos. 359 and 365 are intended for the general reader; no. 358 for the student with some knowledge of literature; no. 361 is the easiest of the specialized studies.

358 BODKIN, MAUD. *Archetypal Patterns in Poetry, Psychological studies of imagination.* Oxford University Press, London, 1934; Oxford paperback, London and New York, 1963.

359 CIRLOT, J. E. *A Dictionary of Symbols.* Translated by Jack Sage with introduction by Herbert Read. Routledge and Kegan Paul, 1962.

360 FREUD, SIGMUND. *The Interpretation of Dreams* (1900). Translated by James Strachey. Allen and Unwin, 1954: Basic Books, New York, 1955.

361 FROMM, ERICH. *The Forgotten Language: an Introduction to the understanding of dreams, fairy-tales and myths.* Holt, Rinehart and Winston, New York, 1951; Grove Press (Evergreen Books), New York, 1957: Gollancz, 1952.

362 JUNG, C. G. and KERENYI, C. *Introduction to a Science of Mythology, the Myth of the Divine Child and the Mysteries of Eleusis.* Translated by R. F. C. Hull. Routledge and Kegan Paul, 1951: Harper and Row (Torchbooks), New York.

363 KERENYI, C. *Prometheus, Archetypal Image of Human Existence*. Translated by Ralph Mannheim. Bollingen Foundation, New York, 1962: Thames and Hudson, London, 1963.

364 RANK, OTTO. *The Myth of the Birth of the Hero, a Psychological Interpretation of Mythology*. Translated by F. Robbins and Smith Ely Jeliffe. Robert Brunner, New York, 1952; Random House (Vintage Books), New York, 1959.

365 USSHER, ARLAND and VON METZRADT, CARL. *Enter these Enchanted Woods, an Interpretation of Grimm's Fairy Tales*. Illustrated by Tate Adams, with a preface by Padraic Colum. Dolmen Press, Dublin, ?1957: revised edition, Dufour, Chester Springs, 1966.

Studies of development in literature

Nos. 366 to 370 are large, fairly specialized critical works; no. 366 is humane and perhaps easier than the others.

366 BOWRA, SIR CECIL MAURICE. *Heroic Poetry*. Macmillan, London and New York, 1952; Macmillan paperback, London and New York, 1965.

367 BUSH, J. N. DOUGLAS. *Mythology and the Renaissance Tradition in English Poetry*. University of Minnesota Press, Minneapolis, 1932: Oxford University Press, London, 1932. Revised edition, Norton, New York, 1963.

368 —— *Mythology and the Romantic Tradition in English Poetry*. Harvard University Press, Cambridge, Massachusetts, 1937: Oxford University Press, London, 1937. Revised edition, Norton, New York, 1963.

369 KER, W. P. *Epic and Romance, Essays on Mediaeval Literature*. Macmillan, 1897, revised edition 1908: Dover paperback, New York.

A comparative study of the whole of traditional literature from Homer to the Arthurian romances. Not outdated as literary criticism: very sensitive to the kind of thing each writer was trying to do.

370 STANFORD, W. B. *The Ulysses Theme. A Study in the Adaptability of a Traditional Hero*. Blackwell, Oxford, 1954, revised edition 1963: Barnes and Noble, New York, 1964.

Addendum, 1977

The following list contains some of the more important books of or about myth and legend published between 1974 and 1977.

BAUMANN, HANS. *Hero Legends of the World.* Translated by Stella Humphries; illustrated by Herbert Holzing. Dent, 1975.

Collection of stories from many cultures excluding Greek and Norse legend: useful because it gives heroic and quest stories from peoples whose fables and comic folklore are more easily found in children's books. Includes Gilgamesh.

BEACHCROFT, NINA. *Under the Enchanter.* Heinemann, 1974.

Realistic, often humorous novel for older children, touching legend and magic not so much in narrative line as in the young heroine's reliance on her reading of fantasy.

CARPENTER, HUMPHREY. *J. R. R. Tolkien: A Biography.* Allen and Unwin, 1977.

Authorized and probably definitive.

CLAIR, ANDRÉE and HAMA, BOUBOU. *The Enchanted Savannah: Tales from West Africa.* Translated by Olive Jones; illustrated by Béatrice Tanaka. Methuen Children's Books, 1974.

Magic tales often giving African versions of motifs familiar in European folklore: unusual in not concentrating on animal fables and in being designed for older readers than many African collections envisage. Lively storytelling and illustration.

Gawain (Sir) and the Green Knight, Pearl, and Sir Orfeo. Translated and introduced by J. R. R. Tolkien; edited by Christopher Tolkien. Allen and Unwin, 1975: Houghton Mifflin, New York, 1975

This translation in the original metre supersedes others, as might be expected: parts could be read to older children. Critical introduction taken from earlier talks and essays contains much in little space.

GRIPE, MARIA. *The Glassblower's Children.* Translated by Sheila la Farge; illustrated by Harald Gripe. Delacorte Press, New York, 1973; Dell Publishing Co., New York, 1974: Abelard-Schuman, 1974; Wyndham Publications (Target Books), 1976.

A highly shaped, romantic, penetrating tale in the Andersen tradition: original treatment of images in *The Snow Queen* and many archetypes of wishes and of light and shadow.

Index

This index includes a selection of names and subjects, the most important of which are printed in capitals. Figures in bold type refer to numbers of items in the Short List and may indicate subjects or stories to be found in particular books. Other figures refer to pages in the text.